1989

University of St. Francis
GEN   821.1 W867
Wood, Chauncey.
The elements of Chaucer's Troi

S0-BRF-622

The Elements of Chaucer's *Troilus*

Triomphe de Vénus. Paris, The Louvre, #16824. First half of the fifteenth century. Photo from Lauros-Giraudon (Art Reference Bureau).

The Elements of Chaucer's *Troilus*

Chauncey Wood

Duke University Press   Durham, N.C.   1984

LIBRARY
College of St. Francis
JOLIET, ILLINOIS

Permission to quote has been granted for the following:

The Works of Geoffrey Chaucer, ed. F. N. Robinson
(Boston: Houghton Mifflin Company, 1957). © 1957
by Houghton Mifflin Company.
The Filostrato of Giovanni Boccaccio, trans. Edward
Nathaniel Griffin and Arthur Beckwith Myrick
(Philadelphia: University of Pennsylvania Press, 1929).

© 1984 Duke University Press, all rights reserved

Printed in the United States of America on acid-free paper

Library of Congress Cataloging in Publication Data

Wood, Chauncey.
The elements of Chaucer's *Troilus*.

Includes bibliographical references and index.
1. Chaucer, Geoffrey, d. 1400. Troilus and
Criseyde.   2. Chaucer, Geoffrey, d. 1400. Troilus and
Criseyde—Sources.   3. Boccaccio, Giovanni, 1313–1375.
Filostrato.   4. Love in Literature.   I. Title.
PR1896.W66   1984   821'.1   83-16397
ISBN 0-8223-0498-8

821.1
W867

To
Sarah, Stephanie, and Jennifer
"of ladies ek so fair a compaignie"

139,852

Contents

Preface

There are three basic ways in which one can interpret Chaucer's *Troilus and Criseyde*: it is either a poem that praises the love affair that is its main subject, condemns it, or offers a mixed or qualified judgment. Since the closing stanzas of the poem disparage "blynde lust" (V, 1824) and "feynede loves" (V, 1848), those critics who find the poem approving the affair between the lovers prior to the epilogue have had to introduce some qualifications about the ending.[1] Thus C. S. Lewis, who argued that the *Troilus* was meant to be a "great poem in praise of love," treated the concluding stanzas as a frightened recantation of what had gone before, and Walter Clyde Curry saw it as "detachable at will."[2] Strictly speaking, then, critics see two forms of qualified praise of love or see condemnation of it.

Perhaps the most common approach in recent years is one in which the epilogue is not so much discarded as discounted, so that the praise of divine love at the close of the poem does not obviate the verses that seem to praise the human love that has been the subject of the poem thus far, but show only that human love, great as it is, is ultimately second best. An early proponent of this school was H. R. Patch, who felt that Lewis was rash to think the poem praised the affair of the lovers, since it had to be judged "illicit." Yet, Patch later calls the same event "this blessed moment" and seems to want the best of both worlds when he says that the love of Troilus is "a good as far as it goes but is not to be confused with the 'blynde lust' . . . which he later condemns, to which Troilus and Criseyde yield in their longing for each other."[3] A somewhat similar approach has been taken recently by John McCall. He finds classical images in the poem that are "hellish" and that deal with treachery on the one hand, but finds "joyous mythical allusions which suggest that earthly love is like paradise" on the other. Unlike some critics, however, McCall sees the imagery of joy undermined. He writes that "as the paradisiacal imagery accumulates in the last part of Book Three . . . the reader is regularly reminded of the inconstancy of earthly affections."[4] A much less qualified estimate of the central love affair has been made by Monica McAlpine, who sees it as providing a kind of objective correlative against which one may judge its participants. Thus for Troilus, who is ennobled by and faithful to his love for Criseyde, love leads to a comedy; for Criseyde, who is unfaithful, love leads to a tragedy.[5] Such are the problems of dealing with a poem that says two different things; yet it seems that some version or other of this approach is perhaps more widespread today than that taken by Root, Shanley, Robertson, and Sharrock, who read the condemnation of love in the closing stanzas of the poem as an open statement of what has been implied or said indirectly throughout.[6] To these three basic interpretations a fourth has recently been added: this approach argues that Troilus and Criseyde actually marry one another. The nuptial theory raises very different problems with the epilogue. At any rate, it seems to be an approach that is unlikely to attract as many followers as those already in vogue.[7]

At the heart of the debate over the meaning or meanings of this poem is a disagreement over matters of tone and mood. While the epilogue's hortatory straightforwardness does not occasion any doubt about its tone, the combination of humor and pathos throughout the body of the poem does. The question of the degree to which our sympathies are engaged, or are meant to be engaged, is difficult to respond to, for as one of the most perceptive students of the poem, Ida Gordon, has noted, "the text taken at its face value is not always the safest guide to Chaucer's meaning."[8] Obviously, the best way to approach problems of meaning dependent upon problems of tone is to bring to bear a variety of internal and external parallel texts for comparison and contrast. It is remarkable, though, how seldom this is done, and how often the poem is read as though it existed all by itself, as though its separate parts, separate speakers, separate images, all projected the same tone, with no room for nuance, let alone irony. C. S. Lewis noted that in the language of the stable one could say that Chaucer's poem was by Boccaccio out of the *Romance of the Rose*, which seems a promising avenue for studying the comparisons we need to make. Yet, in the more than twenty articles on the poem that appeared in the *Chaucer Review* from its inception to the late seventies, fewer than half glanced at Boccaccio's *Filostrato*, while only one undertook a careful look at the *Romance of the Rose*. The present study is intended in part to remedy this deficiency, and in part to explore some other elements of the poem.

The elements of the *Troilus*, as I see them, are the images and actions, along with their nuances, that Chaucer uses to express the love affair between Troilus and Criseyde. In order to determine which of these are important and how we should assess their tone, we must first examine the oddly neglected poem by Boccaccio which is the source for Chaucer. We should then examine the extent to which love ennobles Chaucer's Troilus, the central preoccupation of much twentieth-century comment, and look at the images of Cupid, Venus, the God of Love, Fortune, and blindness, all of which are best understood from a perspective wide enough to include the writings of Boccaccio, John Gower, and, most important, the *Romance of the Rose*. Because of the degree to which I rely upon the *Romance* for illustrative material, I must record my debt to the major modern interpretations of it by Dahlberg, Robertson, Tuve, and above all by John Fleming. Without their labors my own would have perforce been twice as long, and I could not have hoped to have achieved their depth.[9] If I were to imagine an ideal reader of this work, it would be someone who had read these critics on the *Romance of the Rose*, and who had also read Robert Hollander's book on Boccaccio and the two Venuses—would that I had had it when I began my own study of the *Filostrato*.[10]

These, then, are the elements of the poem that are discussed at length in the chapters that follow. By the nature of the task I have set myself, the book does not constitute a "reading" of the entire *Troilus*. Rather, I hope to clarify certain basic issues in order to provide a background out of which sequential readings of the whole might naturally arise. Because the elements in which I am interested are not distributed regularly throughout the poem, I not only neglect some features of the work, but also return to several key passages more than once—not, I hope, in a tiresome way. In this eclectic approach the present work is somewhat similar to Ida L. Gordon's book *The Double Sorrow of Troilus: A Study of Ambiguities in Troilus and Criseyde*.[11] While I do not find as much ambiguity in the poem as does Gordon, we nevertheless often concur on which passages in the text are crucial, and our readings frequently dovetail.

In order that the argument be as unimpeded as possible, I have used translations of foreign languages for longer passages wherever possible. Where not possible, because of the nature of the text or the argument, I have used both a translation and the original. For the ubiquitous *Romance of the Rose* my practice has been to use its Middle English text where possible, Dahlberg's modern English translation elsewhere, and in one instance the original. I refer to it variously as the *Romance of the Rose* or the *Romaunt*, and frequently refer to the lover as Amant when discussing the ME text, even though he is named regularly only in the original French version.

No study of Chaucer's *Troilus* can attempt to cope in any detail with the extant scholarship on the poem. There are streams of books, torrents of articles. Or, to change the metaphor, the student of the poem who begins to survey the writings on it soon finds that "The increasing prospect tires our wandering eyes, / Hills peep o'er hills, and Alps on Alps arise!" If one tried to note every point of disagreement and agreement with other critics, the footnotes would soon outweigh the text, and the argument would be hopelessly impeded. I have, therefore, been entirely eclectic. I have traced opinion chronologically when it seemed desirable; I have selected only a typical quotation where that seemed expeditious. As a result, the absence of reference to an article or book by no means is an indication that its contents were not considered. The basic text of this work was written in the academic year 1974–75, but the scholarship that has appeared from 1974 to about 1980 has been noted whether it has been in agreement or disagreement with my own interpretations. I must add that my not infrequently documented disagreements are with ideas and interpretations, not with individuals, as, for that matter, are points of agreement.

McMaster University supported much of the research for this book through its former program of summer stipends, and I wish to express my gratitude. I am also grateful to The Canada Council for a Leave Fellowship, during which most of the writing was done. My thanks go as well to the University of Victoria, which appointed me Visiting Professor during the tenure of my Leave Fellowship. My friends David Jeffrey and Tony Edwards helped my stay in Victoria go pleasantly and were also of great assistance in solving the problems of scholarship that arise when one is on unfamiliar territory. My visits to the Huntington Library permitted access to materials that would have otherwise been unavailable, and I am indebted to the Library's ever-gracious staff. I am grateful to the Houghton-Mifflin Company for permission to quote from *The Works of Geoffrey Chaucer*, ed. F. N. Robinson (Boston, 1957), and to the University of Pennsylvania Press for permission to quote from the *Filostrato of Giovanni Boccaccio*, trans. Nathaniel Edward Griffin and Arthur Beckwith Myrick (Philadelphia, 1929).

No part of this work has been previously published, but a paper on "Troilus and Saint Venus," based on the materials in chapter 4, was read at the University of Victoria in 1975, and at the University of Texas at Austin in 1977. A short paper based on the final section of chapter 1 was read at the first congress of The New Chaucer Society in April 1979 in Washington, D.C. An essay on "Blind Cupid—Blind Troilus," based on part of chapter 5, was delivered at Princeton University in 1980. Most of chapter 1, on the *Filostrato*, was read by Robert Hollander in 1976, and I am deeply grateful to him for his valuable comments, corrections, and suggestions. Very special thanks are herewith tendered to Edmund Reiss, who read the entire manuscript, and whose sharp and tireless eye noted more infelicities of form and content than I altogether care to remember. My loving thanks go to my wife Sarah for her help with this manuscript and her patience with its author.

My particular debt to D. W. Robertson, Jr., is both intellectual and personal. I began my study of the *Troilus* in his graduate seminar some twenty years ago, and across these two decades he has been a continual source of encouragement to me in my Chaucerian endeavors. In letters and conversations he has offered me help on everything from medieval history to modern stylistic usage. His numerous books and articles have supplied me with both basic information and directions for study, so that not only have I been influenced by Robertson's views on the *Troilus*, but, as my footnotes record, I am indebted to him for all kinds of medieval perceptions. I certainly did not set out to write *A Preface to Troilus*, but the ubiquity of Robertson's name in the text and notes may indicate a "failing" in that regard. Of Robertson's abundant insights one can only echo the Man of Law and marvel that "if he have noght seyd hem, leve brother, / In o book, he hath seyd hem in another."

The Elements of Chaucer's *Troilus*

Chapter I

The Tone of Boccaccio's *Filostrato*

Interpretation, *Quellenforschungen*, Autobiography

Boccaccio's *Filostrato* has undeniably been studied more for what it contributes to distant objectives than it has been for itself. For Chaucerians it has been more often described than really analyzed, usually seen as a simple poem that gives birth to Chaucer's complex one. On the other hand the scholars of Italian literature have examined the poem much more for what it can contribute to the complex mosaic of Boccaccio's art and life than for the way it works within its own limits as a poetic entity. Nor is this neglect altogether surprising, for by stating in his *Proemio* that the poem was written "as a mask for my secret and amorous grief," while addressing himself to a "most noble lady"—a "nobilissima donna"—who has departed the city where the poet resides, Boccaccio seems to have done the job of critic for us.[1]

Who, after all, knows better the author's meaning than the author himself? Because of this authorial self-nomination as exegete, the *Filostrato* has widely been assumed to mean no more nor less than what Boccaccio says it means, and the possibility of authorial playfulness has not been raised. The genre having been accepted, the overall tone seemed unnecessary to investigate with any more precision. Chaucerian scholars who disagreed about important elements of Boccaccio's poem nevertheless agreed on its basic genre—the serious love poem—and subordinated their disagreements as students of Boccaccio to their interest in their disagreements as Chaucerians. We may note, for example, that C. S. Lewis says that Boccaccio commits errors against the code of courtly love, while in contrast Thomas Kirby finds the *Filostrato* to be a typical poem of courtly love. Similarly Sanford Meech argues that Criseida in Boccaccio's poem is "not protected from our scorn," while Robert apRoberts contends to the contrary that she is a lady ideally suited for what he calls a "perfect affair."[2] apRoberts commendably investigates Boccaccio's poem in more detail than is customary with Chaucerians, and surely we would do well to follow his lead. Before we can confidently assert, with Root, that Boccaccio's poem exhibits "tender sentiment and ardent passion," while Chaucer's shows "wise and thoughtful irony," we would do well to inquire into what Boccaccio actually does in his poem as well as into what he says he will do.[3] There is no guarantee that Chaucer will always follow Boccaccio's lead; he might modify, reject, or even misunderstand what he finds there, but we should not rush to judgment about Chaucer's intentions when it is clear that we are not in agreement about Boccaccio's meaning.[4]

A complementary problem that has led scholars away from Boccaccio's text rather than into it is the intriguing autobiographical element therein, which has preoccupied students of Boccaccio the man and Boccaccio the precursor of Chaucer. While biographical speculation about Boccaccio is as old as study of his works, most modern discussions derive from Vincenzo Crescini's nineteenth-century account, in which the sequence of the life is evolved from presumably autobiographical references in the works.[5] In particular, it is argued that from six youthful writings, the *Filocolo*, *Filostrato*, *Teseida*, *Fiammetta*, *Ameto*, and *Amorosa visione*, we can discern the outlines of Boccaccio's love affair with Maria d'Aquino, whom he styled as Fiammetta. She was, we learn, the illegitimate daughter of Robert, King of Naples and the Two Sicilies. She was married to a nobleman in spite of some misgivings, and she had arranged before the wedding that if the union proved distasteful she could return to her life in the convent, where she had been raised. This return in fact took place, and accordingly Boccaccio met her in the church of San Lorenzo at Naples. She withdrew from Naples for a time, perhaps to test Boccaccio's constancy, and it was during this absence that the *Filostrato* was written. Some time after her return Boccaccio became her lover, but later she deserted him for another. From subsequent works in the canon we learn that Boccaccio had a religious experience later in life that turned him against the licentiousness of his youth and made him into a grave and moral scholar given to writing mythographies, tragic histories, and other suitable works.

The persistence and pervasiveness of this romantic biography is considerable. Not only has it given rise to something of a Boccaccio industry in the form of breathy biographies based on the premise that all the world loves a lover, but the conception of the man, drawn from the works, has been taken back to them as a tool of inquiry—always a potential danger in the Hermeneutical circle. Particularly among students of Chaucer the image of Maria / Fiammetta has burned persistently—if not with a hard, gem-like flame, at least with the fascination of the candle for the moth. From Rossetti in 1873 to Howard Schless in 1975 scholars have discussed Maria / Fiammetta in their analyses of the *Filostrato*, sometimes peripherally or incidentally (as Schless does), sometimes centrally.[6] The latter approach is very common. For example, F. N. Robinson, in his edition of Chaucer's works, credits the passionate intensity of Boccaccio's poem to his having written it as an expression of his devotion to Maria, while Robert P. apRoberts suggests that Boccaccio's praise of furtive love was intended to persuade Maria that because love outside of marriage is more delectable than wedded love, she should accept him as her lover.[7]

We see, then, that an autobiographical element pervades the criticism of Boccaccio's *Filostrato*, sometimes contributing prominently, sometimes incidentally, but almost always used by scholars who come to Boccaccio's poem by way of Chaucer. There are, however, reasons for more caution than has been shown. In the first place, the *Filostrato* is not, in fact, addressed to Maria d'Aquino, nor to her in her name of Fiammetta. Rather, the poem is addressed to an unnamed "nobilissima donna," and it has been observed by Vittore Branca that the details of this "donna" differ significantly from those of Maria / Fiammetta set down elsewhere. Moreover, the various poems present her as having a romantically protean ability to remain forever young that, coupled with the genealogists' inability to discover any trace of her in historical record, has led several Italian and German scholars to reject the whole idea of Maria / Fiammetta as historically derived and to see in her instead an expression of romantic daydreams or literary tropes.[8]

None of this information is news. Billanovich was attacking the autobiographical approach in the forties, Branca soon thereafter, and by 1964 the latter could feel that he had been successful to the extent that "the supposed autobiography of the romances has not any longer been able to deceive any serious student."[9] Branca not only demolishes the myth of Maria / Fiammetta; he also offers some good suggestions for critical approaches to replace the autobiographical ones. For example, the sufferings of the young protagonist of Boccaccio's early romances may be understood as stylized and contrived, owing much to Ovid and Andreas Capellanus.[10] This promising approach will be followed here, with the inclusion of the *Romance of the Rose* as one of the more important literary influences on Boccaccio insofar as it, too, is a supposed autobiography of the lover / narrator's amorous adventures.[11] Indeed, there is reason to think that the erotic pseudo-autobiography was a fairly well understood genre in medieval European literature, as G. B. Gybbon-Monypenny has persuasively argued.[12] Once we have recognized the existence of this genre we have a fresh perspective for studying a work like the *Filostrato*, which, although it lacks the interpolated songs usually found in the pseudo-autobiographies studied by Gybbon-Monypenny, nevertheless can better be studied in terms of conventions, tropes, and *topoi* than in terms of an actual declaration of amorous intention.

If Boccaccio is not in earnest in his *Proemio*, if the poem is not really written as part of a grand, seductive plan for the advantage of the real-life Boccaccio, then we may properly ask whether the poet should be taken at face value at all. Just how far one is justified in proceeding in this direction is difficult to know, especially without a full-scale analysis of the other romances, but the tone of the *Filostrato* may be more that of a jeu d'esprit than the autobiographical critics have allowed. Any poet who can have Troilo address Venus as "bella luce eterna" (III, 89), a phrase that Boccaccio elsewhere uses for the Virgin Mary, invites our close scrutiny of his tone. Is this blasphemy, is it a reminiscence of the *dolce stil nuovo*, as Branca would have it, (and if so, what in turn does *that* tell us?), or, is Boccaccio having a joke at Troilo's expense?[13] It is this sort of possible humor that leads one to agree with Carlo Muscetta in categorizing the poem as a "romanzo comico-elegaico."[14]

Certainly the poem's internal contradictions cry out for explanation. Boccaccio's closing (VIII, 29) abjuration to youths to refrain from following the "evil passion" ("appetito rio"), flies in the face of his supposed desire for Maria and his enthusiastic account of the bedroom scenes between Troilo and Criseida. One critic has seen the moralistic condemnation at the close as a "sop to the Christian teaching that all passionate love is wicked," but it is at least as plausible to find the passages in praise of love as ironic as to identify the moral remarks as sops.[15] The same critic makes much of Pandaro's enthusiasm for the "alto appetito" (II, 26) that lovers may follow if they observe secrecy.[16] Leaving aside the question of whether "alto appetito" might not be a joke, since the appetites are regularly associated with lower, not higher, urges in the Middle Ages, certainly the "alto appetito" claimed to exist by Pandaro contrasts precisely with the "appetito rio" finally condemned by the narrator; yet both appetites describe the same thing. We must ask whether Pandaro speaks for the poet more than does the narrator.

Chaucer, of course, would not have risen so quickly to autobiographical bait as so many moderns have done. In Boethius' *Consolation of Philosophy*, which he translated, biography is mixed with allegory, and in his own writings Chaucer amusingly presented himself as the opposite of what he was, thus, the great storyteller of *The Canterbury Tales* includes himself in the work as a tale-teller who knows no stories. This ability of a medieval author to present himself as a laughable narrator should be borne in mind when we later discuss passages Chaucer took from Boccaccio. Moreover, for the analysis of Boccaccio's poem we should note that Boccaccio's idol, Dante, in the *Vita Nuova* wrote a work that gently satirizes his own youthful passion, and there are numerous reminiscences of the *Vita Nuova* in the *Filostrato*.[17] To be sure, Dante's *Vita Nuova* has generally been regarded as an entirely serious treatment of love, but we need not emend the religious imagery of its text as did the redactor of the *editio princeps*, nor find its author capable only of "grimly" smiling as did Tennyson in "The Palace of Art." Dorothy Sayers has taught us to see Dante the artist delicately mocking Dante the character in the *Commedia*, and more recently Mark Musa has commented on the excesses of the protagonist of the *Vita Nuova*.[18]

When three spirits appear to the lovestruck Dante of the treatise, and one announces to him in mock-solemn Latin that he can expect his digestion to suffer from all this, Musa is undoubtedly correct in arguing that Dante the author is poking fun at Dante the lover.[19] Another important feature of the work is the egregious nature of the love poems that Dante selects from his own canon. As Musa observes, anyone who will examine Dante's *Rime* will quickly see that some of the poems placed in the *Vita Nuova* are those that represent a lover at his hysterical worst.[20] Thus, it is not unreasonable to imagine that Boccaccio, responding to Dante's use of himself as a somewhat unsympathetic character in a treatise on love, might decide to create a literary persona himself, but instead of one who is timid, using "screen ladies" and so forth, one who is more forward. Of course, the differences between the *Vita Nuova* and the *Filostrato* are far more striking than their similarities, but the humorous treatment of the narrator of the *Vita Nuova*, who bears the author's name and worships a most virtuous lady, should be remembered when we encounter Boccaccio's similarly love-struck persona rather differently testifying to his grief and urging his "nobilissima donna" to listen to the story of the easily-seduced Criseida. That Boccaccio divides his poem into nine parts would be in keeping with his sense of humor, for he takes nine, the perfect number of the chaste Beatrice, and uses it as the structural base for a poem claimed to be an inducement to seduction! Either Boccaccio wanted to shock people, or, more likely, he intended the various incongruities of his work to militate somewhat against its nominal intention.

Just how people reacted to "personal" poems in former times is very difficult to ascertain. However, J. B. Leishman has suggested that we have taken John Donne's light poems too seriously because we have let a "too-commonly exaggerated autobiographical element" interfere with our distinguishing between what is jest and what is earnest.[21] This pronouncement on Donne could usefully be applied to Boccaccio, for it reminds us of the very limited autobiographical element to be found in the Middle Ages, from St. Augustine's *Confessions* to Petrarch's account of his ascent of Mt. Ventoux. Let us, then, consider some of the possible jests of the *Proemio*. Boccaccio begins by styling himself as desperately saddened because the "nobilissima donna" to whom the work is addressed has departed from Naples to Sannio. Fearing that if he completely bottled up his grief it eventually would rush forth with such force that it would kill him, he decided to give his grief "issue from my sad heart in some suitable lamentation, in order that I might live . . ." (p. 125). The means for this occurred to him at once: in the person of an impassioned one, such as he was and is, he would relate his sufferings in song. The story he selected to be a "mask for my secret and amorous grief" was the story of Troilo "to whose life in so far as it was filled with sorrow by Love and the distance of his lady, . . . after his much-beloved Criseida was returned to her father Calcas, mine, after your departure hath been very similar" (p. 127).

Problems immediately arise: Troilo had been quite happily enjoying his lady's favors before their separation, and not only missed her accommodating self, but was also annoyed that she had rapidly acquired another lover. Neither Criseida's first extramarital liaison nor her second is a very promising source of complimentary comparison, so that the speaker of the *Proemio* (who is not necessarily the real-life Boccaccio) is now in the awkward position of having to modify his comparison between the "nobilissima donna," the object of his own desires, and Criseida, the object desired and won by Troilo and Diomede. This he does by claiming that, of course, he could not hope to enjoy his lady the way Troilo did his: he wrote the work "not because I desire that anyone should believe that I can glory in a like felicity . . . but for this reason have I written it, because when happiness hath been seen by anyone, much better is understood how great and what sort is the misery that followeth after" (p. 127).

Unhappily for the speaker, though, this disclaimer gets him deeper into self-contradictions. In order to avoid an unseemly bluntness he is required to say that he doesn't really hope to get what Troilo got, but few readers of the *Proemio* have been content to take the speaker strictly at his word here, or later when he chastely claims that he drew "from your eyes no less pleasure than Troilo derived from the amorous fruit that fortune granted him . . ." (p. 127). Similarly, if all he wants is the sight of his lady, why praise her discernment and ask her to turn that discernment toward the interpretation of his desires? "And if you are as discerning as I hold you to be, you can from these things understand how great and of what sort are my desires, where they end, and what more than anything else they ask for . . ." (p. 129). One would assume that a discerning lady would not find the interpretation of this writer's great desires a particularly difficult task of textual interpretation. Also, "where they end" and "what they . . . ask for" seem very different from what the speaker claims. The closing lines of the *Proemio* ask that Love "enkindle" in the lady's heart "that desire which alone can be the occasion of my welfare" (p. 131). The tone of the statements about desire is unmistakably sexual, as is the implied analogy between the lady and Criseida, so the disclaimer of hope for a "like felicity" is awkward, unconvincing, and consequently amusing.[22]

There is a further difficulty introduced by the narrator's disclaimer. In saying that he writes the work not because he hopes for a "like felicity" but because people can understand misery only when they see the happiness that goes before, he had adduced an unmistakable if somewhat jarring Boethian echo. In the second book of *The Consolation of Philosophy*, Lady Philosophy is trying to show Boethius that his position on Fortune's wheel is a relative thing. She says, "if you think yourself unfortunate because you have now lost the things which *seemed* to make you happy before, still you should not make yourself miserable, because this sorrow will also pass."[23] Boethius, however, cannot yet accept this, and protests that it is the memory of former happiness—very real happiness to him if only supposed happiness to Lady Philosophy—that makes him sad: ". . . in the midst of adversity, the worst misfortune of all is to have once been happy" (p. 27). Lady Philosophy does not agree that Boethius has really been happy or that he is now desperately unhappy. Rather, she says, "you are being punished for having misjudged your situation" (p. 27). "If," she goes on to counter his complaint, "you are so impressed by this rather silly notion of happiness based on good fortune, let us consider how very well off you are" (pp. 27–28). The point is clearly that Fortune can bring only *supposed* happiness, although real albeit not entirely justified misery. When Boccaccio says he writes the *Filostrato*, a poem about sexual joy followed by separation and misery, in order to show people something about happiness and misery, he is (purposely, I believe) making the same error that the character named Boethius makes: he confuses true happiness with the false happiness (in this case the joy of illicit love) that comes from the gifts of Fortune. Worse, instead of discovering the gifts of Fortune in the persons of a "chaste wife" and "fine sons" (p. 26) as did Boethius, Boccaccio says that he cannot hope to "glory in a like felicity"—that is, in an extramarital love affair—because "fortune never was so kind to me." [24] The whole passage is not a cri de coeur but rather a bit of bookish humor.

Not only is Criseida's easy availability a somewhat indelicate subject for direct comparison, but also her inferior birth (IV, 69) is troublesome if Boccaccio's "nobilissima donna" is assumed to be most noble in birth as well as most noble abstractly. In fact, Boccaccio has, with the story of Troilo and Criseida, chosen a very unsuitable vehicle for the presentation of his grief, and is driven to special pleading for the interpretation of it. Thus, as we have seen, Boccaccio is caught between the horns of a dilemma. He hopes that the lady will understand what "more than anything else" his desires seek, but he dares not draw too many analogies, since the heroine of his story is finally condemned. The narrator is in a desperate predicament, and he knows it. In a hopeless attempt at escape he asks the lady to understand only the nice things about Criseida—beauty, morals, and other praiseworthy things—as applicable to herself, but "as to the other things, which in addition to these are many," she should understand that not one pertains to him but is set down because the story requires it! We could argue that this floundering is the sign of artistic incompetence, but I think that to do so would be a mistake. Rather, we should see Boccaccio creating a love-struck persona so eager to convey his grief (after all, he claims to fear that his anguish is potentially fatal), that he seizes upon the wholly inappropriate story of an inconstant and easily seduced girl, complete with a moral condemning lust, and then dedicates it to his lady of "chaste mind" with a flood of verbal camouflage designed to disguise its unsuitability. The end result is that the *Proemio* emerges not as a love letter nor as a poorly managed literary introduction, but as a witty, cleverly manipulated artifice in which Boccaccio the man presents Boccaccio the literary character as a fervent lover and a consequently bemused poet. With these possibilities for the *Proemio* in mind, let us move on to consider some of the issues of the work as a whole.

The *Filostrato* and Courtly Love

Without doubt one of the areas offering greatest potential for clumsiness in approaching the *Filostrato* is its analysis in terms of courtly love. When Nathaniel Edward Griffin wrote his introduction to his translation of the *Fi-*

lostrato in 1929, he included a twenty-five page essay on the *Filostrato* as a courtly love document, with Boccaccio himself a "past master in the manipulation of a body of conventions." However, only three years later C. S. Lewis was arguing that Chaucer's main object in his redaction of Boccaccio's poem was to bring its teachings more nearly in line with those of courtly love. This longstanding disagreement as to the quantity and quality of courtly love teachings in the *Filostrato* is perhaps not surprising in view of the protean nature of the subject but should stand as a caution against reliance on courtly love as an analytical tool. Even so, as recently as 1964 Vittore Branca, in the introduction to his edition of the poem, called attention to Boccaccio's "omaggio insistente all'ideale arbitro e legislatore della cortesia amorosa, cioè a Andrea Cappellano." [25] One of the weaknesses of appeals to courtly love by way of Andreas Capellanus, its supposed *arbiter amantiarum*, is that Andreas often does not say the things that are accepted as commonplaces of the subject. For example, Meech speaks of humility as among the "virtues that were a man's passport to amour courtois." [26] Yet if we take Andreas as an authority on the subject, humility is nowhere advocated, while its opposite, pride, may be observed frequently in the dialogues of the first book.

Because Branca is more restrained than some critics in his enumeration of points of similarity, influence, or reflection between Boccaccio and Andreas, it is instructive to examine his specific claims. The general drift of Andreas is passed over in silence by Branca, who mentions only precise correspondences. Thus when it is said in *Filostrato* I, 36, that "love disclosed to many bringeth vexation in its train," Branca notes the thirteenth rule of Andreas, "Amor raro consuevit durare vulgatus." [27] In I, 48, Criseida is said "to care for Troilo and for the love he bore her," which Branca says indicates that she obeys rule 14, "facilis perceptio contemptibilem reddit amorem." The previous stanza, describing Troilo's sleeplessness, anxiety, lack of appetite, and pallor, is related to rules 15 and 23, "Minus dormit et edit quem amoris cogitatio vexat," while stanza 46, describing Troilo's desire to please Criseida, is thought to echo rule 25, "Verus amans nil bonum credit nisi quod cogitat coamanti placere." The third part, stanza 38, on the inferiority of riches compared with love, is said to be affirmed by Andreas' tenth rule, "amor semper consuevit ab avaritiae domiciliis exsulare," while part IV, 49, Pandaro's comment that new love "ever driveth away the old" is compared with rule 17, "Novus amor veterem compellit abire."

Perhaps the most obvious barrier to the discovery of insistent homage to Andreas in these notes is that Boccaccio seems to have made specific reference to only a few of the 31 rules listed in Andreas, not to mention the other list of twelve rules and all the precepts that are encompassed without strict codification. Moreover, while this is not the place to enter into a detailed analysis of the meaning of the whole of Andreas' treatise, surely the whole must at least be considered. If we do so we find many points of agreement between the third book and the *Filostrato* that have little to do with the rules of love. Surely Boccaccio's vehemence against fickle women is reminiscent of Andreas' *disuasio* where he says "woman is commonly found to be fickle, too, because no woman ever makes up her mind so firmly on any subject that she will not quickly change it on a little persuading from anyone. A woman is just like melting wax, which is always ready to take a new form and to receive the impress of anybody's seal." [28]

More of a direct objection, though, is that several of the illustrations Branca gives do not fit very well. For example, rule 13, which says that love made public seldom endures, is not precisely the same as *Filostrato* I, 36, where it is maintained that love disclosed brings vexation rather than termination.[29] Similarly, the idea of Andreas' rule 14 that the easy attainment of love makes it of little value does not accord very well with *Filostrato* I, 48, where it is said only that Criseida did not seem to care for Troilo. As for Pandaro's assertion in IV, 49, that the new love ever drives away the old, it is true that the statement is in perfect accord with rule 17, but we should remember that the protagonist of the poem rejects utterly Pandaro's thoughts: "The gods send me death before I commit such a sin." Even so seemingly straightforward a connection as between rules 15 and 23 and Troilo's eating and sleeping but little because of love is somewhat undermined by his identical behavior when suffering from sorrow rather than love (VII, 19, 21).

The most interesting of imperfect connections between the two works is that between rule 10 and *Filostrato* IV, 49. Branca notes that Boccaccio was insistent throughout his writings in his disdain for avarice, and Andreas' rule 10 says that love is a stranger in the home of avarice. However, in Andreas' other set of rules, the list of twelve, the first rule is stated in such a way as to give us more insight into Andreas' meaning: "Thou shalt," he writes, "avoid avarice like the deadly pestilence and shalt embrace its opposite" (81). It is the embracing of the opposite that is dangerous, for as Andreas points out in his third book, "From love comes hateful poverty, and one comes to the prison of penury. For love inevitably forces a man to give without regard to what he should give and what he should not; and this is not generosity, but what ancient common sense calls prodigality, a vice which sacred Scripture teaches us is a mortal one." [30] "Generosity" is the "Catch-22" of medieval arguments on love, for the lover must always be generous yet never grow poor. Since this cannot be, medieval authors showed the absurdity to point up the moral. For example, in the garden in the *Romance of the Rose* Wealth is shown guarding the door, Poverty the exit, and *Fole Largesce* ruling within. Even if we overlook the presumed joke involved with Andreas' "rule" about avarice, the stanza in Boccaccio is at best an imperfect match. While the "rule" requires one to be prodigal, Boccaccio's stanza says that love gives more pleasure to lovers than money does to the avaricious. As a final note, we should remember that while Boccaccio shows Troilo spending money (II, 84) and disdaining avarice (III, 93), he also shows him disdaining power, wealth, arms, horses, dogs, birds, wild beasts, the studies of Pallas, and the feats of Mars (III, 88). In other words, Troilo is as quick to forego wisdom and valor as he is avarice, a fact that may be taken as a tacit comment on the value of Troilo's love.

Precise correspondences, then, between the rules of Andreas and Boccaccio's poem are very hard to come by. Moreover, it is as easy to discover "violations" of the rules as adherence to them. For example, Criseida's often-noted sensual abandon is hard to square with rule 8 of the short list, enjoining modesty. Moreover, rule 11 in the long list and rule 4 in the short one say that one should not love anyone whom a natural sense of shame forbids one to marry; yet Troilo himself admits that Criseida's low birth makes her an unlikely marriage partner for him (IV, 69). Rule 2 of the long list, which maintains that love cannot exist without jealousy, is not discoverable in the *Filostrato*. The love between Troilo and Criseida flourishes very well without jealousy before Criseida's departure; yet Troilo's jealousy of Diomede can scarcely be said to stimulate his love. When he discovers Criseida's affair, he calls on Jove to "put an end to her in whose bosom are lies and deceits and betrayals and deem her ever more unworthy of pardon" (VIII, 18).

It would be easy enough to multiply instances of divergences between Boccaccio's *Filostrato* and Andreas' *Ars honeste amandi*, but the point has been sufficiently made. There is no doubt that Andreas influenced Boccaccio, but both the nature and extent of that influence need investigation that will take into account the contexts of the resemblances. The recollections of Andreas can be observed on the surface of the text, but their meaning requires a deeper look.

Biblical Echoes

Perhaps the most easily recognized bit of humor in the *Proemio* is Boccaccio's amusing exploitation of scripture. Because his "nobilissima donna" has departed for Sannio from Naples, Boccaccio styles himself as smitten with grief, wandering the streets of the city, and repeating "that verse of Jeremiah: 'O how solitary abideth the city that before was full of people and a mistress among the nations!'" (pp. 119–21). Surely Boccaccio's readers would have been amused at the inappropriate comparison of the "dilettevole città di Napoli" to the empty Jerusalem. Naples had lost but one donna, Jerusalem had lost thousands into slavery; Naples remained the same, Jerusalem was held captive by the Babylonians. A young lover temporarily deprived of the sight of his lady is no Jeremiah. However, Boccaccio does not wish to denigrate scripture but rather through overamplification to show how ridiculous and extravagant are the actions of his persona.

Doubtless the inspiration for this inapposite citation of the prophet came from Dante, who used the same kind of joke twice in the *Vita Nuova*. Early in that work, when the first of the ladies he used as a screen for his love for Beatrice had departed for another city, Dante expressed his grief by paraphrasing Jeremiah's Lamentations 1:12, "O vos omnes qui transitis per viam, attendite et videte si est dolor sicut meus." This cry of the stricken Jerusalem for pity is taken by the self-centered young lover of the *Vita Nuova*, who is lamenting not the departure of his loved one, but only of his screen lady, and is paraphrased "o voi che per la via d'Amor passate, / attende e guardate / s'elli e dolore alcun, quant 'l mio grave." [31] Surely Dante's intention here is to show the self-indulgent young lover at his worst. The second time Jeremiah is quoted in the *Vita Nuova* is much more difficult to assess. If we agree with Musa that Dante the young lover does not, in the period of time covered by the treatise, come to understand Beatrice truly—that understanding belonging to the more mature Dante the author, who writes, he tells us, a "commentary on the book of memory"—then the later quotation may also be ironic. When Beatrice dies, the young lover is understandably bereaved, and, he tells us, "poi che fue partita da questa secolo, rimase tutta la sopraditta cittade [Florence] quasi vedova dispogliata da ogni dignitade; onde io, ancora lagrimando in questa desolata cittade, scrissi a li principi de la terra alquanto de la sua condizione, pighando quello cominciamento di Geremia profeta che dice: Quomodo sedet sola civitas." [32] Insofar as Beatrice is allegorically a miraculous representation of the Trinity, then her death might appropriately be broadcast to all the princes of the earth in terms of the lamentation of Jeremiah. But insofar as the young lover still thinks of her as a lady of Florence, it is excessive.

Boccaccio's use of Jeremiah is more boldly inapposite in all respects than Dante's. He is not concerned with death or with a lady who serves as a screen for his real interests. Rather he is talking about a lady whose "chaste" mind he hopes to move to be less chaste. As Robert Hollander has observed (in a note to me), Boccaccio may be imitating Dante only to underscore the silliness of his speaker, whose goal in the New Life is to be an Old Man! Not only is the literal meaning of the first verse of Lamentations grotesquely inappropriate to express Boccaccio's feelings, but the spiritual interpretation of the verse gives us a meaning that reflects even more unfavorably on the eager lover of the *Proemio*. Rabanus Maurus explicated the verse in terms of the soul of a faithful man. The faithful man, like Jerusalem, was once full of virtues, but he is now dominated by the concupiscence of the flesh, kindling the flame of the libido.[33] The young lover who compares Naples to Jerusalem, then, might better see himself as being empty not of people but of virtues.

Immediately following the quotation from Lamentations, Boccaccio introduces what may be an equally jarring echo of the Psalms. With reference to his eyes, which have been denied the vision of his lady, he says, "I will not indeed say that everything hath made them sad to an equal degree, but I do affirm that there is but one direction that somewhat qualifieth their sadness, and that is when they survey those countries, those mountains, that part of the heavens among which and under which I am persuaded that you are." The idea that the eyes are turned to the mountains or the heavens in order to benefit the observer seems a deliberate recollection of Psalm 120 (121), "Levavi oculos meos in montes, unde veniet auxilium mihi," and Psalm 122 (123), "Ad te levavi oculos meos, qui habitas in caelis." The difference, of course, residing in that for the Psalmist it is God who inhabits the heavens, and his "auxilium" comes "a domino," not from a donna.[34] We need not imagine some phenomenon like the sometimes posited "religion of love" to account for the extravagant use of Psalmistic phraseology here. Rather we can see in the grandiloquent address of the narrator to his donna a foreshadowing of the plangent apostrophes of Troilo in the narrative that follows. The religious borrowings, both direct and echoic, are there not to illustrate fact (a religion of love), or to satirize religion, but to underscore the power of love to dominate the lover and to serve as a kind of debased religion.

Not only does the narrator use scriptural allusions that make his amorous state more meaningful to him (if more ridiculous to the reader), but also the characters in the poem allude to Scripture with much the same effect. Criseida, for example, when debating whether or not she should go ahead with the proposed affair with Troilo, turns to Proverbs 9:13–18 for a justification of her actions by an analogy with the stolen waters of the proverb: "'Water acquired by stealth is sweeter far than wine had in abundance. So the joy of love, when hidden, ever surpasseth that of the husband held perpetually in arms. Therefore with zest receive the sweet lover . . .'" (II, 74). Now it is true that the Bible emphasizes the sweetness of stolen water, but certainly not to encourage lechery. On the contrary, the image of stolen water is used as a symbol of that which is outwardly sweet but inwardly corrupting. In the seventh through ninth chapters of Proverbs, Wisdom is styled as a woman who has built a house with seven pillars, who has set out a feast with wine, and sent out her handmaidens to invite those needing wisdom to eat the bread and drink the wine. Her enemy is another woman, attired like a harlot, who also seeks those without wisdom, but to ensnare rather than to enlighten them. The latter woman lures men to her perfumed bed with flattery, and many go like the ox to the slaughter. Whereas Wisdom says "Come, eat of my bread, and drink of the wine which I have mingled" (9:5), the "foolish woman" says "stolen waters are sweet, and bread eaten in secret is pleasant" (9:17), but as the Psalmist observes, the man who responds "knoweth not that the dead are there; and that her guests are in the depths of hell" (9:18). Criseida, therefore, in misusing Proverbs, is tacitly compared with the foolish woman, the harlot who opposes Wisdom.

The last biblical echo that deserves mention occurs in *Filostrato* III, 86.

Troilo, having spent the night with Criseida, utters a hymn to Venus, and then proclaims his inability to praise his lady satisfactorily:

If there were an hundred tongues in my mouth and each were vocal, and if I had the cunning of every poet in my breast, I should never be able to express her true virtues, her lofty gentleness, and her abundant courtesy.

〜〜〜   〜〜〜   〜〜〜

> Se cento lingue, e ciascuna parlante,
> Nella mia bocca fossero, e 'l sapere
> Nel petto avessi d'ogni poetante,
> Esprimer non potrei le virtù vere,
> L'alta piacevolezza e l'abbondante
> Sua cortesia.

This extravagant inability *topos* is funny first of all for its prime image. A hundred tongues in one mouth would not assist but impede the young man in his attempt at praise. Secondly, we find here a juggling of some ideas that may come from the first verse of the thirteenth chapter of I Corinthians, where St. Paul uses an inability *topos* for somewhat different purposes. Paul says that even if he could speak with the tongues of men and angels and had the knowledge of the prophets, he would be nothing without charity. The tongues of men and angels become a hundred tongues in one mouth, the prophets become the poets, and instead of the superiority of charity, we are directed by Troilo to the supposed virtue, pleasantness, and courtesy of his lady. The similarities are sufficient to recall the biblical analogue to mind, the differences more than enough to make us smile. St. Paul felt obliged to emphasize the importance of charity to the Corinthians because they had been jealous of each other's spiritual gifts. These, he points out, are nothing without charity. Troilo, on the other hand, is not concerned with speaking in tongues and prophesying—gifts of the spirit—but with praising the virtue and courtesy of the lady he has recently seduced. Hence his metaphor uses physical tongues and the writings of the poets, and finds that even they are insufficient to praise what appears to him to be virtue. If we remember that there was fornication among the Corinthians, then the significance of Troilo's appropriation of Paul's imagery is further enhanced.[35]

Hercules

Before we examine the progress of the love affair itself, there is one other literary allusion worth our inspection. In the same section of the third part of the *Filostrato* in which Troilo is rhapsodizing about Venus, he recalls his former opposition to love so strikingly in contrast to his current servitude. Lest anyone comment unfavorably on this, he calls on the example of Hercules:

"Let the strong Hercules in this be my strong defense, for he could not shield himself from love, for which every wise man commendeth him. And he who doth not wish to involve himself in falsehood shall never say that what was once becoming to Hercules is unseemly for me" (III, 80). This little *apologia pro vita sua* probably makes a better impression on a modern reader than it would have on a medieval, for while the modern Hercules merely represents strength in a kind of general way, the medieval Hercules could symbolize many things, depending on which aspect of his career was referred to. And Hercules in love is Hercules at his weakest. Chaucer, in the *Knight's Tale*, portrayed on the walls of the Temple of Venus all those who were caught in Venus' "las" causing them to cry "allas." Hercules is there, following, in Chaucer's description, the "folye" of King Solomon. In other words, an appeal by a lover to the figure of Hercules-as-lover is not a valid justification for the "wisdom" of yielding to love. We can, however, come even closer to Boccaccio's probable meaning in this passage. Chaucer based his *Knight's Tale* on Boccaccio's *Teseida*, a work composed about the same time as his *Filostrato*. Moreover, Boccaccio wrote a series of notes (*Chiose*) for it, and in them he tells us something of Hercules the lover. The incident Boccaccio has in mind to justify the inclusion of Hercules in Venus' Temple is Hercules' infatuation with Iole. She, wishing to demonstrate her power over the strong Hercules, makes him discard his lion skin in favor of a purple garment, has him comb his hair, wear a ring on his finger, and, finally, she sets him to spin. In short, she turns Hercules into a woman, and Boccaccio did not intend by this to show the civilizing power of the spinning wheel, but the ultimately feminizing reduction of lust.[36] Certainly it is lust and nothing else that brings Hercules to this ignominy, for this whole section of the *Chiose* on the Temple of Venus is prefaced with a distinction between the good Venus, who symbolizes matrimony and who is not the subject of the poem, and the other Venus, who is the goddess of every lascivious thing desired. The evidence strongly suggests that Boccaccio's meaning in having Troilo call upon Hercules is neither to vindicate Troilo's action nor to magnify the power of sexual attraction, but rather to illustrate the befuddlement of Troilo in his rapture, wherein he tries to justify his carnality by an appeal to the exploits of Hercules, whom, he says, every wise man praises. Every wise man does not.

The *Filostrato* and Dante's *Sacro Poema*

Because Boccaccio's *Filostrato* is ostensibly a poem in praise of extramarital love, a phenomenon universally regarded as a sin in the Middle Ages, it is astonishing to discover literally scores of quotations, borrowings, echoes, and parallels of Dante's "sacro poema," the *Commedia*, in such an unlikely setting. Even if we disregard the vast majority of the parallels listed by Branca in the notes to his edition as accidental, coincidental, or stemming from a common source, it seems impossible to rule out all, and it is very difficult to explain the significance of the borrowings that remain. Branca notes that one of the parallels seems "quasi deformata eco grottesca," but does not attempt to explain why Boccaccio might want to use such an echo when and where he does.[37] Similarly Carlo Muscetta remarks of one of the quotations from Dante that "il sacro poema dantesca è utilizzata per l'erotica commedia," but does not explore the precise nature of the utilization.[38]

If we accept, as I think we must, that Boccaccio at times intentionally borrows from Dante's *Commedia* for his *Filostrato*, then it seems logical enough to assume that these borrowings were intended to serve some function in the poem, either to underscore the "sacred" nature of the seduction of Criseida, or, as seems much more likely, to create humor through the use of incongruity. This sort of thing is not uncommon in medieval literature: in its broadest form, for example, Chaucer has January in the *Merchant's Tale* use the language of Canticles to address his wife, but the disparity in their ages and the literal application of the borrowing from Scripture combine to create a kind of uneasy humor. Chaucer also draws upon Canticles for some of Absolon's lines in the *Miller's Tale*, where Absolon's adulterous intentions and priggish personality are at comic variance with both the literal and figurative meaning of the biblical story.[39] Indeed, in one of his additions to Boccaccio's *Filostrato*, Chaucer borrows St. Bernard's prayer to the Virgin from the thirty-third canto of the *Paradiso* and puts it most incongruously indeed into Troilus' encomium of the "heaven" of Criseyde's person.[40] Boccaccio may have had something similar in mind in the *Filostrato*'s corresponding hymn to Love, wherein Troilo addresses Venus as "O luce eterna" (III, 74), which Boccaccio uses in his sonnets as a metaphor for the Virgin.[41] If in fact it is a traditional metaphor, Boccaccio's employment of it in these unvirginal circumstances may well have been designed for humorous effect.

Several of Boccaccio's uses of the *Commedia* are arresting enough to invite this sort of interpretation. For example, in *Filostrato* II, 72, the line "Non odi tu la pieta del suo pianto" ("Hearest thou not the pitifulness of his plaint?") is word for word the same as *Inferno* II, 106. The circumstances, though, are considerably different. In the *Filostrato* Criseida is debating with herself whether or not to love Troilo. When she asks herself whether she does not hear the pitiful plaint of Troilo, we must remember why Troilo is sad and what it is that will make him happy. In the *Inferno*, on the other hand, the line belongs to St. Lucy, who, at the bidding of the Virgin, tells Beatrice of Dante's plight at the outset of his journey (having lost the way in the Dark Wood). When Lucy asks Beatrice if she does not hear the pitifulness of Dante's plaint, it is one of the first steps in the operation of Grace, which will eventually lead Dante to the Beatific Vision. Criseida, so unlike Beatrice, will nevertheless also listen to the plaint of someone who loves her. But it will all lead elsewhere than the sight of God.

Just six stanzas beyond this spot in the *Filostrato* occurs another quotation from the second canto of the *Inferno*, and this one too seems chosen for its very incongruity. While Criseida is debating the proposition in her mind, Pandaro is satisfied of her ultimate acquiescence, and goes to hold out some promise to Troilo. His hopeful speech causes the dejected Troilo to bloom like a flower in the morning sun.

> Quali i fioretti dal notturno gelo
>   Chinati e chiusi, poi che 'l sol gl'imbianca
> Tutti s'apron diritti in loro stelo;
> Cotal si fe' di sua virtude stanca
> Troilo allora, e riguardando il cielo,
> Incominiciò come persona franca:
> Lodato sia il tuo sommo valore,
> Venere bella, e del tuo figlio Amore.   [II, 80]

As little flowers, bowed and closed by the chill of night, when whitened by the sun, open all and straighten upon their stems, so at that moment did Troilo recover from his weary spirits, and glancing heavenward began as one enfranchised, [I would translate "set free."—C. W.] "Praised be thy supreme power, fair Venus, and that of thy son Love."

Troilo, hearing that his "gran disire" is in "gran parte" already accomplished, warms up quickly enough and praises Venus and her son Love. Dante, in the second canto of the *Inferno*, is also dejected, but suffers from fear rather than from love-longing. The awesome journey that Vergil proposes leads Dante to reflect about his own insignificance, and he deprecatingly muses that he is neither Paul nor Aeneas, and perhaps should not attempt the pilgrimage. Vergil then tells him of the complicated operations of Grace that resulted in Beatrice's sending him as Guide, and it is the knowledge of this divine inspiration that revives Dante. Thus the pilgrim's fear is overcome by divinely inspired courage, which compares almost ludicrously with Troilo's lovelorn vicissitudes. Nor does Pandaro make much of a substitute for Vergil. Note too, that whereas Troilo closed his speech by praising Venus and Love, Dante closes by praising Beatrice and Vergil. Yet for all these profound differences, the actual wording of the two passages is so close as to leave little room to imagine anything other than that Boccaccio is deliberately copying Dante.

> Quali fioretti dal notturno gelo
>   chinati e chiusi, poi che 'l sol li 'mbianca,

si drizzan tutti aperti in loro stelo,
tal mi fec' io di mia virtude stanca,
e tanto buono ardire al cor mi corse,
ch'i' cominciai come persona franca:
"Oh pietosa colei che mi soccorse!
e te cortese ch'ubidisti tosto
a le vere parole che ti porse!"   [*Inf.* II, 127–35]

ᜠᜠᜠ ᜠᜠᜠ ᜠᜠᜠ

As little flowers, bent down and closed by chill of night, straighten and all unfold upon their stems when the sun brightens them, such in my faint strength did I become; and so much good courage rushed to my heart that I began, as one set free, "Oh, how compassionate was she who helped me, and how courteous were you, so quick to obey the true words she spoke to you!"[42]

The curious persistence of echoes of the second canto of the *Inferno* in the second part of the *Filostrato* may be significant itself, but the significance of the whole will have to await a better understanding of the meaning of the parts. In any case, there is a third parallel, albeit less precise than the others examined here, to be found between stanza 105 of part two of the *Filostrato* and *Inferno* II, 36. Troilo is writing to Criseida at Pandaro's suggestion, urging her to give his "painful affliction surcease" through her "tender ministrations" (II, 101). In the course of his appeal he notes that in her wisdom she will understand that if he does not speak adequately it is because he is not by nature a talker: "Or tu se' savia, s' io non dico appieno. / Intenderai assai me' ch' io non ragiono." By the same token, he continues, he hopes that her acts will be "migliori" and "maggiori," better and greater, than he deserves. There is a fairly close precedent for the idea and some of the wording in Dante's line, "'se' savio; intendi me' ch'i' non ragiono.'" The differences between the speakers, the persons they address, and their intentions, though, is considerable. Dante is the speaker of the line in the *Inferno*, and he is again telling Vergil of his fears about the journey. Thus the pilgrim Dante (not the real-life Dante) truly has difficulty in speaking, but because of doubt and fear rather than love-longing. The adjective "savio" of course fits Vergil, the representative of the rational life, somewhat better than "savia" fits the rather superficial Criseida—a woman who unwisely yields to Pandaro's urgings to take a lover while she is still young and beautiful. And, finally, the concerns of the two speakers are almost diametrically opposed. Dante, for all his self-doubt, ultimately seeks the right way, the way he lost in the Dark Wood. Troilo is lost too, in a sense, but does not realize it, and what he seeks is pleasure.

In addition to the several echoes of the *Inferno* already discussed, Boccaccio also borrows in provocative ways from the *Purgatorio*. One such instance may be found in Boccaccio's use of the proverbial idea that the wiser a person is the more he will be displeased at losing time. While proverbial utterances are hard to pin down to one specific source, nevertheless the wording by these two authors is almost identical. Boccaccio's rendering is "che 'l perder tempo a chi più sa più spiace" (II, 135), while Dante's is "ché perder tempo a chi più sa più spiace" (*Purg.* III, 78). The circumstances in which the proverb is uttered, however, could not be more different. Pandaro is using this argument to urge Criseida to embark on her affair with Troilo, although she is still protesting that all she will do is to love him like a brother, whereas in Dante's *Purgatorio* the proverb is uttered by Vergil on the first terrace of the "ante-purgatorio" as he eagerly inquires the way up the slope. Both Pandaro and Vergil are guides, although Vergil must ask the way, yet the goals of their shepherding are in opposite directions. This "deformed, grotesque echo," as Branca has called it, is accurate enough in form, but grotesque in its different meaning.

The last of the parallels that is sufficiently striking to attract our attention is in the eighth part of the *Filostrato* and has to do with God's justice. Troilo has suspected the absent Criseida of having found a new lover, and when the gold brooch he gave Criseida is brought back by Deifebo on a garment snatched from the wounded Diomede, Troilo knows his suspicions are confirmed. In his rage he curses her treacherous lying, vows to kill her new lover, Diomede, if he can, and asks Jove why he has not killed Criseida with a thunderbolt. It is into this questioning of Jove that Boccaccio inserts Dante's questioning of divine justice. Troilo asks:

> O sommo Giove, in cui certo riparo
> So c' ha ragione, e da cui tutta inizia
> L' alta virtù per cui si vive e muove,
> Son li giusti occhi tuoi rivolti altrove?   [VIII, 17]

O highest Jove, in whom I know that justice hath a sure refuge and in whom beginneth entirely the noble virtue by which men live and move, are thy just eyes cast elsewhere?

Dante is also concerned about where God's eyes are cast, but he is not threatening to murder a former lover. Rather, he asks in a much more rhetorical, less literal and emotional way, whether God's justice has missed punishing the internecine strife of the Italian cities.

> E se licito m'è, o sommo Giove
> che fosti in terra per noi crucifisso,
> son li giusti occhi tuoi rivolti altrove?
> [*Purg.* VI, 118–20]

And if it be lawful for me, O Jove supreme that on earth wast crucified for us, are Thy just eyes turned elsewhere . . . ?

Dante, though, is not really doubting or questioning God's providential order. In the very next verse he continues, in a rhetorical way, to ask whether, on the other hand, God has not some plan that is not visible to human eyes. As with the other parallels, the verbal similarities are strong, while the meanings are markedly opposed. Troilo's wrath, after all, is a sin, and his assumption that Criseida has violated some universal law by taking a new lover shows that he is still oblivious to the essentially illicit nature of their affair. What Criseida has vowed to be faithful to is a relationship condemned by the professed morality of the Middle Ages, so that breaking such a vow is substantially different from breaking, say, a marriage vow. While Dante is overtly using "sommo Giove" for the Christian God, Troilo's Jove functions much the same way even if we assume a more or less pagan background, for surely Boccaccio has inserted the lines from Dante in order to underscore the Christian idea of divine justice as normally understood in the Middle Ages. Even were we to divorce Troilo's speech entirely from medieval contexts we should have to ask why he wants to see Criseida killed by some sort of higher power.

The analysis of these borrowings from Dante must be tentative until we know more about the meaning of the several works that comprise the early period of Boccaccio's writings. In the meanwhile, it behooves us at least to ask why Boccaccio borrowed from the "sacro poema" for his erotic comedy. What I have argued is that the borrowings for the most part heighten the comedy.

The *Alto Appetito*

The precise nature of the love affair in the *Filostrato* is more clearly delineated than it is in Chaucer's *Troilus*, and it behooves us to examine it with some care, both for its own sake and for what light it may shed on Chaucer's poem. Boccaccio's work has often been called "cynical," and in a sense one must agree, for the principals of the action seem to agree on the immorality of the seduction of Criseida but do it anyway. The import of this cynicism of the *characters*, however, need not necessarily be imputed to Boccaccio as well.

In the second part of the *Filostrato*, Troilo admits his love for Criseida to Pandaro, but not without some scruple, since she is Pandaro's cousin. Although Pandaro has asked him to name the lady he loves, Troilo says there is an honorable reason ("cagione assai onesta") for his reluctance to name the lady: she is a relative of Pandaro's (II, 15). What we must assume from Troilo's concern for honor is that what he has in mind he considers to be dishonorable. He is considerably embarrassed by this particular object of love, and says to Pandaro that love does not decree that man love lawfully ("per legge"), from which we must assume that right from the start he considers his interest in Criseida to be unlawful as well as dishonorable (II, 19). He has already protested that he would rather be dead than be in the situation to which love has driven him (II, 19), but now he tries unsuccessfully to defend his own love by appealing to, of all things, incest. We are not to suppose that Boccaccio imagines the love of Pandaro's cousin to be sufficiently consanguineous as to constitute incest, since there is no evidence that Troilo is related to her at all. Rather, Boccaccio shows the irrational attempt at self-justification Troilo grasps at. "'Others, as thou knowest, are wont to love their sisters, and sisters their brothers, and daughters sometimes their fathers, and fathers-in-law their daughters-in-law, and even, as is wont at times to happen, stepmothers their stepsons'" (II, 20).

Pandaro is not upset by Troilo's guilty admission. He knows what honesty is, knows that Criseida has it, but sees it only as an inconvenient impediment to the accomplishment of Troilo's dishonest designs. Criseida has "'Only one trait, somewhat troublesome to thee, . . . that she is more virtuous than other ladies, ["è più che altra donna onesta"] and holdeth matters of love more in contempt'" (II, 23). However, Pandaro counts on his "parolette" to find a way around her morality. So much for "onesta": it is only "'una cosa alquanto a te molesta.'" Pandaro develops this line of thought in a subsequent stanza. He is well aware that a worthy lady ought not to become a lover ("'non convenirse a donna valorosa / Sì fatti amori . . .'"), and knows that there would be some backlash if it became known that through their folly ("'per follia di noi'") this worthy lady, who had once been honest ("'dove esser solea / Onor'"), were to turn from honor, honesty, and worthiness to love. It is at this juncture that Pandaro interjects his praise of the "alto appetito," previously discussed. Although he has spent several stanzas agreeing with Troilo that the particular kind of love they are discussing is not virtuous, is dishonorable, and so forth, Pandaro nevertheless now argues that if desire is checked in its action and everything kept secret, then every lover can follow "'il suo alto appetito'" without "'causing any shame to those to whom shame and honor are matters of concern'" (II, 26). This facile vindication of lovers' appetites does not in fact answer either of the objections to love that Pandaro himself had raised in the previous stanzas. Secrecy may prevent others from scorning the corrupters, but what of the corrupted themselves? Or is it to be assumed that after becoming a lover, the "donna valorosa" would no longer trouble herself with the issue of "onesta"? Pandaro knows that a worthy lady should not become a lover, and that should she so become, then the report of his and Troilo's involvement could redound to their and her discredit, but neither problem is really answered by Pandaro's urging of secrecy. Her honesty is still compromised, and if others do not scorn them they still have their own consciences to deal with. Pandaro's caveat that in addition to secrecy desire should be checked in its action seems a vain hope in view of the whole nature of the love affair that is being proposed.

Were we to accept the autobiographical approach to the *Filostrato*, Criseida's initial reluctance yet rapid acquiescence could be explained by imagining Boccaccio's drawing Maria d'Aquino first as she was and then as he would like her to be. Without this convenient explanation, however, we are required to look elsewhere for an interpretation. It would seem that Criseida's acting so swiftly against her own judgment underscores the power of love to prevail over reason, and that in presenting this phenomenon, Boccaccio is in fact warning against it. Criseida's question, who has any right to every pleasure, "piacere intero" (II, 45), of her without first becoming her husband, is significantly left unanswered, although it raises an issue both logical and plausible in a medieval context. We need not summon up sops to Christianity to account for Criseida's question here, or for her distress a few stanzas later when she wonders what others might do when her blood relation counsels her to have an affair. Since the protection of widows was one of the touchstones of knighthood all over Europe in the Middle Ages, the exploitation of a widow by her cousin must have been correspondingly shocking. What is most disturbing about this section of the poem is that Criseida's very real objections to the affair—she is not married, Pandaro should protect, not encourage her, and these affairs are evanescent ("'love changing as thought changeth'" [II, 50])—are dismissed without refutation when Pandaro summons up the old bromide of age withering unused beauty. "'Alas,'" says Criseida "'thou speakest the truth. Thus do the years little by little bear us forward. . . . But let us now stop thinking of this, and tell me whether I may still have solace and joy of love . . .'" (II, 55). Criseida never looks back after this, and her concern that "piacere intero" should only be enjoyed by her husband is ironically counterpointed in the fourth part, when Troilo admits to Pandaro that he thought of asking for her in marriage, but knew that his father would declare that she was not of a sufficiently high station but was "diseguale" (IV, 69).[43] Thus marriage, instituted by the church precisely in order to deal with burning desires like those of Troilo and Criseida—for, Paul said, it is better to marry than to burn—is forgotten by one of the principals and discarded by the other because of a cold assessment of the situation. The "alto appetito" turns out to be the familiar appetite of carnality, decorated with words by Pandaro, who knows he cannot change its unattractive substance.

Persons and Images

Criseida's easy rejection of her own caveats, her susceptibility to others' arguments, her willingness to gather roses while they bloom, have been remarked upon more than once. She is an easily seduced woman, all things considered, and although the same pliancy is the cause of both her affair with Troilo and her later trifling with Diomede, critics have tended to praise her first affair and condemn her second. However, her unreasonable abandonment of her own arguments before her episode with Troilo does not seem calculated to win the reader's sympathy. Criseida is not a very nice person in this poem, and Troilo's chilly assessment of her birth does not endear him to us either. The excesses of both his passion and his grief may have been intended for our instruction rather than our delight. Among the principal characters, then, only Pandaro is left for our sympathy. However, he not only gives his cousin immoral encouragement, but lies to her as a matter of course.

For example, early in the second part of the poem, the narrator tells us that Troilo was alone in his room, engaged in thought, when Pandaro happened by, and little by little Troilo's story of his passion for Pandaro's cousin emerged. However, Pandaro fabricates an entirely different version for Criseida's benefit. " 'The day before yesterday, while things were quiet because of the truce then made, Troilo desired that I should go with him for amusement through the shady woods. When we were seated there, he began to talk with me of love and then to sing to himself' " (II, 56). The changes are not so important for their substance as for the gratuitous way in which they are introduced. Pandaro has perhaps little to gain by styling himself as an intimate of Troilo's in affairs of the heart right from the start, but whatever advantage there may be, he wants to have, the more expeditiously to arrange his cousin's seduction.

While Pandaro lies to Criseida, he offers scant consolation to Troilo. When Pandaro has learned that Troilo's sadness is caused by love, he volunteers his assistance, but Troilo observes that since Pandaro himself has been sorrowful from love, it is doubtful that he can bring joy in love to another (II, 9). Pandaro immediately responds with three proverbs to support his case: the man who cannot protect himself from poison can often safeguard another, the one-eyed (or myopic) man can walk where the man of full vision falters, and although a man does not take good counsel, he can give it (II, 10). The last of these is a version of the still-current admonition to do as a man says rather than as he does, but the previous two are very dubious. Are we really to believe that the man who does not know how to guard himself knows how to guard others? And do we accept on mythical if not medical grounds the idea that the man with poor sight can guide the man with perfect vision? Surely not. Chaucer saw the potential for humor in these lines, and broadened the tone somewhat to make the whole thing even more ridiculous. In Chaucer, the blind rather than half-blind man is said to guide, and a fool counsels the wise man. Even if one argues that some of these ideas are proverbial, they are used for a bad end. Pandaro turns out to be an effective guide, to be sure, but not a good one. For his friend he brings physical joy in love but ultimate sorrow, and for his cousin he traduces any sense of familial love to encourage her seduction. When Pandaro tells Troilo that for his sake he has cast his honor to the ground and corrupted his sister (III, 6), we are not meant to admire the depth of his friendship but rather to wonder that Troilo silently concurs in this corruption only to sing the praises of Venus as the goddess who expels "viltà" (III, 77).[44]

Some of the imagery used to describe Troilo in the course of his passionate attachment can be examined with profit, for the contrasts involved may have been intended by Boccaccio to outline the disturbingly erratic course the lover often follows. Boethius speaks, in Chaucer's translation of his *Consolation of Philosophy*, of the "maladye of perturbacion" (Bk. I, pr. 6), which is well illustrated by Troilo's emotional vicissitudes. For example, when Pandaro informs Troilo that Criseida will soon be his, Troilo's rapture is described in terms of the burgeoning of spring: "And just as the fresh spring suddenly reclotheth with leaves and with flowerlets the shrubs that were bare in the severe season, and maketh them beautiful, revesteth the meadows and hills and every river bank with grass and with beautiful fresh flowers, just so did Troilus, full at once of new joy, smile with calm visage" (III, 12). Then, just as the seasons change, Troilo's fortunes change, and when the news is brought to him that Criseida is to go to the Greek camp, an image of flowers is again used to describe Troilo: "Ev'n as the lily, after it hath been turned up in the fields by the plough, droopeth and withereth from too much sun and its bright color changeth and groweth pale, so at the message brought to the Greeks by the council . . . did Troilo 'neath so great load of harm and peril fall in a swoon . . ." (IV, 18). Flower imagery is employed to describe both the joy and the grief of Troilo, thus reminding us that there are the two sides to the same coin of love.

A similar variation is encountered in the animal imagery associated with Troilo. In part three he "went fowling, holding falcons, gerfalcons, and eagles. And sometimes he hunted with dogs, pursuing bears, boars, and great lions. All small prey he disdained" (III, 91). Nevertheless, in part four he neither hunts imposing animals nor disdains the small ones; rather he himself behaves like an animal in its death throes. "Not otherwise doth the bull go leaping, now here now there, when once he hath received the mortal thrust, and bellowing in his misery maketh known the pain he hath conceived, than did Troilo, casting himself prone, and in a frenzy beating his head against the wall . . ." (IV, 27). Finally, in VII, 80, Troilo the erstwhile hunter, later a mad bull, is now envisioned as a raging lion, hating the Greeks. There is not much imagery of any kind in the *Filostrato*; hence these few, clearly linked images should command our attention. The interpretation of their significance seems straightforward enough. It is the same passion that brings joy and despair; consequently one should treat it with cautious respect. That

133,852

College of St. Francis Library
Joliet, Illinois

Troilo is inconsistent in singing the praises of life-giving Jove, whose earthly deeds are inspired by Venus (III, 76), then later in condemning "cruel Jove" along with Fortune (IV, 121), is no reason the reader should similarly err.

One of the more astounding exchanges in the *Filostrato* occurs when the two lovers, lying in bed, the better to think, are discussing their predicament now that Criseida must leave. Troilo has proposed that they run away together, but Criseida, addressing him somewhat inappropriately as "marito" (IV, 146), fears for his reputation for valor and hers for honesty and chastity! This insistence on the appearance and not the reality of things, on her presumed reputation (we hear of her honesty only from Pandaro and herself) rather than on her actual deeds, points up the hopelessly superficial nature of her thinking. Her status as an unchaste widow is real enough; her status as a paragon of honesty, if real, is illusory. Yet she would sacrifice the real, which she entered into knowingly and without much hesitation, for the deceitful continuance of renown. Note too, that this lack of chastity, which has inspired Troilo to lengthy utterances in praise of Venus and her beneficence, emerges now as meaning less to Criseida than her reputation for honesty, something Pandaro saw as an inconvenience, and which has troubled the principals not at all. In a sense, Troilo and Criseida are in a dilemma of their own making, not altogether unforeseen by either, and characteristic of the problems generated by passion outside of marriage.

A message of this sort was probably on Boccaccio's mind when he had Criseida reject flight, which would bring the relationship into the open, on the grounds that passion flourishes when it is sporadic and secret, the one adding spice, the other sauce. "'But if thou wilt have me freely,'" she argues, "'soon will be extinguished the glowing torch which now enkindleth thee— and me likewise'" (IV, 153). Of course, as we have already noted, the institution of marriage was created precisely in order to deal with Venus' burning torch, not by fanning the flames, but by putting them out. The usual appeal to Andreas' treatise on courtly love, where one can find that secrecy is a "rule" of courtly love, begs the question even if we believe in that insubstantial phenomenon. It is true that one of Andreas' twelve "rules" of courtly love says that "thou shalt not have many who know of thy love affair," but does Boccaccio have Criseida conform to the rule, or do both authors, by emphasizing the necessity of secrecy to keep the fires stoked, subtly suggest that passion, if not fanned, will burn itself out?

Truth, Falsehood, and Self-Delusion

Two interesting falsehoods will delay us before we look at the conclusion of the poem. In the sixth part, stanza 29, Criseida tells Diomede that she has never loved anyone since her husband died—neither Greek nor Trojan. This either means that she didn't love Troilo, or, much more likely, is a lie of convenience to help turn aside Diomede's pursuit. Although easily accounted for, Criseida's lie perforce reminds us of all the other untruths uttered throughout the poem. Troilo lies about being in love, Pandaro lies to Criseida, Criseida to Diomede, etc.[45] The other curious falsehood is Troilo's evasion of his sister Cassandra. In the seventh part, stanza 87, Cassandra utters a scornful opinion of the love affair: "'And since, albeit, matters were thus to be, would that thou wert enamored of a noble lady, instead of having brought thyself to wasting away on account of the daughter of a wicked priest, man of evil life and of small importance.'" It is easy enough, in these democratic times, to take exception to Cassandra's elitist remarks, but one must wonder why Boccaccio included them. Was he trying to show up Cassandra for a biased snob, or was he putting a provocative comment on the true nature of the love affair into the mouth of a woman noted for telling the truth—but not for being believed? In either case, Troilo denies that he has loved Criseida, and then, disastrously, goes on to defend her nobility, so scorned by Cassandra, in the familiar terms of virtue: "'Nobility is to be found wherever virtue is'" (VII, 94). The admirable idea that virtue constitutes true nobility is a medieval commonplace. It may be found in Boethius' *Consolation of Philosophy*, in Dante's *Convivio*, and in Jean de Meun's section of the *Romance of the Rose*, just to mention a few of the possible sources for Boccaccio's poem.[46] However, although the idea was well known, the quality of virtue is notable for its absence in the poem. As we have observed repeatedly, all the principals agree that Criseida should not lose her honor, should not be corrupted, but she is corrupted and does lose her honor. No virtue, no nobility. The triviality of Troilo's lie is lost in the pathetic inaccuracy of his defense of Criseida's virtuous nobility, at the very time that she is continuing her unvirtuous ways with Diomede.

It is ironic enough that Troilo should at this unfortunate time praise Criseida's nobility on account of virtue. It is almost cruelly ironic that Boccaccio has him select a whole series of specific qualities to illustrate his claim—qualities she obviously does not possess, but which Troilo as yet either does not know or cannot recognize. For example, she is said to be the woman of greatest "onesta," to be "modesta," and "vergognosa" (VII, 95), this in spite of her rapid abandonment of her widow's continence in favor of the torrid affair with Troilo himself. Moreover, her modest and retiring nature as envisioned by Troilo accords poorly both with her two seductions and with the uninhibited first night she spent with Troilo, when, in a scene much quoted by the autobiographical critics of the poem, Criseida exhibits only the most transient modesty about removing her last garment, which is quickly cast aside at Troilo's request (III, 32).

A similar tacit comment on Troilo's almost limitless ability for self-delusion about Criseida is to be found in the following stanza, where Troilo defends

Criseida's virtuous nobility on the grounds of her discretion (discrezione) and judicious speaking (ragionare). "'In her behavior appeareth her discretion and in her speech, which is so sound and judicious and full of all reason. And this year I saw in part how much she had of it in the excuse she made for the perfidy of her father'" (VII, 96). This statement represents a proper approach on the face of it—forgiveness for perfidy constituting an example of reasonable discretion—but the statement is at odds with the facts of the matter. Criseida never excuses her father; on the contrary she holds him up to scorn throughout the poem. In our very first encounter with Criseida, the townspeople have been outraged by Calchas' treachery, and are threatening to burn down his house. Criseida, not wishing to be a martyr to Calchas' cause, throws herself at the feet of Hector, and "excusing herself and accusing her father, ended her speech by imploring mercy" (I, 12).[47] Later in the poem, when it is proposed that she be exchanged for Antenor, Criseida is described as one "who had come by now to hold her father no longer in esteem" (IV, 79). Even more forthrightly, when she and Troilo are concocting schemes to overcome their enforced separation, Criseida proposes that she maneuver Calchas back to Troy by playing on his greed. "'He is, as thou knowest, old and avaricious and here he hath that which, if he prizeth it, may make him pay heed to what I shall tell him, to have me brought back here as best he may . . .'" (IV, 136). The most violent outburst, however, occurs a few stanzas earlier in the poem. How Troilo could speak of Criseida's "excuse" of her father's perfidy is difficult to imagine in light of what she said to Troilo about her father's avarice and her characterization of him as a wicked traitor (IV, 128). However, what Troilo does not hear is even less forgiving. When Criseida is alone, she damns her father in the most violent outburst in the entire poem. "'O father mine, wicked and faithless to thine own land, accursed be the moment when into thy heart came evil as great as was thy wish to join the Greeks and desert the Trojans! Would God thou wert dead in the vale of Hell, wicked old man, who in thy life's declining years hast wrought such guile!'" (IV, 93). Troilo has not heard this, but we have, and Boccaccio wants us to judge Criseida's claim to virtue accordingly. Whereas Pandaro and Criseida utter untruths, Troilo does not delude others but rather himself. So much for the inspirational power of this kind of love.

The *Perfetta Donna*

At the end of the *Filostrato*, quite unlike Chaucer's *Troilus*, Troilo's love for Criseida turns to hate, she comes to love Diomede, and Troilo not only wishes to kill Diomede and die himself, but hopes for Criseida's death as well (VIII, 16, 18, 20). This all leads rather abruptly into the "moral" that Boccaccio offers at the end of the poem. The difficulty with the "moral" is that it contains so many qualifications that its real meaning can be perceived only if we do not jump to conclusions. This crucial part of the poem begins straight-forwardly enough. "Such was the end [i.e., death] that came to the ill-conceived love of Troilo for Criseida . . . such was the end of the vain hopes of Troilo in base Criseida" (VIII, 28). By specifying that this disastrous love affair was "mal concetto," Boccaccio is doubtless referring to the corruption of a widow and the rejection of marriage as an alternative: both matters discussed already. He then goes on to warn youths against the "appetito rio" or evil passion, which is understandable enough in view of the havoc that passion has wrought in the poem (VIII, 29). In that same stanza, however, there is a further caveat. Boccaccio says that if his verses are "read aright" then young folk will not "lightly have trust in all women" ("Non di leggieri a tutte crederete"). And there follows a miniature diatribe in the antifeminist tradition against young women, who are fickle, and noble ladies, who are uncivil. What does all this mean? The attack on noble ladies cannot refer to Criseida, since her lack of high birth is an important attribute in the poem. And the attack on young ladies for their fickleness, while closer to the mark, does not precisely apply to Criseida either, for we remember that it was her fear for her passing youth that Pandaro played upon in order to further Troilo's proposition.

If we back up a bit and heed Boccaccio's plea to read his verses aright, we may find a better perspective. It is easy to assume that when Boccaccio says that young men who read his poem aright will not lightly trust in all women, he means that by seeing the false Criseida they will not trust *any* woman. This is the standard judgment on the ending of the poem as an attack on women because they are fickle. However, the readers are not advised to distrust all women but rather not to trust all women; this does not preclude trusting some. The moral of the poem is not that all women are like Criseida, but rather that the ones who are, *and* the young, fickle ones, *and* the supercilious, noble ones, *and* those who are not wise because of advanced age (VIII, 32) are to be avoided.

In other words, the seeming dichotomy between the evil woman ("ria donna") and the perfect woman ("perfetta donna") is a false one. Boccaccio's final plea, that the reader be granted "the boon of loving so wisely" that he "not die in the end for an evil woman," suggests that a woman like Criseida, whose fickleness led Troilo to death, is the archetypal "ria donna." How-ever, Boccaccio's "perfetta donna" is perfect only insofar as she has a "stronger desire to be loved" than does the supercilious, noble lady of the previous stanza and in that she "looketh to the fulfilment of her engage-ments" unlike the fickle woman of two stanzas before. Note too that Boccac-cio qualifies his advice to follow such a perfect lady by saying that the choice of one "should not be made in haste, for they are not all wise, because they may be older and age lesseneth worth." The supposedly perfect lady, then, turns out to be one who is eager for love—but not necessarily matrimonial love, and who keeps her promises—but not necessarily promises one ought to keep! What Boccaccio is describing in this young, eager, constantly illicit woman, whose love may or may not be morally admirable, is only a Criseida who is constant in illicit affairs. This constitutes not perfection but rather a joke about perfection.

The ninth part of the poem is a sort of coda that steps outside of the story of Troilo and Criseida, and the author in that part of the work is imagined as a sentient being voyaging to see the "donna gentil della mia mente." Since we now know that this lady is nothing more than a lady of his poetic imagination, the ninth section, along with the *Proemio*, must be interpreted on other than biographical grounds. As suggested earlier, this tiny section may have been included primarily to supply the poem with nine parts, thus parodying the idea of nine as the symbol of chaste love as found in Dante's *Vita Nuova*. In any case, the poet's presentation of himself as hoping eagerly for a "happy response" is more than a bit ridiculous in view of the moral the poet drew from the story. If the "nobilissima donna" is to see herself as a "perfetta donna," eager in love, young, and yet constant, there is still the little problem of morality: everyone in the poem has agreed that love outside of marriage is wrong, so that the poet's hope that the poem will elicit a "happy response," for which understand an extramarital liaison, is no more than wishful thinking. The poet carefully aligns himself with Troilo in the *Proemio* in spite of his studied disclaimer of any parallel with his ultimate success, and makes it very clear that he hopes to gain what Troilo gained. We should not forget that what Troilo managed to do was not altogether admirable because of its illicit nature and ultimately led to his grief. The contention that Boccaccio presents "what he regards as a perfect affair," with its supreme "sensuousness which love *paramours* affects and marriage cannot" is impossible to agree with.[48] It is a contention that overlooks all the unhappiness, betrayal, and corruption upon which the poem insists in order to concentrate on the sensuality that caused these things, and it treats that sensuality as an end in itself rather than as the vehicle for all the misfortunes that transpire.

There is, then, a strong case to be made that the *Filostrato* is not what its immediate narrator claims it to be: a poem of seductive encouragement. Indeed, if we concentrate upon the work itself and ignore the presumed autobiographical element therein, it can be argued that Boccaccio takes a clearly disapproving attitude toward illicit passion. His use of scripture, of Dante, his imagery, the narrative framework—all these debase rather than exalt the seduction of Criseida. The affair between Troilo and Criseida is only momentarily enjoyable and leads to great unhappiness, besides being very dubious morally. The affair with the "nobilissima donna" proposed by the narrator of the poem, who should be conceived of as a persona and not the real-life Boccaccio, does not promise much better. Boccaccio is able to see the comic possibilities of illicit love, and he can write convincingly about the delights of the flesh, but a careful study of the poem shows that he is much more detached from the subject than has been thought. Boccaccio keeps illicit love in perspective in the *Filostrato*, and our own perspective on this will be improved if we separate the fictitious narrator of the *Proemio* and of the ninth part—the narrator whose life has been spent in the service of love—from Boccaccio the man.

What Chaucer Really Did to *Il Filostrato*

It is clear both from my preface and from this chapter that I do not agree with C. S. Lewis, who maintained that Chaucer approached Boccaccio's poem as a poet of courtly love and corrected the errors that the Italian had committed against the code. Courtly love is a red herring that has been dragged too often across the trail of comparison of the two poems, and Lewis' description of Boccaccio's poem as a series of "cynical Latin gallantries" is sufficiently accurate and sufficiently paradoxical as to arouse rather than stifle critical inquiry. Lewis seems to have overlooked the tension between cynicism and gallantry in his own remarks, but he was certainly on the right track when he tried to recreate the historical, social, and literary circumstances under which Chaucer first encountered Boccaccio's poem. These circumstances indeed caused Chaucer to modify the Italian poem, but they should be understood in a historical context emphasizing English literary concerns rather than the ideals of courtly love emphasized by Lewis.

If we accept Root's *terminus ad quem* for Chaucer's *Troilus* of 1386, then it is reasonable to assume that most of the work of composition of the poem went on in the several years prior to that date. Thus, if Chaucer became acquainted with Boccaccio's poem during or just after his first Italian journey of 1372–73, or after his second in 1378, his decision to rework it for his own purposes may well have owed much to the disturbing social and political events of the extraordinary decade of the seventies. Certainly other poets were affected by them. The author of *Piers Plowman*, in revising his poem at the end of the decade, particularized his figure of Lady Meed with a sly reference to Alice Perrers, the unsavory mistress of the aging Edward III, and introduced the allegory of the mice who would bell the cat as a commentary on the power of John of Gaunt and the vacillating nature of parliament. He also evinced concern in this allegory over the accession to the throne of the young Richard II in 1377, a topic that Bishop Brinton had preached upon publicly.[49] In a similar way one may trace the dispiriting course of England's fortunes and its effect on Chaucer's friend John Gower. As John H. Fisher puts it, "Gower's interest in kingship can be traced from his disillusionment with Edward III in the *Mirour*, through his concern for Richard II in the *Vox Clamantis*. . . ."[50]

If Fisher is correct in his conjecture that parts of *Vox Clamantis* were written in the late seventies and the dream-vision added after the Peasants' Revolt of 1381, then we might envision Chaucer and Gower working on *Troilus* and *Vox Clamantis* in the turbulent years from 1375 to 1385—influencing each other, perhaps, and being influenced by the course of history.

If the events of the seventies influenced others, why should they not have influenced Chaucer as well? Lewis' judgment that Chaucer was, at the time of the composition of the *Troilus*, "the great living interpreter in English of *l'amour courtois*" envisions a Chaucer curiously detached from the vital concerns of his day. Surely Fisher's conclusion that John Gower's "moral earnestness and social conscience may have influenced Chaucer's artistic development in the 1370's" is more believable.[51] Indeed, so persuasive is Fisher's argument that one wonders why he assumes that *only* the "moral dimension" of the *Troilus* is dedicated to Gower, since the "courtly love" element Fisher identifies he finds to be "blended" with the moral dimension.[52] Fisher finds Chaucer turning to social criticism like Gower's only after 1386, the date of the *Troilus*, but there are good reasons for thinking that Chaucer intended the *Troilus* itself to be a kind of social document.

If we imagine Geoffrey Chaucer, who between 1376 and 1381 seems to have been occupied mainly as controller in the port of London but also as an ambassador, diplomat, and esquire to the king,[53] casting about for a poetic subject, Boccaccio's poem would have had for him a strong and novel attraction it had not had for Boccaccio himself or for any of the earlier redactors of the tale. Because London was thought of as "New Troy" in an identification dating as far back as Geoffrey of Monmouth's *Historia Regum Britanniae*, a Trojan story offered Chaucer a built-in analogy with London. Moreover, at perhaps the same time that Chaucer was writing his poem of Troy and Troilus, his friend Gower was using "New Troy" as the name for London in his account of the Peasants' Revolt of 1381 in *Vox Clamantis*.[54] If Chaucer read *Il Filostrato* as a satire upon passion, his own involvement as a statesman and Gower's poetic influence might well have combined to suggest to him that he transmute the story from a disparagement of illicit passion amusingly ill-fitted to the narrator's ostensible motives to a tale with social as well as individual criticism. As McCall has noted, the name Troilus means "little Troy," and in medieval interpretations the fall of the city was ascribed to foolish pride and criminal lust, while Boccaccio's poem itself was insistent that the love of Troilo for Criseida was the same love that led to the destruction of the city.[55] Even more significantly, Gower was—at about the same time—attributing England's problems to moral decay generally and to the service of Venus specifically. "Thus the Mistress of the people renders tribute to sin . . . she who once was holy is becoming the goddess Venus herself" (p. 285). Gower, for all his concern with the evils of New Troy, either neglected the idea of a symbolic Troilus, or did not know of the stories in which he was featured as an unhappy lover, for he refers to Troilus only as a type of faithfulness in love (p. 252). All Chaucer had to do to effect a double level of meaning was to change the narrative strategy somewhat, make the moral more explicit, and make the reader or auditor more aware of Troilus not as just an individual who succumbs to Venus and Cupid but as a prince of the realm.

These are, of course, precisely the changes he did make. Chaucer's awareness of the symbolic role of the king in national affairs is easily seen in his little poem "Lak of Stedfastnesse," in which the "up-so-doun" affairs of the people are to be redressed by proper moral and social behavior in King Richard. The king is addressed significantly as "O prince," and is exhorted to be "honourable," to cherish the folk, to fear God, love truth, and to "wed thy folk agein to stedfastnesse." The king should use both precept (in the form of "castigacioun") and example; he must himself love truth and worthiness while simultaneously marrying his people to the ideal of steadfastness. It follows that moral decay in the nobility generally, but in the ruling house especially, would serve a general cautionary purpose, and sexual license among the nobility was considered such a problem by Bishop Bradwardine, Bishop Brinton, and John Gower.[56] Chaucer did not have to do anything to have his audience think of the relevance of Troy to London, but he carefully modifies the *Filostrato* to emphasize that Troilus is the king's son. His goal is not to attack the royal family, but to create a paradigm or emblem showing moral failing—in this case lust—in a high-born person—in this case a prince—leading to personal downfall while the realm falls simultaneously. Although Troilus himself cannot be blamed for the fall of the city—indeed he fights well before, during, and after his affair—nevertheless his similarity to Paris, whose service of Venus *is* the cause of Troy's downfall, reminds the audience of the parallel between Troy and Troilus. Perhaps it is because of the inevitable analogies between Troy and London that Chaucer did not want to make the prince's downfall the direct cause of the city's doom but only an emblem of it, lest his general concern be mistaken for a personal attack. Certainly some of Chaucer's additions to Boccaccio are intended to emphasize the parallels between Troy and Troilus, such as the poignant statement that Fortune "Gan pulle awey the fetheres brighte of Troie" (V, 1546), which is echoed by bird and feather imagery applied to Troilus.[57]

The changes Chaucer makes from Boccaccio's narrative strategy are both obvious and crucial. Instead of casting himself as one in the service of Love (Proem), Chaucer styles himself as the servant of the servants of Love (I, 15), and instead of posing as a would-be seducer he says he could not love "for myn unliklynesse" (I, 16). The abandonment of Boccaccio's immediacy opens more distance between the narrator and the subject matter, and introduces a more dispassionate tone to the whole.[58] Similarly, whereas Boccaccio in his invocation rejects Apollo, Jove, and the Muses of Parnassus for "thee, my lady," Chaucer somberly invokes Tisiphone, the "cruwel Furie" some-times associated with carnal love in a pejorative way, and regards himself not as an actor in the drama but as "the sorwful instrument, / That helpeth lov-eres" (I, 10–11).[59] Again the effect is to remove the narrator from the action, to introduce more room for the reader's perspective, and, consequently, to invite judgment. Certainly Chaucer's change of Boccaccio's prayer to lovers (I, 6) accomplishes this, for while Boccaccio asks lovers to pray for him to Love, so that his fortunes in love can ameliorate, Chaucer asks lovers to pray first for Troilus and then to pray for him in order that he might show "Swich peyne and wo as Loves folk endure" (I, 34).

In addition to these changes in narrative strategy, Chaucer is very much concerned to show Troilus as a prince. While Boccaccio has only a passing reference to Troilus as "son of Priam, most noble king of Troy," buried in some eight pages of *Proemio*, Chaucer selects this detail to open the entire poem, thus giving it maximum prominence: "The double sorwe of Troilus to tellen, / That was the kyng Priamus sone of Troye, . . . My purpos is" (I, 1–5). Nor does Chaucer let it drop there; in the scene wherein Troilus first sees Criseyde and is struck by the arrow of Love, Chaucer adds a long anal-ogy in which Troilus is compared with Bayard the horse, and in which it is insisted that Troilus is struck "Though he a worthy kynges sone were" (I, 226). At the same time that Chaucer is at pains to emphasize Troilus' noble birth he is also concerned to show his abandonment of responsibility as soon as he is struck by Cupid's arrow, and this, too, is an innovation beyond his source. For example, while Chaucer repeats Boccaccio's comment that the "fiery flames of love spared not the royal blood" (I, 40; cf. *T&C*, I, 435–36), he prefaces this with an image of Troilus renouncing his princely birth in favor of the state of a humble servant:

> "For myn estat roial I here resigne
> Into hire hond, and with ful humble chere
> Bicome hir man, as to my lady dere."   [I, 432–34]

In other words, Chaucer's poem shows a hero whose noble birth and ignoble servitude in love are equally insisted upon. These twin stresses have no counterpart in Boccaccio and serve to emphasize that it is indeed "a sorwful tale." A very similar scene of self-abasement is added by Chaucer to the con-fession scene in Book I, where instead of Boccaccio's restrained comment by Troilo to Pandaro, "'I put myself in thy hands'" (II, 33), Chaucer has the more abandoned "'My lif, my deth, hol in thyn hond I leye'" (I, 1053).[60]

Another instance of Chaucer's greater emphasis on Troilus' noble birth is to be found in his handling of Boccaccio's disclosure scene, in which Pan-daro, after building some suspense, tells Criseida the name of her suitor. Boc-caccio's Pandaro notes that Troilo is a citizen, not of the lesser order, and his great friend (II, 46), while Chaucer thrice insists on his high birth. Troilus is "'the kynges deere sone,'" he is "'the noble Troilus,'" and "'that noble gentil knyght'" (II, 316, 319, 331). Later in Book II the same sort of intensification occurs again.[61]

It is in the seduction scene that the differences between Chaucer and Boccaccio in regard to Troilus' status and actions are most clearly to be found. As many critics have noted, in Boccaccio's version of the story there is really not much buildup at all, since Criseida has clearly made up her mind in advance, if indeed she was ever in any doubt about what she would ultimately do. As Rossetti drily put it more than a century ago, "perhaps we are to understand that her previous resistance was not quite so doughty as in her words it appeared."[62] At any rate, Chaucer creates a self-abasing Troilus who accepts Criseyde's "up-so-doun" put-downs; yet Chaucer is careful to insist simultaneously that this is, in spite of what he is doing, a king's son. The additions begin with Troilus' elaborate self-humiliation in which he wishes to be under Criseyde's "yerde" (III, 137), an instrument normally used for the correction of children. Criseyde's response to Troilus' grovelling involves an overturning of a standard medieval hierarchy. Commoners were expected to acknowledge the prerogatives of the monarchy, and after the disastrous affair of King Edward III and Alice Perrers, it is hard to imagine a London audience finding anything uplifting when Criseyde uses her sexual desirability to put Troilus under her power:

> "But natheles, this warne I yow," quod she,
> "A kynges sone although ye be, ywys,
> Ye shal namore han sovereignete
> Of me in love, than right in that cas is;
> N'y nyl forbere, if that ye don amys,
> To wratthe yow. . . ."   [III, 169–74]

Chaucer continues this motif of Troilus' extravagant humility by having him kneel at Criseyde's bedside (III, 953, 962), which is an addition to Boccaccio, and by having Troilus kneel to Pandarus (III, 1592), whereas in Boccaccio's version Troilo embraces Pandaro.[63] Toward the end of Book III Chaucer seems to sum up this series of additions to the source when he writes: "And thus Fortune a tyme ledde in joie / Criseyde, and ek this kynges sone of Troie" (III, 1714–15). Salter, who finds Book III of the poem to be a "celebration of 'suffisaunce . . . blisse . . . singynges . . . (III, 1716)'" thinks this is the only line that suggests that "all may not ultimately be well."[64] Rather, in this motif of a prince subjecting himself to Fortune by subjecting himself to a woman, Chaucer has been at some pains to sketch a situation in which nothing *can* be well.

What Chaucer really did to *Il Filostrato* turns out to be an issue that has not in fact been investigated in much detail, or, where it has been, the significance of the changes has sometimes been colored by an impressionistic criticism—the sort of thing that led Karl Young to speak of the "charm of humility" found in Chaucer's Troilus and lacking in Boccaccio's Troilo.[65] Perhaps more to the point is to ask *why* Chaucer modified Boccaccio's poem, and here I think that the influence of Gower is crucial. Consider, for example, just two of the additions to Boccaccio that have been discussed in this section: Troilus' putting his life and death in Pandarus' hands and his being caught with birdlime. Both of these may be compared, allowing for minor variances, with Gower's *Vox Clamantis*, Book V, chapter 3, in which he assails the knight who is ensnared by a comely woman.[66] Gower's condemnation of people like Troilus is very clear, and if we accept Fisher's contention that the moral dimension of the poem is dedicated to Gower, then it seems reasonable to assume that the moral comments at issue are those on knights who succumb to passion, against whom Gower inveighs for hundreds and hundreds of lines in the *Vox Clamantis*. Fisher's belief that the moral dimension is "blended" with courtly love, is based to a large extent upon his belief that "the love of Troilus and Criseyde [is] a manifestation of the universal creative urge. . . . Destiny in Troilus is only partly a metaphysical Boethian concept. Partly it is simply another manifestation of the primal sexual urge man shares with all sensible creatures."[67] We shall have much to say in the next chapter about the relationship between sexual impulses and the will, but suffice it to say that the thrust of Gower's attitude towards passionate involvement seems the same as that found in the *Troilus*, and when Fisher finds Chaucer recognizing a connection "between human and divine love," when he finds Chaucer using "this spiritualized conception of courtly love as the vehicle for [the poem's] moralization," I cannot follow him.[68] Rather, the changes Chaucer makes from Boccaccio's story seem to be designed to create a negative exemplary pattern in which a prince becomes subject to Fortune by subjecting himself to a woman. Chaucer was surely thinking along the same lines as was Gower, who wrote that "no ancient writings about kings show that an appeased Venus and a kingdom stand together for long" (p. 240).

In the *Vox Clamantis* Gower clearly distinguishes the love he denigrates from "virtuous love," and in a significant passage he notes that the foolish knight has only himself to blame:

> But if a knight chooses a woman's love for himself, then he will pay for it more dearly than with his wealth. He will give up so many good things for it—his body, his soul, his property. . . . Nevertheless, when he shall have done with his troublesome doings . . . and when neither the prattling talk of the world reaches his ears nor virtuous love bestows its treasures upon him, then the dupe will say, "Alas, how wicked Fortune is!" . . . The man who laments for himself in this foolish way is too late, for he himself is the cause of his suffering, and not another.   [p. 202]

Whether Chaucer knew Gower's exact words before he came to redact the *Filostrato*, or whether he only shared a general point of view with Gower is not important. What is important is that both Boccaccio's Troilo and Chaucer's Troilus complain of their loss to Fortune ("'Fortune, allas the while! / What have I don?'" [*T&C*, IV, 260–61]). I do not detect any difference of tone in this outcry between Chaucer and Gower, or indeed among Chaucer, Gower, and Boccaccio. However, the changes from Boccaccio seem to be designed to sharpen the "Gowerian" emphasis on the lover's subjection to Fortune. For example, Chaucer prepares the reader for the hero's expostulation against Fortune with the important addition to the source we have already adduced: "And thus Fortune a tyme ledde in joie / Criseyde, and ek this kynges sone of Troie" (III, 1714–15). Gower would have understood what Chaucer was driving at. And he would have approved.

Chapter II

Love and Will

Love is he that alle thing may bynde

One of the most significant changes that Chaucer makes from the *Filostrato* is to introduce, in Book I, nine stanzas on the process of Troilus' falling in love. The lines in question first describe how Troilus is hit by the God of Love's arrow, then compare the lover's state with that of proud Bayard, the horse, and finally reflect upon the power of love. Boccaccio had contented himself with a passing reference to Love's dwelling with his darts within the lady's eyes, and he had noted with regard to Troilo's scorn of lovers that things often do not turn out as planned. Chaucer treats the whole event very differently. He introduces the element of pride into Troilus' contempt for lovers, and indeed has Troilus ask archly "'Loo! is this naught wisely spoken?'" (I, 205). Chaucer also expands Boccaccio's remarks on the irony that contrary effects often follow our intentions, and, most important for our present purposes, Chaucer introduces four stanzas in which the narrator lectures the audience on the nature and power of the God of Love. We are told to take Troilus as an example teaching us not to scorn Love, for Love can enthrall us quickly. Indeed, Love's power is part of the law of nature:

> For evere it was, and evere it shal byfalle,
> That Love is he that alle thing may bynde,
> For may no man fordon the lawe of kynde.   [236–38]

Chaucer goes on to say that neither wit, strength, worth, nor degree is sufficient to protect one against Love. Indeed, he continues, that is a proper thing, for Love can comfort those in woe, appease cruel hearts, make worthy folk worthier, and cause people to renounce vice and shame. The whole addition to the source concludes with the narrator's advice not to refuse to be bound to Love, since Love cannot be withstood anyway, and indeed is "a thing so vertuous in kynde" (254).

This rather substantial addition to the *Filostrato* was obviously important to Chaucer, and the stanzas have not gone unnoticed by critics. However, love's inevitability and its ennobling power, while plainly attested to in these stanzas, nevertheless require for their understanding more context than they have customarily received. Love's ennobling power will be discussed in chapter 3. Here I should like to examine the issue of the God of Love's power and his function as a natural force, an ineluctable phenomenon.

The major editors of the poem, Root and Robinson, have accepted Chaucer's statements about Love's power at face value, and they refer the reader to various other medieval poems, Robinson noting that the idea is "too commonplace to be traced to a particular source." Critics have also seen nothing untoward in the remarks, and, to select a few from fairly recent writings, P. M. Kean notes that love "as an ennobling power . . . ought not to be resisted even if it were possible," and further maintains that Chaucer underscores the impossibility of resisting Love by "the introduction of the idea of the relation of love to the freedom of the will" in the previous stanza. While it might seem that introducing the freedom of the will would go some distance towards showing the possibility, rather than the impossibility, of resisting Love, let us delay discussion of the issue. In a vein similar to that of Kean, Elizabeth Salter has argued with reference to one of the later stanzas of the group under scrutiny that "the tone of the passage is not ironic: advice is plainly given, and it bases its argument on the power and virtue of love," for which she quotes the lines "Now sith it may nat goodly ben withstonde, / And is a thing so vertuous in kynde . . ." (I, 253–54). Another critic, Peter Heidtmann, who also wrote in the 1960s, quarrels with D. W. Robertson's view that Troilus "allowed" himself to fall in love, and contends that it happened "involuntarily." Finally, Donald Rowe has recently put forth again the idea that love is irresistible.[1]

It is readily apparent that the critics cited who have declared that people inevitably succumb to Love's arrows have done so because the poem says so. Only Salter has raised the possibility of there being some irony here, although she counters this by declaration rather than refutation. However, the question remains: can Love bind everyone as the text states? Or, since Chaucer chose to introduce into the poem a good deal of Boethian material regarding the freedom of the will, is he in fact asserting Love's irresistibility with amusement or irony? In order to answer the question we need more than just Chaucer's text; we need to examine some other medieval literary treatments of Love, his arrows, and the interesting process of falling in love. What we shall find is that although it is regularly said that one cannot avoid Cupid's arrow, the statement is usually embedded in a context suggesting exactly the opposite.

We may begin with a series of comments on the heart's affections that Chaucer might well have known: the interpretations of Mars and Venus that Boccaccio appends as *Chiose* to his *Teseida*, the poem Chaucer redacted as the *Knight's Tale* at about the same time he was writing the *Troilus*. Boccaccio begins by saying that "in every man there are two principal appetites," which he defines as the concupiscible and the irascible. The former of these carries no modern connotations of lubricity, but rather is the appetite "whereby man desires and rejoices to have the things which, according to his judgment—

whether it be rational or corrupt—are delightful and pleasing."[2] What we desire, in other words, may or may not be worthy of desire and our judgment can lead us astray. The other appetite, the irascible, is simply the response to any hindering of the concupiscible appetite. It is the appetite "whereby a man is troubled if delightful things are taken away or impeded, or when they cannot be had." This appetite can be held in check "by a very strong effort of reason," which suggests that neither appetite is anything like an elemental, destinal force.

Mars, of course, represents this irascible appetite, and Venus the concupiscible. However, our desires can be good or bad depending upon our judgment (not upon our stars), so that Boccaccio introduces the idea of two Venuses to accommodate proper and improper desires. While he confines himself to defining the two Venuses in terms of sexual inclinations that are worthy of praise or blame, nevertheless an extrapolation to all desires is clearly possible. His precise wording is worth quoting: "just as Mars, as was said above, consists in the irascible appetite, so Venus consists in the concupiscible. This Venus is twofold, since one can be understood as every chaste and licit desire, as is the desire to have a wife in order to have children, and such like. . . . The second Venus is that through which all lewdness is desired, commonly called the goddess of love." If we put the two passages on Mars and Venus, the irascible and concupiscible appetites, together, the process Boccaccio envisions is very clear. Insofar as falling in love is concerned, a man (or woman) can exercise proper or corrupted reason and either marry or follow lewdness. There is no suggestion that some people are spared and others condemned to follow the illicit Venus.

Boccaccio assures the reader that his argument in the notes is confined to the illicit Venus, for of the other he says "this Venus is not discussed here." This distinction is crucial, for in the long analysis of the Temple of Venus that follows, Boccaccio concentrates upon the effects of the illicit Venus with only occasional references to the possibility of choosing the other Venus. Thus, those who follow the Venus of lewdness and worship in her temple commit themselves to a certain course of events, and once committed seldom escape. This is well illustrated by the series of remarks leading up to and following from his description of the arrows of Cupid.

In discussing the Temple of Venus in detail, Boccaccio says that the author of the poem describes two kinds of stimuli: those which can "according to natural forces, provoke anyone to the sexual act," and those "which stimulate some whom we call lovers." Again the distinction is clear enough: it is natural to have sexual feelings, but one may choose to act upon those impulses within marriage or outside of it. Those called "lovers" follow the latter course. He continues to characterize these provocations "some as natural and some as stimulating causes," and we should observe the difference. One, he says, is

Yearning, and by this the author "means that natural desire, which every man or woman has, to see and to possess or acquire some beautiful and precious things. . . ." This, of course, is the same as the concupiscible appetite he has already defined. Yearning, he goes on, draws young men to "places where ladies are gathered together." At this juncture, though, the stimulants of lovers come in, and Boccaccio says the author includes among "these stimulants . . . Beauty, Youth, Grace, Nobility, Charm . . . [and] others that are almost strengtheners of the appetite, that is, excited by the above mentioned." Among these stimulants of a natural appetite "he places Cupid, which is commonly called Love." Thus it is natural to yearn, but this desire can lead either towards the good or the bad Venus. When the stimulations stimulate, people become lovers. When Boccaccio goes on to say of Love that "since one cannot escape very serious harm from Him, anyone who speaks of Him says that He is armed with arrows," we need not assume that a wound from Cupid's arrow is inevitable but rather that it is inevitable, by definition, for those who permit stimulations to lead them to act in a certain way in response to natural impulses. Lest anyone misunderstand this aspect of Cupid's power, Boccaccio glosses the significance of the arrow by saying it was tempered by Voluptuousness in the fountain of false esteem.

Such a delight as this tempers the arrows of Love, that is, makes them strong to be able to impassion the heart well. And Voluptuousness tempers them in the fountain of our false esteem, when, through this delight born of Love and Hope, we judge that the pleasurable thing is to be placed above every other thing, whether temporal or divine.

The "fountain of our false esteem" explains the whole process. Our judgment seeks that which appears delightful and pleasing, but can err. Clearly, when we choose to follow the illicit Venus, our judgment, which can be "rational or corrupt," is the latter. By wrongly esteeming voluptuousness we give Cupid power over us. Thus his arrows are supplied him by us and are strong because we make them so. Cupid is not an ineluctable power, only the emblem of a habit-forming choice. Everything else in this lengthy comment bears out this conclusion. Boccaccio always leaves open the possibility of following the good Venus, or of not entering the temple at all. For example, of the lover's sighs he remarks that they "are not born, nor do tears come, before a man is within the temple, that is in love, and touched by Jealousy." Similarly he says of those who want to preserve their chastity that they should avoid human consorting (the natural result, we remember, of Yearning), and also idleness, "for these two things, if what has been said above is clearly understood, are very great causes of falling into the snares of Venus." If Venus can be avoided she cannot be unavoidable. The snare will catch only those who walk in Venus' ways. And so when he speaks of the apple in Venus' hand in the temple, he says it represents "the foolish choice of those who place this kind of life over every other." There is no doubt in Boccaccio's mind that one has a choice, and that the choice of the illicit Venus is an egregious blunder. Her temple, he says, is dark "because those who practice evil hate the light," and she is shown naked because appearances "attract the souls of those whose thought cannot penetrate reality." Finally, he notes that the temple is perfumed "since the act is of itself so fetid that if the sense of smell were not appeased by aromas, it would easily impede the stomach and the brain and consequently the whole operation."

Boccaccio was by no means alone in suggesting that one could choose to follow or to avoid the kind of love symbolized by a certain Venus or by Cupid and his arrows. A very similar approach may be found in the *Romance of the Rose*, which was known to both Boccaccio and Chaucer. In the Middle English version most pertinent for a study of Chaucer, the *Romaunt*, most of the references to love's power are to the God of Love rather than to Cupid or Venus, but there is no significant difference since Cupid is identified as the God of Love in *RR*, 3702–03. When the dreamer enters the garden, he soon meets Sir Myrthe, Gladnesse, Curtesie, and the formidable God of Love, who is described in terms very similar to those Chaucer was to use in *Troilus*:

> And next hir wente, on hir other side,
> The God of Love, that can devyde
> Love, and as hym likith it be.
> But he can cherles daunten, he,
> And maken folkis pride fallen;
> And he can wel these lordis thrallen,
> And ladyes putt at lowe degre,
> Whan he may hem to proude see.   [*RR*, 877–84]

The God of Love is accompanied by Swete-Lokyng in this poem, who carries not one but two bows, the one for use with the arrows that initiate love (Beaute, Symplesse, Fraunchise, Compaignye, and Fair-Semblaunt), and another five that are inimical to this kind of love (Pride, Vylanye, Shame, Wanhope, and Newe-Thought). This garden contains the Well of Love, which also has power over lovers. This well is the "mirrour perilous" in which Narcissus saw his face and fell in love with it, and indeed

> . . . whoso loketh in that mirrour,
> Ther may nothyng ben his socour
> That he ne shall there sen somthyng
> That shal hym lede into lovyng.   [*RR*, 1605–08]

Both the God of Love and the Well of Love are powerful, and just as we were warned against the "snares" of Venus in Boccaccio's *Chiose*, here we are alerted to Cupid's "gynnes" (*RR*, 1620) that are set around the well, and the

lover is later caught in a "snare" (*RR*, 1647). The scene is set for Love's con-
quering of the dreamer, which is accomplished as soon as the latter looks in
the mirror, chooses a rosebud, and moves toward it. The God of Love, with
his bow, has been stalking the dreamer / lover, "And whanne he saw hou that
I / Hadde chosen so ententifly / . . . He tok an arowe full sharply whet"
(*RR*, 1719–23). It is important to note that the dreamer has to choose before
the God of Love can act, because without that final decision the God of Love
cannot really have power over him.

When the arrow is shot, significantly through the eye and into the heart,
the God of Love rushes up in triumph over the lover, baldly stating his irresistible power:

> "Yeld thee, for thou may not escape!
> May no defence availe thee heer;
> · · · · · · · · · ·
> Be meke, where thou must nedis bow;
> To stryve ageyn is nought thi prow."   [*RR*, 1930–40]

The dreamer concedes readily enough to Love's claims of power, and states
"hombly" that he will become Love's "prisoner," and will yield governance
of "herte and will," indeed he will place "'My lyf, my deth . . . in youre
hond.'"[3] This extravagant humility, culminating in the lover's attempt to kiss
the feet of the God of Love, may have inspired Chaucer to have Troilus similarly abase himself before Criseyde and Pandarus; certainly the language is
echoed when Troilus says "'My lif, my deth, hol in thyn hond I leye'" (I,
1053). However, the main issue is whether or not the lover could have
avoided the arrow; whether his love is voluntary or involuntary. Not surprisingly, the problem is resolved here much the way Boccaccio was to handle
it later: the God of Love is irresistible once one enters his domain, which is
why he cries out with triumph, "'May no defence availe thee *heer*.'"

The lover, of course, entered the garden of his own free will—indeed, so
eager is he to enter that when he once finds the door he immediately begins to
"smyte" upon it, and continues shoving and hammering with eagerness until
he is answered:

> Ful long I shof, and knokkide eke,
> And stood ful long and oft herknyng,
> If that I herde ony wight comyng,
> Til that the dore of thilk entre
> A mayden curteys openyde me.   [*RR*, 534–38]

The lover's passionate assault upon the garden gate should not surprise us,
for he is just twenty years old, the age "Whan that Love taketh his cariage /
Of yonge folk" (22–23), and many of his actions performed before he reaches
the garden, such as his basting his sleeves, are conventional signs of a general

response to what Boccaccio called "natural" promptings and, more specifically, a tendency to become the sort of person commonly called a lover.[4]

Any doubts we might have about the lover's freedom to enter or to refrain from entering Love's garden are dispelled by Reason, who reverses the image of the walled garden with a door, and tells the lover that *he* has admitted the God of Love rather than the other way around:

> "A sory gest, in goode fay,
> Thou herberedest than in thyn inn,
> The God of Love whanne thou let inn!
> Wherfore I rede, thou shette hym oute."
>
> [*RR*, 5106–9]

If the lover has admitted the God of Love and can, with the encouragement of Reason, shut him out again, then the God's power can scarcely be thought to be inexorable. It is only the hunters who become hunted—only those who look in the perilous mirror who become powerless in front of the God of Love. The lover's first approach to the rose is therefore justly described as an error resulting from ignorance:

> But hadde I first knowen in my wit
> The vertu and the strengthe of it, [i.e., the mirror]
> I nolde not have mused there.
> Me hadde bet ben elliswhere.   [*RR*, 1643–46]

Ignorance, a culpable failure of "wit" or reason, leads in a familiar progression to delight, in this instance in the wrong kinds of things, and finally to the acquiescence of the will. When Chaucer's Parson describes mortal sin he says that a sin cannot come into being unless "it nas first in mannes thought, and after that in his delit, and so forth into consentynge and into dede" (*ParsT*, 297). In the *Romaunt* the progression is from thought—the desiring of the rose, to delight—in its perfume, to consent: "Whanne I hadde smelled the savour swote, / No will hadde I fro thens yit goo" (1706–07).

We are not dealing with irresistible forces in either Boccaccio or in the *Romance of the Rose*. The God of Love is immensely powerful once one enters his purview, but even there escape is possible, essentially through the opposite of the procedure that enthralls one to Love. Proper thinking will lead to a desire for something better than this love, and the will can be strengthened to resist the God of Love. Thus, when Reason comes to the aid of the lover, her first counsel is to oppose his former ignorance with knowledge, which will get him out of the trouble he fell into through improper thinking.

> "For if thou knewe hym, out of doute,
> Lightly thou shulde escapen oute
> Of the prisoun that marreth thee."   [*RR*, 4677–79]

Reason's lessons, though, are not easily learned by those who are already in Love's garden. Although the lover could "lightly" escape *if* he knew the true nature of the God he was dealing with, nevertheless it is a big "if." The lover has arrived where he is through irrationality, and he is not disposed to be reasonable merely because he has been asked to be. The savor of rosebuds still benumbs his senses, and following Reason's distinction between good and "foly love" (5085) all he manages by way of response is to suppose that if he cannot follow foolish love, he must hate (5158). But, as Reason observes, he is a fool (5185).

The God of Love can and should be avoided. This is Reason's message in the *Romaunt* and, without entering into the question of whether or not Reason may be thought of as the spokesperson for either or both of the authors, the text of the poem is sufficiently clear: enter the garden and Love will pursue you and overwhelm you, but decline to enter or flee once inside and you can be safe.

In an important passage that seems to anticipate Chaucer's list of "wise, proude, and worthi folkes" (*T&C*, I, 233) whom Love can enthrall, Reason gives a list of all those who can be "daunted" by Love:

> "For noon is of so mochel pris,
> Ne no man founden so wys,
> Ne noon so high is of parage,
> Ne no man founde of wit so sage,
> No man so hardy ne so wight,
> Ne no man of so mochel myght,
> Noon so fulfilled of bounte,
> That he with love may daunted be."   [*RR*, 4757–64]

An important qualification, however, follows immediately: "All the world holdith this wey; / Love makith all to goon myswey" (4765–66). That is, everyone *may* be overcome by the God of Love because everyone travels "this way"; i.e., the way of interest in the opposite sex. However, the God of Love causes people to go *from* the way or astray ("myswey") when he enthralls them—when sexuality becomes dominant rather than remaining subordinate.[5] Reason's subsequent words make this clear: she says that the God of Love can mislead anyone except those of "yvel lyf," cursed by Genius, who are unnatural—for which understand homosexual. Reason does not love those who are unnatural or those who are Love's servants, and only those who follow what she will define as good love are left to receive her very desirable blessing:

> "Love makith all to goon myswey,
> But it be they of yvel lyf,
> Whom Genius cursith, man and wyf,

> That wrongly werke ageyn nature.
> Noon such I love, ne have no cure
> Of sich as Loves servauntes ben,
> And wole not by my counsel flen."   [*RR*, 4766–72]

Reason's counsel to flee in the last line above is repeated for emphasis and phrased with its converse for the same reason. It is very significant that no one in the poem attempts a refutation or rejoinder to Reason's prescription, "'If thou fle it, it shal flee thee; / Folowe it, and folowen shal it thee'" (4783–84). Rather, the lover is content to pronounce himself "devyaunt" from Reason's "scole" (4789), which merely anticipates her subsequent judgment that he is a fool. Not all ignorance is vincible ignorance. Reason's earlier sarcastic comment on the lover's knowledge of his Lord ("'Lo, there a noble conisaunce!'" [4668]) gives way to her all too reasonable doubt that the lover will listen: "'In veyn, perauntre, I shal travayle'" (5192). And so she does.

It is easy enough to produce passages from medieval literature in which Cupid or the God of Love or Venus is said to be all-powerful, yet these are frequently just rhetorical moments rather than studied conclusions. Chaucer's friend John Gower furnishes us with a good instance of this pattern in *Vox Clamantis*. He heaps Ossa upon Pelion in describing Love's power, only to modify the anticipated conclusion that we might as well give in gracefully. Gower begins by offering a version of the proverbial "love conquers all," which Chaucer was to use for his Prioress, and then reinforces the claim with the rhetorical devices of hyperbole and *repetitio*, so that the reader is forced to see that everything, everyone is subject to love:

> Thus love conquers everything—whatever nature has created—yet love itself remains unconquered throughout everything. . . . it subjugates everything to itself yet is unrestricted to all. . . . It militates against everyone; its rule excepts scarcely anyone, for it often causes even saintly people to be sinful. There is no one who can calmly go against its laws, but love itself bears everything calmly. . . . Love wounds the whole human race, but suffers no wound itself.[6]

But Gower is no Roman poet, and "Omnia vincit Amor," rendered by Gower as "amor omne domat," is not followed by the logical "et nos cedamus Amori." Rather, Gower prefers Reason's ploy and counsels lovers "when love is brandishing its piercing dart" to "fly a safe distance away from it." Flight is possible, struggle is not: "There are no arms which prevail in combat with love."[7]

Gower habitually repeats himself, and his comments upon the irresistibility of love are no exception. Within a few lines of the passages quoted above he returns to the topic without much alteration and says that it is inescapable *except* by divine aid or flight.

Neither brawn nor brain can escape its burden. No one can avoid this innate disease, unless it be that divine grace alone watch over him. . . . You will conquer if you shun love, and you will be conquered if you resist it. Lest you be conquered like a lion, you must flee like a hare.

[p. 200]

The last lines on the necessity of flight might well have been inspired by the *Romance of the Rose* wherein the message is, as we have seen, of central importance.

Gower is never ambiguous or equivocal about stating a point of view in the *Vox Clamantis*, so that we do not have the problem so prevalent in Chaucer of deciding which, if any, of the characters in the work speaks for the author. Nor is there much doubt that the authorial voice is Gower's, although the relationship of speaker and poet is often disputed when we deal with Chaucer. If Gower wrote *Vox Clamantis* at approximately the same time that Chaucer wrote the *Troilus*, and indeed only an approximation is necessary since undoubtedly there was considerable literary communication between the two men from 1376 onward, clearly the two would have discussed their views on love and its employment in poetry. It is of course possible that they profoundly disagreed with one another, but it is not very plausible that Chaucer would write a poem presenting a view of love diametrically opposed to that of Gower and then dedicate the poem to him. When reading Chaucer's *Troilus* we would do well to remember that Boccaccio and the *Romance of the Rose* were powerful influences, and that good and bad love, a good and a bad Venus, are distinguished by them. Gower too wrote of "carnal love" and "virtuous love," "voluptuous lust," and "chaste love" found in marriage.[8] He revered one and despised the other and scorned the man who allowed himself to be ensnared by Cupid: "The man who is once free and subjugates himself voluntarily ought to be reckoned more idiotic than an idiot. It is practical for a knight to avoid battles in which he might be made captive, when he cannot win" (Bk. V, chap. 1, p. 197). It is some measure of the distance between our own century and the fourteenth that this series of chapters in *Vox Clamantis* condemning lust and exalting wedded love, both attitudes shared widely throughout England and Europe in the Middle Ages, should be regarded by the translator of the *Vox* as "the low point of the entire poem. . . ."[9]

Thus far we have examined statements about the inexorability of love in several writers who might have furnished Chaucer with inspiration, but we must also look at Chaucer himself for treatments of the idea outside of the *Troilus*. Of course, the characteristic that distinguishes Chaucer from, say, Gower, is his fondness for indirection and irony: to say one thing and mean another. Thus we shall have to be alert to the context, the background, and the tone of Chaucer's comments on Love, Cupid, and the arrows.[10] Perhaps the best place to begin, for both chronological and critical reasons, is with

Chaucer's description of Cupid in the *Parlement of Foules* wherein he is seen with his usual paraphernalia and his daughter Will:

> Under a tre, besyde a welle, I say
> Cupide, oure lord, his arwes forge and file;
> And at his fet his bowe al redy lay;
> And Wille, his doughter, temprede al this while
> The hevedes in the welle. . . .   [*PF*, 211–15]

Because this whole section of Chaucer's poem has long been known to be heavily indebted to Boccaccio's *Teseida* and the *Romance of the Rose*, we should expect that the attitude expressed about love's power will be the same. Although a good deal of scholarly ink has been expended in the discussion of whether or not Chaucer misread Boccaccio's "voluptade" as "voluntade," thus making Cupid's daughter Will rather than Voluptuousness, Robertson and Huppé have pointed out that "Will" makes excellent sense, since although Cupid's arrows come from outside, it is man's own will that gives them the temper or edge to harm him. This insight is to a degree anticipated by Bennett, who argues that a deliberate substitution of Will for Voluptuousness would put the passage in the tradition of the opposition of Wit and Will. However, although Bennett cites the remarks from Boccaccio's *Chiose* discussed above, in which Voluptuousness tempers the arrows of Cupid in our false esteem, he does not seem to think this should modify our assessment of Cupid, whom he styles as signifying a "civilized, courtly emotion." [11] Whatever we may think of the extent to which Cupid is civilized, certainly Chaucer's presentation of him in the *Parliament* does not suggest that he is omnipotent. The relationship of reason, delight, and consent of the will are clear enough in both Boccaccio and the *Romance of the Rose*, and Chaucer's substitution of Will for Voluptuousness merely eliminates a step in the familiar process. Will is depicted as the not-unwilling accomplice, indeed the daughter of Cupid. Anyone unwise enough to get close to Cupid's well, the perilous mirror around which he sets his snares, may find his or her will transferring allegiance to Cupid.

Chaucer drew again upon Boccaccio's *Teseida* for remarks about the seemingly inexorable power of love, this time styling love as Venus in the temple of the goddess in the *Knight's Tale*. Having described the "sacred teeris," and the "firy strokes of the desirynge" that lovers endure, and having imported from the *Romance of the Rose* the porter "Ydelnesse" and the figure of Narcissus, Chaucer then enumerates those who have been conquered by Venus, such as Solomon, Hercules, and Croesus, from which he concludes:

> Thus may ye seen that wysdom ne richesse,
> Beautee ne sleighte, strengthe ne hardynesse,

Ne may with Venus holde champartie,
For as hir list the world than may she gye.

[*KnT*, 1947–50]

The description as a whole in Chaucer's poem seems, to Dorothy Bethurum Loomis, to place its emphasis on the power of Venus, and of the lines just cited Loomis writes "the account ends with seven lines saying that nothing can withstand the power of love. *Venus vincit omnia*."[12] It is true, of course, that the line says that no one may hold "champartie" with Venus, but the reference to champarty suggests the deceitfulness rather than the power of Venus. Throughout the fourteenth century statutes were passed forbidding champarty, and so widely was the outlawed practice used and abused that a "champertor" was assumed to be a cheat—a court officer who entered into a legal case involving land in order to steal it for himself.[13] To say that no one may hold champarty with Venus is to say that she is like a crooked lawyer. When one tries to do business with her, "as hir list the world *than* may she gye." There is no implication here that no one can withstand the power of Venus. Rather, the prudent, law-abiding person would not want to hold champarty with her. Small wonder that the next lines refer to those who have dealt with Venus as people who were "caught" by her. "Lo, alle thise folk so caught were in hir las, / Til they for wo ful ofte seyde 'allas!'" (*KnT*, 1951–52). Lest anyone forget that there is a choice to be made about entering into agreements with Venus, Chaucer introduces into the passage the figure of "Ydelnesse," the porter of the gate, from the *Romance of the Rose* (noted by Skeat but not mentioned by Robinson) to remind the reader that one need not enter the door at all. Indeed, the remedy for lust was Idleness' opposite, Industry—a medieval commonplace expressed by the Ovidian "Otia si tollas periere Cupidinis arcus."[14] Though one be strong, rich, wise, or hardy, it is in the nature of things that those who idly approach close enough to Venus to worship in her temple have, in a sense, already lost the struggle by "champartie."

Chaucer's deliberate addition of the character Ydelnesse to his principal source is a signal that the *Romaunt* was very much on his mind while he was writing the *Knight's Tale*. Indeed when we consider his treatment of passionate love with the French poem in mind, it is plain that he expresses much the same sort of attitude. Just as the God of Love assured the lover that nothing would avail him *here*—that is, within the garden—so in the Temple of Venus no one can deal successfully with Venus for *then* she may control anyone. Reason in the *Romaunt* urged the lover to flee love, which he declined to do, while Chaucer recasts the scene more dramatically and more amusingly and has Arcite, deeply wounded by Love, declare after that occurrence that "'A man moot nedes love, maugree his heed. / He may nat fleen it, thogh he sholde be deed'" (*KnT*, 1169–70). Indeed, although Chaucer does not mention either an arrow or an archer, Palamon is said to be "'. . . hurt right now thurghout myn ye / Into myn herte . . .'" (*KnT*, 1096–97), the precise path of the God of Love's arrow in the *Romaunt* (indicating, we remember, suggestion and delight), and this detail is probably added from the *Romaunt*; it is not to be found in the *Teseida*. Finally, Reason's judgment that the lover is a fool is echoed by Theseus, who sets lovers up as the prime examples of fools: "'Now looketh, is nat that an heigh folye? / Who may been a fool, but if he love?'" (*KnT*, 1798–99).

When Theseus' speech on love is read with the *Romance of the Rose* in mind, it becomes difficult to agree with Muscatine that it is a "mature appraisal, not an adverse criticism, of courtly love. . . ."[15] Rather, the invocation of the God of Love by name, the reference to lovers as fools even while they think they are wise, the emphasis on being a servant of Love (cf. *RR*, 1947), on its pain, and the image of being caught by the God's "laas," reminiscent of Cupid's "gynnes" and "snare" (*RR*, 1620, 1647), combine to make the speech appear indeed to be an adverse criticism of the God of Love. Moreover, while Theseus' speech begins with the now familiar statement that the God of Love is irresistible, it nevertheless concludes with Theseus' reference to his own love-service in the past tense—proof that at least some can heed Reason's advice to flee even after they have entered the garden:

> "The god of love, a, *benedicite*!
> How myghty and how greet a lord is he!
> Ayeyns his myght ther gayneth none obstacles.
> He may be cleped a god for his myracles;
> For he kan maken, at his owene gyse,
> Of everich herte as that hym list divyse.
> Lo heere this Arcite and this Palamoun,
> That quitly weren out of my prisoun,
> And myghte han lyved in Thebes roially,
> ·
> And yet hath love, maugree hir eyen two,
> Broght hem hyder bothe for to dye.
> Now looketh, is nat that an heigh folye?
> Who may been a fool, but if he love?
> Bihoold, for Goddes sake that sit above,
> Se how they blede! be they noght wel arrayed?
> Thus hath hir lord, the god of love, ypayed
> Hir wages and hir fees for hir servyse!
> And yet they wenen for to ben ful wyse
> That serven love, for aught that may bifalle.
> ·
> But all moot ben assayed, hoot and coold;
> A man moot ben a fool, or yong or oold,—

> I woot it by myself ful yore agon,
> For in my tyme a servant was I oon.
> And therfore, syn I knowe of loves peyne,
> And woot hou soore it kan a man distreyne,
> As he that hath ben caught ofte in his laas,
> I yow foryeve al hoolly this trepaas." [*KnT*, 1785–1818]

The entire sarcastic praise of Love and his power is an addition to Chaucer's source, and while Boccaccio refers to the folly of the young men, and to Theseus' own former folly, many of the details, such as the "laas," are additions.

Love, for Chaucer, was certainly an elemental force, but scarcely an irresistible one. "Maistrie" in marriage, so sought after by the Wife of Bath, is sufficient to drive away this kind of love, if we may believe the Franklin, who assures us that "Whan maistrie comth, the God of Love anon / Beteth his wynges, and farewel, he is gon" (*FranklT*, 765–66). Of course, if Chaucer had in mind the kind of distinction Boccaccio made between a Venus of marriage and procreation as opposed to a Venus of lascivious delight, it would be clear enough that the two could not coexist, and that indeed, "maistrie" would drive away the God of *that* Love. Lip service is paid to the god's power throughout Chaucer's works, but at the same time Chaucer was at some pains to develop an amusing image of himself as a narrator of love poems who was nevertheless incompetent as a lover.[16] This variation of the familiar inability *topos* in which Chaucer substitutes amorous for literary inability perhaps reaches its peak in the *Legend of Good Women*, in which the narrator Chaucer appears to the God of Love as "nothyng able" (*LGW*, G, 246). Obviously the God of Love's oft-mentioned omnipotence is useless against impotence— whether it be physical or literary. The *Legend of Good Women* is a complex series of ironies layered over ironies, and is far too subtle to be considered here.[17] However, insofar as we are concerned with the power of the God of Love we should remark that the god himself submissively hands over the bridle to Alceste, and with regard to Chaucer's mock forgiveness and penance says to her, "'Al lyth in yow, doth with hym what yow leste'" (*LGW*, G, 439). The narrator Chaucer, who, like Theseus, is said to have kept Love's estate in his youth (*LGW*, G, 400) is significantly accused as his greatest crime of having translated the *Romance of the Rose*, which, the God of Love feels, not without considerable justification, causes "'wise folk fro me [to] withdrawe'" (*LGW*, G, 257). In his defense Chaucer does not plead ignorance, which Alceste had offered on his behalf, for ignorance is no excuse. Rather, he pleads that his intention was "'To forthere trouthe in love and it cheryce'" (*LGW*, G, 462), which, if we heed Reason's distinctions about love in that poem, is precisely what a translation of it would accomplish.[18]

Love's Power in the *Troilus*

If in general statements about the God of Love's or Cupid's power in Chaucer and in other medieval literature need to be taken with appropriate caution, it behooves us to look carefully at the *Troilus* to see whether the general rule holds for this specific instance. Troilus' first appearance in the poem is at the Feast of Palladion, during which he walks up and down with his retinue, gazing at the ladies while feeling smugly secure. The God of Love is angered by Troilus' pride, and shoots him with an arrow. Then there follows an interjection about Proud Bayard, to be discussed later. Troilus erroneously "wende nothing hadde had swich myght / Ayeyns his wille that shuld his herte stere" (I, 227–28). Yet, in language reminiscent of the eye and the heart in the *Romaunt*, Troilus' sight of Criseyde leads to an effect on his heart, and his will is overthrown:

> Yet with a look his herte wax a-fere,
> That he that now was moost in pride above,
> Wax sodeynly moost subgit unto love. [I, 229–31]

Chaucer has, rather carefully I think, laid out the elements of reason, will, pride, and delight (the involvement of the heart) that recall the lover in the *Romaunt* and make Troilus' subjugation inevitable even if they do not make the God of Love's power irresistible. Like the lover in the *Romaunt* Troilus is eager for the aesthetic appreciation of ladies if not so bluntly their enjoyment. In the *Troilus* there is not exactly a "mirrour perilous" of Narcissus, but Troilus' disparagement of "lovers," and his pride in his own detachment, even to the point of asking " 'Loo! is this naught wisely spoken?' " (I, 205), is narcissistic in the extreme. The God of Love in the *Romaunt* humbles lords and ladies "Whan he may hem to proude see" (*RR*, 884), and it is Troilus' pride that arouses the god in this poem. Moreover, just as the lover in the *Romaunt* rues the failure of his "wit," in underestimating the power of the mirror, so Troilus "wende" that his will could not be overthrown by his heart. The masses of rosebuds, we remember, served to stimulate the lover in the *Romaunt*, but after he chose a particular one, the God of Love shot him with his arrow. So with Troilus; he gets away with looking "Now here, now there" (I, 187) until he sees Criseyde, at which point the eye involves the heart. Even though the description of this comes after Chaucer's reference to the God of Love's shooting the arrow, it may be taken nevertheless as a different way of representing what is in essence if not sequence the same phenomenon. Thus Troilus is "On this lady, and now on that, lokynge" (I, 269), until "thorugh a route / His eye percede, and so depe it wente, / Til on Criseyde it smot, and ther it stente" (I, 271–73). He stands there "astoned" (I, 274), and "Therwith his herte gan to sprede and rise" (I, 278). In the *Ro-*

maunt it is choosing a particular rosebud followed by smelling its perfume that leads successively to the lover's having "No will . . . fro thens yit goo" (*RR*, 1707) and to being hit by the arrow, whereas in *Troilus* it is his sight of Criseyde that serves the same function. It is, we must remember, "with a look" that Troilus' heart becomes on fire—"a-fere."

Troilus' reason fails to recognize a danger, because he is blinded by pride. Consequently his eye and heart respond to the stimulus of the beautiful lady, and his will is overthrown in spite of his naive conviction that such a thing could not happen. He thought "nothing hadde had swich myght / Ayeyns his wille that shuld his herte stere" (I, 227–28). All this is so exactly like the irrational behavior of the lover in the *Romaunt*, who to a degree regrets his own folly but cannot withdraw from his predicament, that it is hard to imagine that Chaucer meant to convey a sympathetic portrait. Thus when he goes on to ask "wise, proude, and worthi folkes alle" (I, 233)—i.e., those who are like Troilus in pride if not in wisdom—not to scorn Love, "which that so soone kan / The fredom of youre hertes to hym thralle" (I, 234–35), we are invited to consider the God of Love as a dangerous adversary rather than an irresistible force. To be sure, Chaucer goes on to draw a broader picture when he says,

> For evere it was, and evere it shal byfalle,
> That Love is he that alle thing may bynde,
> For may no man fordon the lawe of kynde.   [I, 236–38]

As with the contradictory examples from Gower examined earlier, we must question whether Chaucer means there is a law of kynde or nature asserting the power of the God of Love to bind everyone, or whether he means there is a law of nature stating that all those who scorn the God of Love may be bound by him? After all, those who treat him with the respect his power properly inspires do not get near enough to him to be caught. Perhaps it would be nearest the mark to interpret Chaucer's passage as saying there is a law in nature that men who watch ladies will not do so dispassionately forever. If one enters the God of Love's purview by "byholding ay the ladies of the town," then suggestion will lead to delight, delight to consent, and the arrow will find one.

It does not matter much, Chaucer goes on, what sort of person you are, for you are not smarter than those who have been overcome by love, and indeed the strongest, the worthiest, and the greatest of degree have also been mastered. The vocabulary here, "wit," "strengest folk," "worthiest," and "greatest of degree" echoes almost word for word the description in the *Romaunt*:

> For noon is of so mochel pris,
> Ne no man founden so wys,
> Ne noon so high is of parage,

> Ne no man founde of wit so sage,
> No man so hardy ne so wight,
> Ne no man of so mochel myght,
> Noon so fulfilled of bounte,
> That he with love may daunted be.   [*RR*, 4757–64]

While it would perhaps be wrong to overemphasize Chaucer's "*may* bynde" and the *Romaunt*'s "may daunten," nevertheless we have already noted that the passage in the *Romaunt* is followed immediately by a remark that the God of Love misleads people from nature's way, indicating that there are other ways. Hence the passage is followed by Reason's counsel to flee the God of Love, which emphasized the element of free choice. The God of Love *may* bind or daunt or he may not.

Chaucer's tactic is very different. Having shown Troilus' subjection to the God of Love and having warned the audience of the god's power, he then uses a strongly ironic verse in which he says that the god's power "was, and is, . . . / And trewelich it sit wel to be so" (I, 245–46). This appears to be so counter to what Chaucer says elsewhere as to constitute an antiphrasis. Then follow some lines to be treated in detail in the next chapter, which say that this power of the god is "so vertuous in kynde" (I, 254). Either Chaucer is being ironic here, as he is when he describes the worldly Friar as "vertuous" (*Gen Prol*, 251), or he is arguing that the love represented by Cupid is virtuous, pace Gower, one of the dedicatees of the poem, who argued the exact opposite.[19] Certainly none of the texts we have examined thus far would suggest that love inspired by Cupid is virtuous, but let us pass on for now to the conclusion of the stanza, in which the narrator enters the poem and counsels the audience, addressed as "yow," to follow Love:

> Now sith it may nat goodly ben withstonde,
> And is a thing so vertuous in kynde,
> Refuseth nat to Love for to ben bonde,
> Syn, as hymselven liste, he may yow bynde.
> The yerde is bet that bowen wole and wynde
> Than that that brest; and therfore I yow rede
> To folowen hym that so wel kan yow lede.
>
> [I, 253–259]

This has to be ironic, granting the poem any coherence whatsoever, for not only has Chaucer not really said that love is irresistible—only that Troilus could not resist it—but his counsel to the audience to follow love is at odds with his disinclination to follow it himself.[20]

The narrator's reluctance to follow Love needs more attention than it has customarily received. As noted earlier, Chaucer was at some pains in his career to develop a narrative persona who was interested in love, indeed enthusiastic about it, but somehow ignorant or unable in matters of love that are practical rather than theoretical. One assumes that this is a literary rather than a biographical joke. This amusing persona, which by no means prevented Chaucer from offering very critical views of the service of love, was probably created to set him apart from both the Ovidian boast "Me Venus artificem tenero praefecit Amori," and the literary commonplace of the teacher who has learned about love at some personal expense—a figure found in Andreas Capellanus, in John Gower of the *Confessio Amantis*, and in Chaucer's own figure of Theseus in the *Knight's Tale*. In creating and modifying this persona Chaucer is consistent in his entertaining division between talking about love and doing something about it, but he varies from time to time the representation of "Chaucer's" relationship to the God of Love. Thus in the *Hous of Fame* and the *Legend of Good Women*, both written in approximately the same decade as the *Troilus*, he styles himself respectively as one who has "served so ententyfly" the "blynde . . . Cupido" (*HF*, 616–17), while as we have already noted he is one who has served the God of Love in his youth, although now at least *appears* to be a renegade (*LGW*, G, 400–401). In the *Troilus*, though, Chaucer is careful to distinguish himself from the servants of Love, not just as one who has outgrown that stage, but as one who is set apart from them. Consequently, while he maintains that he is an unlikely lover, he says that he serves the servants of the God of Love rather than that he serves the god himself. Moreover, he distances himself from the god by saying he could not even pray for the god's assistance, being so far removed:

> For I, that God of Loves servantz serve,
> Ne dar to Love, for myn unliklynesse,
> Preyen for speed, al sholde I therfore sterve,
> So fer am I from his help in derknesse.   [I, 15–18]

The narrator Chaucer dares not pray "godspeed" from Love, but he does pray for those who serve the god

> For so hope I my sowle best avaunce,
> To prey for hem that Loves servauntz be,
> And write hire wo, and lyve in charite.[21]   [I, 47–49]

By separating himself from the servants of the God of Love, by living in charity while they live in "wo," (even though he ironically styles his life of "charite," "compassioun," and soul-advancement as "derknesse"), Chaucer makes it overwhelmingly clear that the God of Love is not irresistible.[22] *He* has resisted (or avoided) him. Chaucer cannot pray to the God of Love for assistance because what he will do in *Troilus* is to show how the servants of Love are unhappy—the kind of thing that caused the God of Love in the *Legend of Good Women* to complain that Chaucer's translation of the *Romance of the Rose* prompted "'wise folk fro me [to] withdrawe'" (*LGW*, G, 257).

Chaucer does, though, pray to lovers that they "preieth to God so dere" (I, 32)—not, we notice to the God of Love—that he will, in the poem, be able to show "Swich peyne and wo as Loves folk endure" (I, 34). This is important, for if it is reasonable to want to be happy, or as Boethius put it in Chaucer's translation "yif blisfulnesse be the soverayn good of nature that lyveth by resoun" (Bk. II, pr. 4), then it is unreasonable to be unhappy, foolish to be a servant of the God of Love. Chaucer did not invent this attitude; it is to be found in the *Romaunt* where Reason says she does not love "'sich as Loves servauntes ben'" (*RR*, 4771), for they follow the kind of loving that will make them "'wrecchis full of woo'" (*RR*, 4775).

Chaucer's stanzas about the power of love are both accurate and important. But they do not absolve either Troilus or the members of the audience from responsibility for their own actions. It is precisely because Love is so powerful, precisely because he cannot be overcome in struggle, that the prudent course, the reasonable course, is to avoid him. The emphasis on the height of Troilus' position as a king's son, and on the depths of his self-abasement in love, both additions to the source as we have seen, are of a piece with Chaucer's use of the story as an exemplum of the general unhappiness of Love's servants, which is also an addition. He asks the audience to take "ensample . . . of this man" (I, 232) not to scorn love, and he also shows the general relevance of Troilus' specific difficulty when he clearly states his intention: ". . . *to shewe*, in som manere, / Swich peyne and wo as Loves folk endure, / In Troilus unsely aventure" (I, 33–35). The function of an example is to be exemplary: to teach. If love were indeed both unavoidable and irresistible, an exemplum about its dangers would be nugatory. Thus, the narrator's later counsel to follow Love who "so wel kan yow lede" can only be ironic. In urging the audience to take the course he does not follow himself the narrator is not forgetful but playful. In the *Romance of the Rose* the lover thinks he can be happy only if he disregards Reason's counsels, whereas exactly the opposite is true. Chaucer presents the same general theme found in the *Romance of the Rose*: service of the God of Love is the unhappy result of the failure of reason compounded by pride. However, he presents it in a very different way, choosing instead of a dialogue between Reason and a lover an exemplary tale with narrative comment. Since the theme was scarcely recherché, Chaucer felt free to have the narrative commentary veer in tone from the solemn to the ironic and back again, apparently assuming that the overall direction of his narrative would be easy enough to follow. However, now that devices like the service of the God of Love have become ancient history rather than living literary conventions, critics have all too frequently interpreted Chaucer's lines in too narrow a context.

Boethius, Destiny, and the Freedom of the Will

Since freedom of the will is an essential ingredient in the service of the God of Love, it is apparent that much of the scholarly lucubration about the "function" of the Boethian elements in the *Troilus* has been somewhat beside the point. Troilus' garbled speculations on the freedom of the will are not included in the poem because of their philosophical profundity nor even because of their lack of it. Nor are they included to call attention to the power of destiny, or the lack of it. Rather, they are included because they are part of the medieval vocabulary of love. What is interesting about them is their form rather than their function, for their function is not new.[23]

The three works that have been used as touchstones thus far in this chapter—Boccaccio's *Chiose* to the *Teseida*, the *Romance of the Rose*, and Gower's *Vox Clamantis*—all concern themselves to a degree with the relationship between romantic love and freedom of the will. By looking at another work, one which is concerned with love much more generally, we may better see why this relationship between love and free will was a commonplace among medieval authors. The work is Dante's *Purgatorio*, in which he introduces a comment on the nature of love in the seventeenth canto: that is, precisely in the middle of the entire *Commedia*. Vergil discourses on love to the pilgrim Dante, with the goal of explaining the nature of sin and punishment. However, the series of distinctions he sets out is very useful for other contexts as well. To begin with, Vergil notes that no one has ever been without love, either "natural" or "of the mind." As Singleton distinguishes the two in his notes, "natural" love is that which each creature has for its own place or goal, which in mankind is for God. This love for God is implanted by God, and as such cannot err. Vergil says this in the text: "The natural is always without error; but the other may err either through an evil object, or through too much or too little vigor." Singleton's felicitous term for "love of the mind" is "elective love," which, he points out, can only occur in mankind in this life, because it presupposes free will and choice. As Vergil observes, this latter love can be directed to the "Primal Good" without sinful pleasure, and it can be directed towards "secondary goods" without sin, provided that it observes the proper measure. However, when it is turned toward evil (which, as Singleton notes, must be evil wrongly perceived as a good), or when it "speeds to good with more zeal, or with less, than it ought," then it errs, and we with it. As Vergil concludes, "Hence you can comprehend that love must needs be the seed in you of every virtue and of every action deserving punishment." In the next canto Vergil describes in more detail the process of love, which begins with the "faculty of apprehension." This faculty "draws an image from a real existence and displays it within you, so that it makes the mind turn to it." Then, if once turned "the mind inclines toward it, that inclination is love." Natural love, directed toward the primal good, is like the bee's innate desire to make honey, and merits neither praise nor blame. Elective love, however, is not always praiseworthy, "because perhaps its matter appears always to be good: but not every imprint is good, although the wax be good." Now it is inevitable, and hence "necessary," that our minds respond in a positive way to those things that please us, because they were created to be that way. As Vergil puts it, "The mind, which is quick to love, is responsive to everything that pleases, as soon as by pleasure it is roused to action." However, most important for our present considerations, that "necessity" is nevertheless overruled. "Wherefore, suppose that every love which is kindled in you arises of necessity, the power to arrest it is in you. This noble virtue Beatrice understands as the free will." [24]

Awareness of the kinds of things someone like Dante had to say about love and free will is very useful for a consideration of romantic love and free will. It explains, for example, why poets commonly said that the God of Love was irresistible, yet ought to be resisted. The "natural desire" Boccaccio wrote of, which he said "every man or woman has, to see and to possess or acquire some beautiful and precious things," is the same thing that Dante has Vergil describe as the responsiveness of the mind to everything that pleases. But, just as Dante reminded the reader of the possibility of loving the wrong object or loving too much or too little, so does Boccaccio introduce the concept of two Venuses to explain why love is not always a good thing. Dante refers to free will, Boccaccio to a judgment that can be either rational or corrupt. The same kind of analogy explains why the arrow of the God of Love is said to enter the eye and penetrate to the heart in the *Romaunt*. Love of all kinds begins with the faculty of apprehension, as Dante calls it, so that the fixing of the eye represents the first step, while the mind's turning toward the object, and then inclining towards it, is called love, which is aptly represented by the heart.

The love of a man for a woman, or of a woman for a man, was not perceived in the Middle Ages to be a unique phenomenon; one explicable only in terms of itself. Shelley's idea that "eternal Love" was the only thing not subject to "Fate, Time, Occasion, Chance, and Change," elevates love to an eminence it did not enjoy in Chaucer's day. Love was a process, not a force, in the Middle Ages, and since romantic love was simply an aspect of the more general phenomenon of love, it is no wonder at all that poets concerned with romantic love not uncommonly introduced the linked topic of the freedom of the will, particularly when they were portraying the passionate love outside of marriage, *fol amour*, which ought to be resisted by exercising the free will one has.

Both Dante and Boccaccio find it useful to introduce free will into their discussions of the processes of love, but for an examination of Chaucer's *Troilus* it is more relevant to inspect some passages in the *Romance of the*

Rose. In Jean de Meun's section of the poem we find a discussion of the freedom of the will embedded in a poem devoted to the examination of kinds of
love, and it has been known from the time of Langlois' edition of the poem
that the discussion, by the character Nature, depends upon Boethius for its
ideas.[25] The function of Nature's speech on free will in the *Romance* is much
the same as that of Vergil's speech on the same subject in the *Commedia*: it
serves to remind the reader of the ultimate responsibility the individual has
for his actions. As John Fleming puts it, "Amant's free will is crucial to the
poem, for it predicates a moral responsibility which cannot be waived by an
appeal either to philosophical or biological determinism."[26] Chaucer could
have gotten the idea of including some comment on the freedom of the will in
his poem of the love of Troilus and Criseyde from any number of sources, but
the particularly Boethian expression of it might well have come from the *Romance of the Rose*, and Jean de Meun's rather oblique introduction of it may
also have inspired Chaucer. Jean, after all, did not, as Dante did, choose a
clearly tutelary figure like Vergil to introduce the Boethian arguments for the
freedom of the will. It is not Reason, as we might expect, who adduces the
arguments, but Nature, and Nature does not understand all of their implications. Nature's complaint, in the *Romance*, is that man alone, of all created
creatures, does not follow her commandment to create further life, but,
through his evil deeds, actually purchases death. "See with what shackles the
miserable creature chains himself. Does he do well to go buying his death by
giving himself to such evils?" (p. 317). As Fleming points out, Nature does
not understand grace, and so thinks that the enemy is death, to be conquered
by procreation, rather than sin, to be conquered by charity.[27] Thus the
Boethian arguments for the freedom of the will are uttered by a character who
is a bit shortsighted—a situation not altogether different from that which
Chaucer effected in his poem, in which Troilus, as both Robertson and
Stroud have noted, presents a challenge or partial argument as though it were
a conclusion or were conclusive.[28] Thus Chaucer's use of Boethius, while it is
an addition to his primary source, is not really a novelty but, broadly understood, may be seen as a commonplace in medieval treatments of love. Neither
the Boethian speeches nor the apostrophes to the power of the God of Love
should be taken at face value. Chaucer, like other medieval writers, invokes
destiny in order to emphasize free will, and Cupid in order to renounce him.

Vox Clamantis and Troilus and Criseyde

Love and the will, the subjects of this chapter, were concepts familiar to
Chaucer from his ventures into literature and philosophy. The additions he
makes to his source involving these subjects—a series of stanzas showing
Troilus' succumbing to the God of Love and an ironic urging of the reader to

succumb too, plus Troilus' inadequate citations from Boethius—combine to point up a moral that would have surprised no one in fourteenth century England. Chaucer tells us that in old Troy a prince was free to choose wisely in love but did not, and the implications for citizens of New Troy are clear enough. Thus as a story the poem is a fairly close rendering of Boccaccio's *Filostrato*. The significance of the story, however, bears a remarkable similarity to the significance of John Gower's *Vox Clamantis*, which has many of the same specific emphases: man's freedom, fortune, destiny, and good and bad love.

Gower begins his poem by asserting that "writings of the past contain fit examples for the future" (p. 49), a medieval commonplace that Chaucer does not adduce, but which clearly applies to any English poem on a Trojan subject. Following the Prologue Gower proceeds with his dream vision, in which the Peasants' Revolt is styled as the revolt of the rabble metamorphosed into beasts, ransacking New Troy. The question naturally arises as to why these unfortunate events should transpire. People, Gower says, "ask why so many strange and highly burdensome evils now attend us almost daily. For nothing on earth happens without cause. . . . Nevertheless, all men commonly say they have nothing to do with cause, as if no one were responsible for things. In fact they now blame fickle Fortune . . ." (p. 99). Gower, however, discounts the influence of Fortune, saying that "whatever other people do, I still cannot believe in fate, at least as long as God is omnipotent" (p. 100).[29] On the individual level, Gower believes, a man chooses his own fate, while on a national level a kind of collective consciousness determines a country's relative prosperity. "Fortune is nothing," Gower asserts, "and neither destiny nor fate nor chance has anything to do with human affairs. But each man fashions his own destiny and opposes chance as he pleases and creates his own fate" (p. 102). This fate is dependent upon what Boccaccio called rational or corrupt judgment, for as Gower puts it "If your will is good, a good fate follows; if your will is bad, through the operation of your mind you cause fate to be bad" (pp. 102–3). Multiplied by the many the same effects follow: "Thus God disposes the times according to our deserts" (p. 103).

When one considers the structure of Gower's *Vox Clamantis* his emphasis on collective responsibility for the ills besetting New Troy is striking. In book 1 of the poem Gower relates the dream of the social upheaval in which the various protesting groups are envisioned as animals. Book 2, significantly, is entirely given over to a justification of the ways of God to man. That is, the whole book is an extended argument in which the power of Fortune is denied, the freedom of the will defended, and the awarding of punishment or reward by a just God is maintained. "In His wisdom He allots all things with just judgment" (p. 111), Gower writes, and he concludes the book by asserting that "nothing is fortunate or unfortunate because of fate; rather, God bestows His gifts according to man's deserts. . . . I truly acknowledge that whatever happens in the world, whether it be good or evil, we ourselves are the cause of it" (p. 112). Although Gower does not avail himself explicitly of the Boethian arguments on the freedom of the will, the sentiments expressed are certainly harmonious with the teachings of the *Consolation of Philosophy*. The tenor of the passage just cited from Gower, which closes his book of commentary, is precisely the same as the tenor of the close of the *Consolation*, which, in Chaucer's translation, reads "'Withstond thanne and eschue thou vices; worschipe and love thou vertues. . . . Gret necessite of prowesse and vertu is encharged and comaunded to yow . . . syn that ye worken and don . . . byforn the eyen of the juge that seeth and demeth alle thinges'" (Bk. V, pr. 6). By devoting an entire book to the denial of Fortune's power and to the assertion of man's ability to effect his own good or bad fate, Gower provides his reader with the basis for a moral commentary on the England of his day. Book 1 portrays the fact of a troubled realm, in which the natural social order is disrupted. Book 2 asserts that this sorry state is the result of God's properly adverse judgment on the collectively free but improper choices of Englishmen. Books 3, 4, 5, and 6 outline what these improper choices have been by listing the failings of people in the three estates, and book 7 tells us what the ultimate error is that has caused so many to have chosen so poorly.

For Gower, England's social problems were the result of the downfall of justice, which was in turn the result of the people's abandonment of righteousness in their eagerness to embrace Venus. "In my opinion," he writes,

> there is now one very bad fact which can be called the source and well-spring of evil. Alas! Because Justice, a fugitive, has withdrawn to afar, her associate Peace has also departed elsewhere. Peace, which in times gone by used to bestow kisses upon Justice, now has fled from the land, because Righteousness has vanished. . . . It is not least of all that adultery is grievous now, for the flesh insists upon everything that is possible. Even if Venus does hold sway in other countries, they make up for this by their good qualities in other respects. For law is well established there. . . .   [p. 284]

It may surprise us that Gower links lawlessness with Venereal promptings, but it should not. Indeed, since love, as Dante put it, is the source of every deed deserving both reward and punishment, Venus as the symbol of sexual love of the wrong sort serves by metonymy as the symbol for all wrong loves. Perhaps because St. Paul said that with his mind he served the law of God but with his flesh the law of sin (Romans 7:25), medieval writers were inspired to portray the opposition of flesh and spirit as an opposition of sexual sin to righteousness. At any rate, what we find in Gower is an insistence on England's lack of any redeeming virtue: "And so to a certain extent, Justice redeems their [i.e., other countries'] sin of the flesh, which falls because of its frail nature. But in this country not only are we mastered by the goad of the flesh, with which man is spurred on, but indeed the law, ignorant of what is right, oversteps its boundaries" (p. 284).

Gower was not alone in his indictment of England as a Venereal nation. Thomas Brinton, in 1375, had said that if the earth did not abundantly render its gifts, it was the result of accidia in the people, and the manifestations of this sin he defined as "rapina, gula, luxuria, incestus, et adulterium."[30] Gower's attribution of England's decline to lust and lawlessness is not much different from Brinton's attribution of it to sloth, gluttony, and adultery. Both pieces must have been very moving to the audiences of the times, considering the shattering events of the seventies. Gower's conclusion particularly, since it was written after the Peasants' Revolt and the last sad days of Edward III, is very poignant:

> Fate, which never used to use us harshly, now overwhelms us guilty people, hard pressed on every side. The earth, which used to be rich with every kind of metal, now does not contain its own weight in lead. . . . Thus my native land, which was once steadfast, is weakened by unjust legal decisions and by denying rights of man. Thus the Mistress of the people renders tribute to sin, and she stands apart from God, almost like a widowed woman. Thus she who used to be moral is now sinful; formerly law-abiding, now she is lawlessly fierce. Thus she who once was generous now suffers poverty; she who once was holy is becoming the goddess Venus herself.   [p. 285]

If Gower and Chaucer discussed poetic themes in the late seventies and early eighties, it may be that each to an extent influenced the other. In spite of their differences in form, in language, and in style, *Vox Clamantis* and *Troilus and Criseyde* have more in common than one might at first suppose. Gower writes a poem in which the troubles of New Troy are attributed to the people's choice of Venus in preference to Justice, while Chaucer writes a poem in which the sorrow of Troilus, a prince of Old Troy whose name stands for the city itself, is attributed to his free submission to Venus and Cupid. At the same time the city's problems derive from the very similar choice by Paris. Chaucer might have been disappointed by Gower's inability to be livelier; Gower might have been disappointed at Chaucer's relative neglect of the failures of justice. As Professor Coffman has so well demonstrated, Gower is always the advocate of a moral order.[31] Because of Gower's expression of the collapse of this order by the elevation of Venus as mistress of the people, it seems almost inevitable that Chaucer's poem about Troilus' celebration of Venus accompanying his capitulation to her son Cupid, should be dedicated to the moral Gower.[32]

Chapter III

The Ennoblement of Troilus

The Discovery of Courtly Love and the Consequent Claims for the Ennoblement of its Practitioners

In the previous chapter an attempt was made to demonstrate that in the *Troilus* love is not an irresistible force, and that the textual claims to the contrary must be construed as ironic. In this chapter we shall deal with the related claim that love is virtuous itself and ennobles lovers. The idea that the hero of Chaucer's *Troilus and Criseyde* is ennobled by his love for Criseyde is so commonly encountered in modern critical estimates of the poem that one tends to forget its relative novelty. Upon examination, however, we find that the idea scarcely exists prior to the present century, and indeed is most regularly discovered in writings of the last thirty-five years. The cause for this new direction in critical analysis is almost certainly the practice of turning to courtly love in order to explain the actions of the protagonists in medieval love poems. Since it was only in 1883 that Gaston Paris introduced the term *amour courtois* into the critical vocabulary of medieval studies, it follows that it was not until the turn of the century that critics of English poetry began to employ the concept of courtly love as a historical phenomenon that would explain the behavior of characters in literary works.

In some ways the appearance of courtly love on the scene of literary criticism must have been greeted with a good deal of thanksgiving, for it enabled critics to surmount what had been very real obstacles to the appreciation of poems like Chaucer's *Troilus*. Thomas Campbell, for example, writing in 1830, had objected to the "inconsistency between the strength and tenderness, and the lawlessness and secrecy of Troilus's passion. The poet represents no sufficient cause to prevent the Trojan from marrying Cresseide. . . ."[1] Courtly love, of course, would be adduced to "prove" that love and marriage were held to be incompatible; therefore the *Troilus* succeeds because of rather than in spite of what Campbell had called adherence to "nature and probability."

In the nineteenth century, then, a critic might praise Chaucer's *Troilus* as "the most beautiful diary of love ever written," as Hartley Coleridge did in 1848, or he might single out touches of "pathetic beauty" for admiration, as did Campbell in 1819.[2] But, before the discovery of courtly love, a critic would not go so far as to suggest that the passionate attachment of the principals, however beautiful, resulted in the ennoblement of one or the other or both.[3] Before the century was over, though, the concept of *amour courtois*, first discussed by Gaston Paris with regard to French literature, was taken up and applied to Italian literature by Lewis Freeman Mott.[4] Hard on the heels of this development, in 1913, came the first major treatment of Chaucer's *Troilus* as a work in the genre of the courtly love poem, written by William George Dodd. Dodd was emphatic about the ennobling power of love affairs in courtly love poetry generally and in the *Troilus* specifically. He wrote: "one of the commonest sentiments in the love-poetry of the troubadours, in that of Chrétien, and in the book of Andreas, was that love is not only good in itself, but is the cause and origin of all good." For evidence Dodd cites Pandarus' words to the love-stricken Troilus:

> "And for-thy loke of good comfort thou be;
> . . . for nought but good it is
> To love wel, and in a worthy place."

Dodd's pronouncement on love as the cause and origin of all good became very much a standard view for the next half century and more. "The ennobling nature of love finds many expressions in the *Troilus*," he wrote, and his loci (which will be examined in detail below) became the touchstones for this approach to the poem for a very long time.[5] To be sure, from very early on in the history of "ennobling" interpretations of the poem there were those who were skeptical. Root, for example, in the preface to his 1926 edition of the poem remarks that Chaucer found "inherent contradictions and fallacies" in the code of courtly love, but the mainstream of criticism of the poem by-passed fallacies and contradictions to dwell upon uplift and ennoblement.[6] For example, Kirby, in 1940, argued that the main difference between Chaucer's and Boccaccio's treatment of the hero was the former's "development of Troilus as a courtly lover," that is, Chaucer's demonstration of the "courtly conception of love as a great spiritual, ennobling, and regenerative force."[7] Similarly, in 1950 Denomy concluded that the love and behavior of Troilus and Criseyde, according to the code of courtly love, were "necessary and praiseworthy, their love a source of ennoblement and growth in excellence."[8]

This strain of criticism continues through the 1950s and the sixties, although there appears to be a greater concern to justify the ennobling powers of love by an appeal to the text of the poem than by recourse to a courtly love tradition. Still, in 1959 Meech argued that while Chaucer could "genially" oppose the absurdity of courtly love to its noble idealism, nevertheless he perfects his hero "by the standards of amour courtois." In comparison to Boccaccio's hero, Meech finds Chaucer's Troilus "ennobled and intellectualized in his responses—improved in all qualities of heart and mind. . . ."[9] Finally, two critics writing in the sixties may be cited to complete this review of opinion. Alfred David wrote of Troilus that "the ennobling of his character" was the result of the humbling of his pride, and while David does not derive the ennoblement of Troilus directly from the precepts of courtly love, he nevertheless argues that "Courtly Love furnishes the antecedents of the concept of love . . ." in the poem. Donald Howard may also be cited as one who takes a somewhat qualified approach to the relationship of courtly love to Chaucer's poem. He writes of "the underlying theme of much courtly literature, that love has an ennobling effect," and seems to link this with the "courtly" element of the poem—so that love has an "ennobling effect on the hero" of the Troilus.[10]

We see, then, that twentieth-century critics have frequently found Chaucer's Troilus to be ennobled by love, and have justified this both with internal proofs and, directly or indirectly, with an appeal to the precedents of courtly love. It would repay us to examine both kinds of evidence, and I propose to begin with the arguments from the conventions of courtly love. Even the briefest investigation shows that general statements about courtly love are almost invariably based on evidence gleaned from the De amore or Ars honeste amandi of Andreas Capellanus, a work that was long accepted as a kind of quasi-historical document, but which in recent years has been frequently interpreted as an ironic attack on passionate involvement.[11] While it would not be appropriate to rehearse the whole controversy surrounding this work here, nevertheless the nature of its impact on a medieval audience is worth examining before we proceed to focus more closely on what it has to say about love's ennobling power, for what it says will depend to some extent on how we assume that it was read.

Andreas, Historical Responses, and the Condemnation of 1277

One clue to the way in which Andreas' treatise might have been understood in the Middle Ages has been noted in passing but not given the prominence it deserves.[12] Andreas defines love in book 1, chapter 1, as an "inborn suffering derived from the sight of and excessive meditation upon the beauty of the opposite sex, which causes each one to wish, above all things, the embraces of the other and by common desire to carry out all of love's precepts in the other's embrace."[13] This definition has been held to be amusingly inadequate by those who maintain an ironic reading of the text, on the grounds that it defines lust rather than love. Some welcome support for this view may be found in a somewhat unexpected quarter: Pietro di Dante's commentary on his father's Commedia. When Pietro comments on the fifth canto of the Inferno, the canto of the carnal sinners, he dwells for some time on the pilgrim's encounter with Paolo and Francesca, the adulterous lovers now suffering eternal damnation. Dante, Pietro says, causes the characters to speak and to tell of their unfortunate love and of their death. Then Pietro cites a definition of this kind of love from "Gualterius," a common name for Andreas' treatise derived from its being addressed to one Walter. And, Pietro cites word-for-word the definition of love that Andreas uses to open his treatise.[14] Here, then, we have a fourteenth century scholar and critic employing Andreas' definition of love to elaborate on the kind of love that leads to damnation. It follows that if Pietro realized that Andreas' definition in the *De amore* was nothing more than a definition of carnal lust, something not quite the same as the kinds of love discussed later in the *Commedia*, he would have recognized it as an inadequate definition of love in its potentially more uplifting aspects, and would not have taken seriously the "benefits" that were supposed to flow from it. Nor would he be much impressed by the arguments about love's ennobling powers advanced by the eager gentlemen in the dialogues of the treatise.

Another clue to the way in which Andreas' treatise might have been understood has been appropriated by those who believe that because it was condemned in 1277 it could not have been entirely ironic, else there would have been no call to condemn it. Reference to the Condemnation of the treatise is widely used as a basis for arguments claiming its serious historical impact, but we may take one recent comment as typical. F. L. Utley, writing against those who would interpret the treatise ironically, draws primarily on the Condemnation for support of his point of view. "At the center of this school's attempt to extend the single rhetorical device of irony to the whole of medieval secular literature there lies a basic paradox, in that the medieval authors themselves seem again and again to have been disappointed at the results of their supposed irony. Andreas tries to be funny, and yet he was condemned for Averroism by Bishop Simon [*sic*] Tempier of Paris in 1277, about a century after he wrote."[15]

It is true enough that Bishop Stephen Tempier issued a Condemnation in 1277, and that Andreas' work was mentioned in it (along with over 200 propositions not related to Andreas); yet the historical circumstances surrounding the Condemnation are so remarkable that it is wrong to go on blandly supposing that the mention of Andreas by Tempier constitutes some sort of official recognizance of the treatise's serious, unchristian utterances.

In the thirteenth century the study of Aristotle at the University of Paris grew from small beginnings and against the ecclesiastical interventions of 1210, 1215, and 1231 until in 1255 all of the known writings of Aristotle were put on the syllabus, and the Arts Faculty became in fact a Philosophy Faculty. The approaches to Aristotle reached across a broad spectrum in the Arts Faculty, and in the middle of the century Aristotelianism began to develop in the Theology Faculty as well. In a very general way one could say that the "left" at Paris was represented by Siger of Brabant, who professed an extreme reliance on rationalism, although he did not contradict Christian faith. On the "right" was the Theology Faculty, particularly the Franciscans, and in the middle was Thomas Aquinas.

On the 18th of January 1277 the newly made Pope John XXI asked the bishop of Paris, Stephen Tempier, to inquire about the errors that he had heard were being spread at the university. Tempier was to investigate and report. Tempier, however, went far beyond his mandate, and on his own authority proclaimed the Condemnation of some 219 propositions less than two months after being charged with the job of inquiry. The propositions, or errors, were so hastily put together by the sixteen theologians appointed to the task that they are sometimes repetitious, sometimes contradictory, and touch upon virtually all sectors of philosophy and theology.[16]

The two biggest losers in the Condemnation were Siger of Brabant (on the left) and Thomas Aquinas (in the center), while the conservative Franciscans were the winners. Historians of philosophy seem mightily unimpressed with Andreas' share in all this, since whatever the *De amore* is about, it certainly has nothing to do with Aristotelianism. However, Grabmann and Denomy, in the articles noted, have suggested that some of the 219 propositions, especially those relating to sexual matters, are in fact citations of Andreas.

Regrettably, the "identifications" require all too often that positions taken by speakers in an argument be taken as representative of Andreas' utterances on the subject, even when the characters contradict one another. Thus, the proposition condemned by the bishop, "quod simplex fornicatio, utpote soluti cum soluta, non est peccatum," is claimed to be from Andreas on the basis of the eighth dialogue, in which a gentleman who hopes to be seductive raises a distinction between "pure" and "mixed" love, the latter being sexual, the former almost sexual. Denomy argues that since mixed love is said to be the source of goodness, Andreas indeed is claiming that "simplex fornicatio" is not a sin. Never mind that the woman addressed replies, "You are saying things that no one ever heard or knew of," never mind that the gentleman in the dialogue is married, that he is a cleric, and that she is a widow, hence there is nothing "simplex" about the issue. The fact remains that he is a special pleader, and he no more necessarily speaks for Andreas than does the lady, who says in the same dialogue that to love carnally is gravely to offend God.[17]

The second proposition "identified" in Andreas is "quod continentia non est essentialiter virtus." Denomy concedes that Andreas never says this, but assumes that it applies to him because he states the opposite: that is, that incontinence is the source of all good works, therefore (Denomy deduces) it must be a virtue. Again, though, this requires us to assume that the lecherous gentlemen in the dialogues speak for Andreas, while in book 3, when Andreas condemns fornication, that he does not speak for himself. The other presumed parallels between Andreas' treatise and various errors listed in the Condemnation are also subject to attack on the same grounds, and it would be supererogatory to argue each case.

Perhaps the most stunning argument advanced by Denomy and Grabmann is that Andreas' use of two approaches to his subject—praising illicit love in the first two books and condemning it in the third, "recalls the so-called double truth used by the philosophers of Latin Averroism." Denomy is careful to claim no more than an analogy between Andreas' methods and the "double truth," since he points out on the last page of his essay that it would have been chronologically "impossible" for Andreas to have been directly influenced by Averroes.[18] However, Denomy's cautious analogy of the nineteen-forties turns into a confident condemnation of Andreas for Averroism in the seventies, as we have seen. The "double truth," which Denomy was careful to call the "so-called" double truth, is simply the proposition that reason and faith can be on an equal footing: that a proposition can be affirmed or denied as well by philosophy as by faith. The idea that Andreas' treatise with its two views of illicit love somehow presents the "double truth" of philosophy and faith is so farfetched as not to merit serious consideration. That it "recalls" the double truth is not much better. Indeed, according to van Steenberghen the charge of a "double truth" laid to Siger of Brabant by the framers of the Condemnation was factitious, and resulted from their own ambivalent feelings about Aristotle on the one hand (whose works they wanted to defend when interpreted in a certain way), and the Christian faith on the other. Averroes believed that there was only one truth—philosophical truth. Siger believed as well in one truth, and said repeatedly that if philosophy and faith disagreed, truth was on the side of faith. Andreas did not concern himself with the matter, hence the only "double truth used by the philosophers of Latin Averroism" is to be found in the Condemnation itself. There is doubtless something to be learned from the appearance of Andreas' treatise in Bishop Tempier's Condemnation, but at present we do not know what the lesson is. At any rate, we should not go on claiming that Andreas preached an unorthodox gospel that had to be condemned by an offended bishop.[19]

The *Fons et Origo Bonorum*

If we may confidently dismiss the idea that the *De amore* was seditiously Averroistic, we must consequently examine its tone without making the prior assumption that it was sufficiently grave as to call down the bishop's wrath. In any case, since much of the treatise is given in the form of dialogues, we must be careful not to assume that a speaker necessarily represents the viewpoint of the author—or indeed that any of the speakers do. With this caveat in mind let us examine the often-encountered claim that Andreas styles love as the source of all goodness—for this is the source of claims for the existence of ennobled lovers.

T. A. Kirby was one of the first to state the position in detail. "A favorite idea that Andreas strives to bring home by frequent repetition," he writes, "is the troubadour notion of love as the source of all good, the fountain of virtues and benefits; 'qui omnium dicitur fons et origo bonorum.'"[20] The idea of love as the "fons et origo bonorum" is indeed mentioned several times in the *De amore*, but it is not put forth by Andreas, as claimed; rather it is advanced by several eager gentlemen in the dialogues as a part of their propositions of seduction. Because of the principle of Ciceronian decorum we would expect that a would-be seducer would present his case with all the arguments he could muster, but it would be naive to assume that those arguments were necessarily true or that they represented the view of the author. The speakers, we shall see, are insistent about the good effects of love, but are forced by their female counterparts in the dialogues to state their views in ever more indefensible situations.

The initial mention of love as the origin of good comes in the first dialogue, in which, it will be remembered, a member of the middle class attempts to seduce a lady from the same class. His first tack is to ask for the lady's love on the basis of his own merit: "Nam si ego tanto meis meritis essem dignus honore, nullus in orbe vivens recte mihi esset coaequandus amator." ("Now if I, by my merits, might be worthy of such an honor, no lover in the world could really be compared with me" [p. 37]).[21] The lady is willing enough to grant him some merit, but rebuffs his advances by introducing details that thicken the plot: the man is elderly and she is young. "Quamvis multa sis probitate laudandus, ego tamen iuvencula veterum horresco solatio" (p. 25). ("You may deserve praise for your great excellence, but I am rather young, and I shudder at the thought of receiving solaces from old men" [p. 39]). Andreas, however, provides the reader with an alternative story line. If the man is young, not old, the lady might decline because he has not yet done many good deeds. To which the man replies that good deeds cannot in fact be performed unless inspired by love—that is, love must precede good deeds and not follow them. Passing over the fact that there is a certain contradiction between this position and the one previously offered, let us look at the precise words the man uses:

Profiteor etenim, quod magnis sunt digna praeterita facta muneribus, verumtamen universis constat hominibus, quod nullum in mundo bonum vel curialitas exercetur, nisi ex amoris fonte derivetur. Omnis ergo boni erit amor origo et causa. [pp. 28–29]

ᨘ ᨘ ᨘ

I admit that good deeds when done deserve great rewards, but all men
agree that no one does a good or courteous deed in the world unless it is
derived from the fount of love. Love will therefore be the origin and
cause of all good. . . .[22]   [p. 40]

The lady explains to the man the contradiction in his position and they proceed to speak of other matters, leaving the reader to reflect upon the significance of the man's claim.

In the third dialogue the idea is restated in somewhat different language.
The lady (from the higher nobility) has just given the man (of the middle
class) a little lecture on the duties of a man who would serve in love's army.
Just how seriously we should take this may be judged by the lady's admonish-
ment to be generous with money—first to the rich and then to the poor!
Moreover, as Robertson has noted, the virtues of a knight cease to be virtuous
when they are performed with the goal of serving in love's army.[23] After the
lesson, the man thanks the lady and affirms that love is the cause of every
good: "Nam quum omnibus, quae fiunt in saeculo, bonis amor praestet ini-
tium, merito in primis tanquam omnium bonorum radix et causa principalis
est postulandus" (p. 69). ("For since love offers everybody in the world an
incentive to do good, properly before everything else we ought to seek love as
the root and principal cause of everything good" [p. 61]). The idea of a *radix
omnium bonorum* might well have reminded medieval readers of the *radix
. . . omnium malorum* of I Timothy 6 : 10, leaving the reader to ponder whether
the man's *amor* could be sufficiently distinguished from St. Paul's *cupiditas* as
to cause opposite effects.[24]

The idea that no one can do any good unless kindled by love is glanced at in
the fifth and sixth dialogues (pp. 87–88, 98, 118), but it is in the eighth dialogue that the significance of the statement can be perceived most clearly, for
there is a kind of progression in this work in which the concept that love is
the source of all goodness is offered to the reader in contexts in which it is
increasingly difficult to accept. Since *amor* had been defined even before the
dialogues began as being nothing more than an innate *passio* leading to one's
desire to carry out all of love's precepts in the embraces of a member of the
opposite sex,[25] the reader of the dialogues might well be amused by the as-
severations of various would-be seducers that *amor*—for which understand
passio—is the source of all goodness. Even so, if we grant that the statement
is "novel" at the least, it is perhaps less intrusive when presented without
close scrutiny of the meaning of *amor* than with it. In the first dialogue we
could almost forget for a moment what kind of *amor* we are concerned with,
as the idea is presented more or less theoretically. In the third dialogue it is
offered again, but with a potentially disturbing biblical echo, while in the
eighth (and last) dialogue it is first presented and refuted, and then given
hard on the heels of a definition of the simple, physical act that constitutes

amor for these dialogues. When we are reminded of the meaning of *amor*, the recurring idea we have been discussing is not so much ambiguous or something to strain our credulity as it is mind-boggling and outrageous. And this ability to utter the outrageous in bland tones is a characteristic of the humor in this essay.[26]

In the last and longest dialogue, already glanced at with regard to its use for expression of Andreas' thoughts on "simplex fornicatio," we gradually learn that the male protagonist is (a) married, and (b) a cleric, and that the female protagonist is a young widow. Since St. Paul had enjoined widows to be chaste or to remarry, (I Corinthians 7:39–40), and since the pursuit of adultery by a cleric is hard to reconcile with the source of all goodness, one may legitimately suggest that the two mentions of the idea here are intended to be humorous.[27] The first comes right at the opening of the dialogue, when the clerk says that women (rather than *amor* per se) cause all goodness:

> Credo quidem et est verum, bonos omnes ob hoc a Deo in hac vita disponi, ut vestris et aliarum dominarum voluntibus obsequantur, et lucidissima videtur mihi ratione constare, quod homines nil esse possunt nilque de bonitatis valent fonte praelibare, nisi dominarum hoc fecerint svadela commoti. Sed quamvis ex mulieribus cuncta videantur bona procedere, et multam eis Dominus praerogativam concesserit, et omnium dicantur esse causa et origo bonorum, necessitas sibi tamen evidenter incumbit, ut tales se debeant bona facientibus exhibere, ut eorum probitas earum intuitu de virtute in virtutem modis omnibus crescere videatur.
>
> [p. 156]

∿∿ ∿∿ ∿∿

> Indeed I believe it is true that God has inclined all good men in this life to serve your desires and those of other ladies, and it seems to me that this is for the very clear reason that men cannot amount to anything or taste of the fountain of goodness unless they do this under the persuasion of ladies. But although all good things seem to proceed from women, and although God has given them a great privilege and we say that they are the cause and origin of everything good, still they are clearly under the necessity of so conducting themselves toward those who do good deeds that by their approval the good character of these men may seem in every respect to increase from strength to strength.   [p. 108]

While it seems clear from the context that the gentleman here is asking for a good deal by way of the ladies' *intuitu* or regard, the statement is still one that permits two meanings. The particular lady appealed to sees it just this way, and replies to the statement in a two-fold manner. Yes, she says, ladies *should* be the cause of good, *but* to exhibit the *amor* in question is to offend God:

Scio ergo, mulieres, ut vestra notavit assertio, esse debere causam et ori-
ginem bonorum. . . . Amorem autem exhibere est graviter offendere
Deum, et multis mortis parare pericula.   [p. 159]

∿∿   ∿∿   ∿∿

I know that women should, as you have asserted, be the cause and origin
of good things. . . . But to show love is gravely to offend God and to
prepare for many the perils of death.   [pp. 109–10]

At this juncture, then, the reader is reminded of other possible definitions of
amor, as well as the contrary nature of the *amor* the men have been seeking so
persistently. Neither this love nor women loved this way are likely to be the
source of all goodness if to exhibit this *amor* is to offend God.

The final mention of love as the source of goodness is so ludicrous that one
can easily see why Drouart La Vache laughed so much upon reading the
treatise.[28] In this section of the dialogue the lover distinguishes between *amor
purus* and *amor mixtus*, the former extending as far as "modest contact with
the nude lover" (p. 122) ("verecundum amantis nudae contactum" [p. 182])
—whatever that may be—but omitting the final solace; the latter includes it.
The lover is careful to condemn neither, but to rank them in a hierarchy.
Both are good, he says, but *amor purus*, which he seeks, is better. However,
his definitions of their worth sound suspiciously similar: from *amor purus*
"totius probitatis origo descendit" (p. 183), while *amor mixtus* is said to
be "origo bonorum" (p. 183), or, as one manuscript has it, "fons et origo
bonorum."[29]

Our last look at the idea in Andreas, then, reveals modest nude contact as
the source of *probitas* and adultery with a clerk as the *fons et origo bonorum*.
Small wonder that the lady replies with contemptuous incredulity: "inaudita
et incognita verba profertis" (p. 184). The humor is broader here than earlier
in the dialogues and is consequently more easily observed. The essential joke,
however, remains the same. Having defined the kind of love being discussed
as sexual, no amount of special pleading would convince a medieval audience
that that kind of love was the source of all goodness.[30] None of the men in the
dialogues is successful with his seductive entreaties, which suggests the essential inadequacy of the positions each is defending.

Of course, part of the joke depends upon the clearly defined categories of
medieval thinking. To suggest in the eighth dialogue that adulterous love is
the source of all goodness is a trifle outré even in our own philosophically
latitudinarian times, but in the Middle Ages the source or fountain of goodness was well known and had nothing to do with fornication or modest nude
contacts. As Lactantius Firmianus pointed out as early as A.D. 304 in his *Divine Institutes*, "fons autem bonorum Deus est, malorum vero ille, scilicet di-
vini nomini semper inimicus."[31] Not long afterwards St. Augustine addressed
himself at some length to the question of the origin of good in *De natura boni*,

in which he says in a variety of ways that God is the source of all goodness.[32] Depending upon how one defined love, then, it could indeed be the source of all goodness, or alternatively, of all evil.

As noted above, in chapter 2, Dante stressed the commonplace medieval idea that love was necessarily the source both of every virtue and of every deed deserving punishment. If Dante could reiterate the idea for tutelary purposes, Andreas could parody it for humorous ones.[33] Indeed, not only was the idea of God as the source of all goodness a commonplace, but also much to the point are the references in Proverbs 31 to the virtuous woman who is more precious than rubies. In a passage of his *Vox Clamantis* depending upon this chapter of Proverbs, John Gower develops the idea that "All good things come from a good woman, whose chaste love provides love's riches."[34] The contrast with the woman in Andreas' dialogues is striking. Gower's woman, who truly could be the source of all goodness, is married and chaste. Moreover, her opposite has opposite effects: "All evils have usually proceeded from an evil woman" (p. 203). Whether we consider love as the "fons et origo bonorum" or womankind as the source, in either case we shall have to remember that for medieval audiences it was good love and good women who were so acknowledged, and the testimonies in Andreas to the contrary should be judged accordingly.

There is, then, a real danger in an approach that interprets Chaucer's *Troilus* by placing it in the genre of the courtly love poem, then analyzes Chaucer's effects by comparison with the presumed guidelines of courtly love. Even if we were to grant the existence of courtly love as a literary if not social phenomenon, there would still be difficulty in relying upon it to demonstrate the supposed ennoblement of Chaucer's Troilus, for even among those who acknowledge the existence of courtly love, there is disagreement about what constitutes "worthy" behavior. Note, as a caution, that Gaston Paris' seminal article on the subject claimed that one of the characteristics of *amour courtois* was the heroine's concern to render the hero "meilleur, à le faire plus 'valoir'," but Paris later confines this "worth" to the sense of "prouesse" and "renommé."[35] The external evidence for Troilus' ennoblement is, at best, tenuous; it remains to examine the internal evidence.

A thing so vertuous in kynde

More than half a century ago Dodd called attention to four passages in the *Troilus* that he felt expressed most emphatically "the ennobling nature of love." Just a few years ago, in 1974, Utley adduced six passages wherein are described Troilus' "heroic qualities," his "virtues," and in some of which "tribute" is paid to "the new Troilus ennobled by love."[36] Since there is only one instance of overlap, the two critics seem to have cast their nets widely,

and by studying the passages they chose we shall come to a better understanding of the issue of Troilus' ennoblement than we would by studying the
many essays that merely glance at the topic or cite only one or two passages
for evidence.[37]

Although he does not say so, it is clear from an inspection of the verses
cited that Dodd's principle of selection was to look for lines of the poem that
asserted that lovers in general or a lover in particular was inspired by love to
turn away from vice. Thus lovers are said "to dreden vice and shame" (I, 252)
in his first selection, "To flemen alle manere vice and synne" (II, 852) in the
next. In the third "vices they resygne" (III, 25), and, finally, Troilus is said to
flee pride, envy, ire, avarice, "and everich other vice" (III, 1806) in the
fourth selection. This is straightforward enough if we do not raise the question of tone, but when reading Chaucer it is always necessary to ask ourselves
about the meaning of a Chaucerian verse as well as its plain statement, for
Chaucer habitually assures us that a thing is true when he means the opposite. In the portrait of the Knight in the General Prologue, for example,
Chaucer uses the words "worthy" and "worthiness" some five times in his
description, and there is widespread agreement that he means what he says.[38]
If he does, though, then he certainly does *not* mean what he says when he
goes on to describe the lubricious Friar as "worthy," when he remarks that
the Friar's acquaintance is with "worthy" women of the town, or when he
adduces examples of sexual activity to illustrate the Wife of Bath's supposed
worthiness:

> She was a worthy womman al hir lyve:
> Housbondes at chirche dore she hadde fyve,
> Withouten oother compaignye in youthe,—
> But thereof nedeth nat to speke as nowthe.
>
> [*Gen Prol*, 459–62]

The passages cited by Utley also invite discrimination for tone, some of
which Utley supplies himself. For example, when he cites the description of
Troilus that Pandarus gives to Criseyde, he recognizes that Pandarus is not an
altogether objective observer and acknowledges that the numerous praises
("goode, wise, worthi, fresshe, free, noble, gentil" [II, 317, 331]) may be
"dramatically discounted." Similarly Utley notes that Criseyde is a "preju-
diced witness," and we must therefore keep in perspective her assertion that
Troilus possesses "grete trouthe, servise, goodnesse" (III, 992, 995). On the
other hand, Utley stoutly maintains that many of the encomia mean exactly
what they say, that "any ironic interpretation cannot cancel out their admiration," and he opposes the presumed view of Chaucer's courtly audience to the
possible interpretations of "strict churchmen" and "strict moralists."[39] One
might object that Utley claims rather than demonstrates the absence of irony,
but that would simply beg the question in another way. The text of a poem is,

in the last analysis, not the easiest but the hardest evidence to evaluate, and one of the inescapable truths of the Hermeneutic circle is that in order to deal with internal literary evidence we regularly have to compare it with external evidence. Nevertheless, these discriminations of tone must be made, and the evaluation of the poem's comments on the ennoblement of Troilus is central not only to this chapter but indeed to this book.

A good perspective on the problem of tone in the *Troilus* is afforded by the *Romance of the Rose*, for scholars have done some very careful work on the earlier poem. Just before the battle between Danger and Franchise, for example, Jean de Meun invites "loyal lovers" to listen to the ensuing battle, "so that the God of Love may help you and grant that you may enjoy your loves!" (pp. 257–58). As Dahlberg points out in his introduction, the passage "shows the voice of the poet and the point of view of the Lover." However, as Jean de Meun develops this section of the poem, we find that he tacitly compares and contrasts two hunts: the hunt of Venus, which pursues rabbits, and the hunt of Adonis, which pursues the boar. In conventional medieval mythographic and iconographic treatments, the two hunts represent the pursuit of concupiscence and charity respectively. The poet, then, teases, amuses, and challenges the reader by varying his address from direct to ironic statement and back again. One moment he offers his poem up to the correction of Holy Church; the next moment he concludes from retelling the story of Venus and Adonis that one should not listen to Reason. On the surface, Jean de Meun seems to endorse both hunts, but since they are traditionally opposed, we must assume that one is endorsed truly and the other ironically. The trouble is, as Rosemond Tuve has put it, "Jean's method is very risky. . . ."[40]

Chaucer's method also combines direct with ironic statement, and the extent of critical disagreement about his meaning shows that his, too, is a very risky method. In chapter 2 we noted that the narrator of the *Troilus* urges lovers to follow the God of Love, even though the narrator does not follow the god himself. If we allow Chaucer a reasonable degree of control over his material, the most straightforward conclusion is that he, like Jean de Meun, varies direct and ironic statement. Moreover, we have noted that service of the God of Love in the *Romance of the Rose*, in the *Knight's Tale*, and indeed in the *Troilus* itself is equated with folly. Troilus himself characterizes lovers as blind fools (I, 202), and the narrator too denigrates them as "fooles" (I, 217). It is difficult to imagine that becoming a fool is the logical first step in the process of banishing vice. By the same token the narrator's careful distancing of himself from the servants of Love by noting that they live in "wo" while he lives in "charite" (I, 49), makes little sense if the road to virtue begins with fleeing vice by serving the God of Love. We must, in fact, question whether concupiscent love is a "thing so vertuous in kynde" (I, 254) as stated, in which case Chaucer would be a major literary innovator to judge from the evidence adduced in the previous chapter. By a careful look at

Dodd's and Utley's examples of the presumably ennobling power of love, placing them in the context of pride leading to Troilus' succumbing to Cupid's arrow, we shall be in a position to distinguish true pride, a vice which gets Troilus into trouble, from nominal pride—a supposed vice that as a lover he later abjures for putative virtues.

Proud Troilus, Proud Bayard

We noted in passing in chapter 2 that the God of Love in the *Romaunt* was aroused to employ his arrows against people "Whan he may hem to proude see" (884), and it is Troilus' pride that stirs up Cupid in this poem too. That two medieval poets should link pride with concupiscence should suggest to us that there was some common ground both drew from, and indeed there is. Both Troilus and the lover in the *Romaunt* ultimately suffer from self-love, which will be examined presently. Interestingly, Chaucer's way of demonstrating the general pride of self-love is through a particular manifestation well-suited to literary purposes. Troilus is not proud of his wealth or his birth, he is not proud of his strength or his good looks, but he is proud of what he conceives of as his ability to withstand temptation. It is his *habit* to lead his colleagues in girl-watching:

> This Troilus, as he was wont to gide
> His yonge knyghtes, lad hem up and down
> In thilke large temple on every side,
> Byholding ay the ladies of the town.   [I, 183–86]

However, Troilus' pleasure is not, as we might expect, solely in the aesthetic evaluation of the ladies themselves, but also is in the discomfiture of those in his retinue who cannot admire dispassionately, but who become emotionally entangled. It is those he denounces as blind fools—ironically, since he himself is blind to his danger—and with his denunciation "he gan caste up the browe, / Ascaunces, 'Loo! is this naught wisely spoken?'" (I, 205). His pride, then, would be familiar to a medieval audience as pride in what Chaucer's Parson was to describe as one of the "goodes of grace," "withstondynge of temptacioun" (*ParsT*, 455). As the Parson further observes of these, "certes it is a ful greet folye a man to priden hym in any of hem alle" (*ParsT*, 456). The wiser course is, as Reason advises in the *Romance of the Rose*, to flee love; rather than seek temptation out one should pray that one not be led into it, as Christ taught in the Sermon on the Mount.

Troilus' pride in his ability to play Love's game on his own terms is insisted upon in this section of the poem. He is compared with a proud peacock, his pride is said to be caught by the God of Love, he is called a proud knight, the

effects of "surquidrie and foul presumpcioun" (I, 213) are outlined, and the
moral of the episode is directed to wise, proud, and worthy folk. All this is
added to the scene in Boccaccio's version in which the events are much the
same, but where pride is not specifically named. As soon as Troilus is struck
by the arrow from the God of Love, the narrator exclaims over Troilus' subjection to Fortune through blindness induced by pride:

> O blynde world, O blynde entencioun!
> How often falleth al the effect contraire
> Of surquidrie and foul presumpcioun;
> For kaught is proud, and kaught is debonaire.
> This Troilus is clomben on the staire,
> And litel weneth that he moot descenden;
> But alday faileth thing that fooles wenden.   [I, 211–17]

Pride, blindness, the staircase of Fortune (suggesting the reversal of pride),
and the assumption that Troilus and other lovers are foes, each plays a role in
the stanzas that follow. Chaucer now draws the analogy between Bayard, the
horse, and Troilus, the prince, both of whom suffer some comeuppances.

> As proude Bayard gynneth for to skippe
> Out of the weye, so pryketh hym his corn,
> Til he a lasshe have of the longe whippe;
> Than thynketh he, "Though I praunce al byforn
> First in the trays, ful fat and newe shorn,
> Yet am I but an hors, and horses lawe
> I moot endure, and with my feres draw";
> . . . .
> So ferde it by this fierse and proude knyght:
> Though he a worthy kynges sone were,
> And wende nothing hadde had swich myght
> Ayeyns his wille that shuld his herte stere,
> Yet with a look his herte wax a-fere,
> That he that now was moost in pride above,
> Wax sodeynly moost subgit unto love.   [I, 218–31]

Patricia Kean has seen in this comparison a relationship between the horse,
which must obey "horses lawe," and Troilus, who must obey the "lawe of
kynde" (I, 238). Thus, she says, "Chaucer goes on to give another reason for
the inevitability of the way in which Troilus' story develops. Love itself is
part of the direction which Nature, by her laws, gives to all living beings."[41]
However, since Kean goes on to develop the idea that love, for Troilus, is
both inevitable and ennobling, it is hard to see why Chaucer would choose to
compare Troilus with the ignoble figure of the horse. If indeed love ennobles

Troilus, then the coherence of the simile breaks down, for as Troilus is "sub-git" to love, so Bayard is subjected to the traces and the whip. And, of course, the comparison of the prince, committed to the love that is said to ennoble, with the fat horse is a trifle ludicrous.

Bayard, as Rowland has noted, was traditionally the name for a blind horse, and this, in turn, "hints at the nature of Troilus' affliction."[42] The comparison of the young prince with a fat, traditionally blind horse, is not a promising beginning for the presumed insistence on the ennobling power of love. The horse, as Robertson has observed, was a common symbol in medieval art for the fleshly appetites.[43] Gordon has granted Robertson's point: that as Bayard obeys horses' law, so Troilus will obey the law of "kynde," which Robertson relates to the fleshly or "horsy" aspect of man. However, Gordon feels that this "can hardly be the whole meaning." Since Bayard is controlled by the whip, she finds that the analogy would signify the "control of fleshly appetite (by Reason)." Developing this idea she argues that "as the horse . . . has to be controlled and directed by the whip, so sexual desire has to be controlled and directed by reason. . . ."[44] While this is true, it should be emphasized that it is not Troilus' reason that pains him, as the whip does the erring horse, but rather the arrow of the God of Love. Thus the main thrust of the analogy is the emphasis on pride and punishment. Proud Bayard skips out of the way and is whipped in accordance with horses' law; proud Troilus also "feels his oats," tries to love without servitude to the God of Love, and is struck by the arrow in accordance with the law of "kynde." Consequently the paradoxes and ambiguities that Gordon deduces from the analogy are somewhat forced. Her subsequent argument that Chaucer is concerned with two kinds of sexual love, one that "blinds and enslaves" and one that does not, contains a most unfortunate omission of qualification, for surely Chaucer and most fourteenth-century men were agreed that the only way in which sexual love could have virtuous effects was when transformed through the sacramental grace of marriage.[45]

Returning to the insistence on pride in the analogy, we may recall the poet's insistence on this element in Troilus. Unlike Boccaccio's Troilo, who remembers his "gran follia" (I, 23) rather than outright pride, Chaucer's hero is a "proude knyght," "moost in pride," and the apostrophe on "surquidrie," and "presumpcioun," following the description of the shooting of the arrow leads directly into the analogy with "proude Bayard." Finally, the analogy itself is expressed in terms of pride of rank. Bayard reminds himself that although he is "First in the trays," he is still subject to the whip, while the proud Troilus, "Though he a worthy kynges sone were," is subject to the arrow.

Stephen A. Barney has taken an admirable step by emphasizing the importance of pride in the sequence concerning Bayard and Troilus, but I cannot agree with him that Troilus is caught like Bayard between interior drives and exterior attractions in such a way that he is "as innocent of these forces as Bayard."[46] The whole point of the comparison between a man and a horse is surely to say something pejorative about the man. If Troilus cannot now resist the God of Love, that is not to say that he was never any better than a horse, but rather that now he is no better than one. If "kynde" cannot be resisted, that is not to say that lust cannot be controlled. Chaucer's emphasis on pride, here specified as pride of rank, is clearly a force that blinds Troilus to the dangers of his situation, as it does blind Bayard.[47] What is less obvious to modern audiences is that the description of a lover as proud carries with it a certain moral connotation, for pride is the prime requisite for idolatrous passion. While one kind of source for this idea might be found in medieval knowledge of human behavior, the likeliest literary source for Chaucer is the *Romance of the Rose*, where the function of pride is illustrated by the episode of the Well of Narcissus.

Because the little exemplum of Narcissus was sometimes placed in the very center of Love's garden by early illustrators of the poem, Fleming has duly noted that it can be considered in a sense to be the central concept of the *Romance*.[48] The interpretation of the Narcissus story is as close to a "universal," perhaps, as one can get: it is the archetypal account of the destructive nature of self-love arising from pride. In the *Romance* it is taken for granted that the expression of self-love will be in sexual gratification: the love governed by Cupid. Since the very name Cupid was derived by medieval mythographers from a fanciful etymological origin in the Latin *cupiditas*, it is not surprising that the link was made between Narcissus' desire to possess himself, and Amant's desire to possess the rose.[49] The whole process is very clearly set forth in the Middle English translation of the *Romance*. There the perilous mirror of the well is first related to *proud* Narcissus, then to the process of loving, to Venus and Cupid, the deities of love, and finally is called outright the Well of Love. The reason the mirror is perilous is the ease of self-love. The generalizations of the text suggest that not only does this particular lover encounter peril at the well, but that all lovers experience a similar process.

> This is the mirrour perilous,
> In which the proude Narcisus
> Saw all his face fair and bright,
> That made hym sithe to ligge upright.
> For whoso loketh in that mirrour,
> Ther may nothyng ben his socour
> That he ne shall there sen somthyng
> That shal hym lede into lovyng.
> . . . .

> For Venus sone, daun Cupido,
> Hath sowen there of love the seed,
> That help ne lith there noon, ne red,
> So cerclith it the welle aboute.
> .   .   .   .
> This welle is clepid, as well is knowen,
> The Welle of Love, of verray right.
>
> [*RR*, 1601–27]

Pride, then, goes before a fall as it has always done, but the specification of the fall is sexual. With this important literary precedent in mind, Chaucer's purpose in introducing the analogy between proud Bayard and proud Troilus is plain enough. When Troilus casts "up the browe" and superciliously asks of this derogation of lovers, "'Loo! is this naught wisely spoken?'" (I, 205), his request for approbation is figuratively the same as admiring his face in the narcissistic mirror. What Troilus does not know is that self-delight is "perilous." But he soon finds out. Troilus' self-approbation indicates that he has metaphorically entered the garden of the God of Love, where, like Amant, he soon becomes the prey. One does not enter the garden innocently; one is not struck by the arrow as a random event. Troilus has indeed "clomben on the staire," and while it is not impossible to escape from the garden, neither Troilus nor Amant is able to do so. Reason's advice to Amant in the *Romance of the Rose* is to flee this sort of love, and this advice implies a measure of freedom even for one already within Love's garden. Paradoxically, the lover is told to free himself by taking the bit between his teeth. This remarkably appropriate image for the passage under discussion urges the lover to exchange a bondage that brings "myche tribulacioun" (*RR*, 3282) for the traditional bridle of temperance. "Tak with thy teeth the bridel faste, / To daunte thyn herte . . ." (*RR*, 3299–3300). Amant declines, and Troilus too remains bound to the God of Love rather than bridling his heart. Lady Philosophy observed that he who desires something (or, in Troilus' case, someone), "enlaceth hym in the cheyne with which he mai ben drawen" (Bk. I, m. 4). Troilus chooses his servitude.

The full meaning of the analogy is now apparent. Proud Bayard skips out of the way because "so pryketh hym his corn," and receives a lash of the whip, reminding him that although he is the first horse in the trace, he is still a horse and must obey horses' law. Proud Troilus, the king's son, watches the ladies with his companions, while displaying pride in his ability to withstand temptation. As Bayard is reminded by the whip that he is only a horse, so Troilus is reminded by the arrow that he is only human. As Robertson has noted, the comparison of Troilus to a horse calls forth the consideration of Troilus' fleshly or concupiscent potential, and in light of the relationship between pride and concupiscence afforded by the *Romance of the Rose*, the analogy between a proud prince and a proud horse would seem to follow most naturally the God of Love's hitting Troilus, "atte fulle."

Fleeing Vices

By his long and well-developed analogy between proud Troilus and proud Bayard, Chaucer stresses a whole series of pejoratives about the prince's behavior. Troilus is at fault morally in his pride, intellectually in his blindness or lack of prudence. Both flaws arise ultimately from self-love, of which a characteristic literary manifestation is sexual desire. Thus far in his additions to the source Chaucer has used direct rather than ironic statement. The next two stanzas after the Bayard group continue in much the same vein. Chaucer urges people not to scorn the God of Love, who is clearly very powerful, and he notes that neither rank, worth, strength, nor intellect is a sufficient guarantee against Love's power. Having made these cautionary statements, having shown the abruptness of Troilus' reversal, and having earlier in the poem sketched the unhappiness of the servants of the God of Love, Chaucer now switches to ironic statement when, as narrator, he assures the audience that not only is the God of Love powerful, but indeed it is appropriate that he should be so, since love comforts, civilizes, and improves. This stanza is the first of the examples cited by Dodd:

> And trewelich it sit wel to be so.
> For alderwisest han therwith ben plesed;
> And they that han ben aldermost in wo,
> With love han ben comforted moost and esed;
> And ofte it hath the cruel herte apesed,
> And worthi folk maad worthier of name,
> And causeth moost to dreden vice and shame.[50] [I, 246–52]

Even taken out of context the verse has some characteristics that signal caution in accepting it as a direct statement of fact. Simply put, the lines quoted are overemphatic. Not just the wisest and the most woeful are invoked, but the "alderwisest" and those "aldermost" in woe, who are comforted "moost," thus inviting comparison with those "moost" caused to dread vice and shame. Of course, read at the close of the sequence of actions and comments that lead up to it, the stanza can be seen to deny much of what has preceded. The narrator argued that "woe" was the characteristic of lovers (34, 49), a sentiment echoed in part by Troilus himself (201), but now love is said to comfort the woeful. Troilus called lovers fools (202), and the narrator called Troilus a fool for permitting himself to be hit by Love's arrow (217), but now we are told that love will please the alderwisest. And, whereas the narrator distanced himself from "Loves servauntz" by not numbering himself among them and living in charity (48–49), now we are assured that love causes people to turn away from vice. That love of one kind has the potential for making worthy folk worthier and causing people to dread vice and shame, there can be no doubt. But it is not the love found in the service of Cupid: rather it is what Gower was to call honest love, a love to be found in marriage. As he put it,

> For evere yit it hath be so,
> That love honeste in sondri weie
> Profiteth, for it doth aweie
> The vice. . . .[51]

The matter of Troilus' pride and his royal blood arises again in Dodd's illustration number four, which is one that Utley also avails himself of. Troilus, at the end of Book III of the poem, has consummated his love with Criseyde and is described with a series of encomia on his might and virtue, both of which are said to derive from his service of Love. Thus he is, "Save Ector most ydred of any wight; / And this encrees of hardynesse and might / Com hym of love, his ladies thank to wynne" (III, 1775–77). He spends the time of truce hunting boars, bears, or lions and foregoing smaller prey, while his speech is "moost of love and vertu" (1786),

> And though that he be come of blood roial,
> Hym list of pride at no wight for to chace;
> Benigne he was to ech in general,
> For which he gat hym thank in every place.
> Thus wolde Love, yheried be his grace,
> That Pride, Envye, and Ire, and Avarice
> He gan to fle, and everich other vice.   [III, 1800–1806]

Utley says "this tribute I find it hard to discount, even by maligning the narrator-persona."[52] However, it must at once be suspect on the grounds we have already examined: the claim that love causes people to flee vice being hard to reconcile with the early conditions of the narrative. Moreover, while Troilus' decision to flee pride, envy, wrath, and avarice is quite closely adopted from the *Filostrato*, nevertheless Chaucer had very different things to say about the relationship of love to these sins elsewhere in his poetry. In "The Former Age" (p. 534), Chaucer describes a golden age of mankind in which the people, "voyd of alle vyce" (l. 50), cherished each other with a consequent absence of "pryde," "envye," and "avaryce" (l. 53). What is important for an analysis of the *Troilus* is that this former age existed before "Jupiter the likerous, / That first was fader of delicacye, / Come in this world" (ll. 56–58). If the absence of pride, envy, and avarice characterizes a society that does not know lust, it is hard to imagine that Chaucer is serious when he suggests that Troilus is successful in banishing vice through his carnal passion for Criseyde. Of course, Chaucer's "The Former Age" probably dates from a period in Chaucer's career long after the composition of the *Troilus*.[53] However, Chaucer's treatment of the former age drew upon Boethius' *Consolation* and heavily upon the *Romance of the Rose* for its details—including the absence of pride, envy, and avarice described in the *Romance*. Chaucer was undoubtedly familiar with Jean de Meun's treatment of the subject at the time he was working on the *Troilus*. It is also worth noting that when Chaucer read the *Romance* he read it carefully, for whereas the lover's *Amis* speaks of the golden age as a time of unbridled promiscuity, *Raison* had earlier described it as a time of chastity. Thus Chaucer took the details from *Amis'* section of the poem, but the correct or standard interpretation from *Raison*'s.[54]

It is necessary to try to put Troilus' banishment of pride, envy, ire, and avarice into some sort of literary context, for in terms of the character of Troilus as drawn in this poem, their banishment does not make much sense. To be sure Troilus does suffer from pride, which is here said to be banished, but there is nothing in the poem to suggest that he is similarly afflicted with avarice, wrath, or envy. Moreover, the same holds true for Boccaccio's Troilo, and we should remember that this series of stanzas at the end of Chaucer's Book III is a fairly close adaptation of Boccaccio. If the poems demand that the heroes resign vices they do not have, we must look beyond the texts for a general statement about lovers and the abandonment of certain vices. Since both Chaucer and Boccaccio knew the *Romance of the Rose*, it is one of the most likely places to look for source material, and as usual we can find provocative parallels.

Even before the lover enters the garden in the *Romaunt*, the poem describes a series of personifications that are painted on the exterior walls of the place. These personifications are of Hate (associated with "wrathe," and "yre" [148]), Felonye, Vilanye, Coveitise, Avarice, Envye, Sorowe, Elde, "Poope-Holy" or religious hypocrisy, and Poverty. Because the God of Love calls his rules "comaundementis" (2133), and assigns the lover a "penaunce" (2355), it is easy enough to mistakenly accept the religious language as valid. One could then jump to the erroneous conclusion that the images outside the garden represent real vices, and that the behavior prescribed for the lover must be an exercise in repudiating the vices outside for virtues within.[55] Thus, Vilanye is painted on the wall, and the lover is abjured to foreswear it "over alle thyng" (2176) as a servant of the God of Love. However, not all the emblems on the walls are vices—indeed something like Poverty was usually considered a condition having the potential for virtue. Nor will it do to argue, as C. S. Lewis has done, that Hate, Covetousness, and Envy are outside the garden because in order to enter "a man still needs, along with certain gifts of nature, and a sufficient fortune, a certain selection of genuinely moral qualities."[56] A better way to envisage these conditions or attitudes would be as complementary qualilities that are causally linked (e.g., Wealth within the garden leading to Poverty without), or as qualities that differ from one another in a direct fashion, but suffer from identical negative moral valences. Thus Avarice is outside the garden, but the equally unpraiseworthy riches and largesse are within; outside we find Envy, the resentful feeling toward others, inside we find the Well of Narcissus representing the unqualified love of self; outside we find in first place Hate, while inside the ruling figure is the God of (carnal) Love.[57]

That Troilus should give up some of the qualities depicted on the outside of the garden in the *Romaunt* does not indicate that he is fleeing vice, as stated, but that he is pursuing carnal delight like the lover before him. Moreover, to give up pride might be a good thing in Troilus' case, considering all the trouble it got him into, but again there are uncomfortable parallels with the lover in the *Romaunt*. That lover is exhorted by the God of Love to give up something *called* pride, but which sounds like prudence. Unlike the pride that Chaucer's Parson styled as the "general roote of alle harmes," (*ParsT*, 388) pride to the God of Love is merely an impediment to his own service:

> And he that pride hath hym withynne
> Ne may his herte in no wise
> Meken ne souplen to servyse.　　　　　　　[*RR*, 2242–44]

The lover in the *Romaunt* is told to banish pride, and Troilus is said to have done so, which is merely a different artistic approach to the same joke: since pride is the general root of all harms or sins, and since carnal delight is a sin, it follows logically that a lover cannot be said to have banished pride. Indeed, since carnal love is linked with narcissistic, cupidinous self-love in medieval thought, one might aver that pride is a characteristic of lovers.

Upon inspection we find that several other passages cited by Utley and others to show Troilus' presumed ennoblement are in fact echoes of the commandments of love laid down for the protagonist of the *Romaunt*. The God of Love begins his instruction with a mock definition of gentility and villainy that is ultimately a parody of Boethius' *Consolation of Philosophy* (Book III, pr. 6 and m. 6). Both works define true gentility as the exercise of virtue rather than as mere lineage, but, as we have noted, true virtue in the garden is impossible since the ultimate goal is vice. For men of the Middle Ages actions do not speak louder than words, intentions do. It follows that the right thing done for the wrong reason is not a virtue but a vice—a moral commonplace that can be found in western culture from *The City of God* to *Murder in the Cathedral*.[58] Thus all the assertions that Troilus has become virtuous through love may be traced to the God of Love's claim that a true "gentilman" is "whoso is vertuous" (2196, 2191). The elucidating details also dovetail well. In the *Romaunt* it is said that villains lack friendship (2183–84), whereas Troilus is "bicom the frendlieste wight" (I, 1079). A servant of the God of Love should be truly "gentil" (2196), "in his port nought outrageous"

(2192), and "not straunge ne daungerous" (2312). Troilus, similarly, is the "gentilest," who has foregone "His heighe port and his manere estraunge" (I, 1080, 1084).⁵⁹ The lover is advised to be "Glad and mery" (2290); Troilus is in "suffisaunce, in blisse" (III, 1716). The lover is to sing, to give cheerfully, to be clad in fresh array, and to joust (2319, 2272–73, 2253, 2314–15), while Troilus

> . . . in singynges,
> This Troilus gan al his lif to lede.
> He spendeth, jousteth, maketh festeynges;
> He yeveth frely ofte, and chaungeth wede.⁶⁰
> [III, 1716–19]

In aligning the behavior of the lover in the *Romaunt* with that of Troilus, only a partial citation of a key stanza in Book I was made in order to emphasize the details. However, the passage deserves quotation in full, for it is an addition to the source and has attracted a substantial amount of critical response.

> For he bicom the frendlieste wight,
> The gentilest, and ek the mooste fre,
> The thriftiest and oon the beste knyght,
> That in his tyme was or myghte be.
> Dede were his japes and his cruelte,
> His heighe port and his manere estraunge,
> And ecch of tho gan for a vertu chaunge.   [I, 1079–85]

The claim that this verse shows how Troilus' "nature expanded, became ennobled," could be maintained only if we did not compare the lines with the other demands of the poem.⁶¹ To be friendly is in itself morally neutral, and becomes a virtue or a vice depending upon one's choice of friends. Since Troilus now surrounds himself with the lovers who were ill-treated by the narrator and by himself, one may judge accordingly about his imagined improvement. His gentility, of course, is not supported by the poem, since to be involved in an illicit passion is by definition not to be virtuous, as we have seen. To be "free," could refer to actual freedom or to generosity. If to generosity, then he is a spendthrift like the lover in the *Romaunt*, while in terms of actual freedom Troilus is *less* free at the close of Book I than he had been at its opening. Whereas he was once largely his own man, now he has given his spirit to the God of Love (422–23), his royal estate to Criseyde (432–33), and his very life into the custody of Pandarus (1053). As John McCall has persuasively argued, the entire movement of the *Troilus* is to some extent an inverted parallel with Boethius' *Consolation of Philosophy*, in which Troilus becomes increasingly circumscribed in contrast with Boethius who progressively gained control over his life.[62] Finally, Troilus' abandonment of "japes" and "cruelte" is virtuous only if we imagine it is a vice to reprove folly. As Pandarus observes, Troilus' "japes" were at "Loves servantz everichone" (912), and at their master, whom Troilus accurately if foolhardily styled as "'Seynt Idyot'" (910).

One characteristic of the enamoured Troilus that does *not* derive from the *Romaunt* is his prowess in battle. As Utley has noted, we are told in Book I that he played the lion in the field (1074), a metaphor repeated in V, 830, while in Book III he is described as "the first in armes dyght . . . And this encrees of hardynesse and myght / Com hym of love" (1773–77). It was sometimes said in the Middle Ages that the servants of the God of Love more typically lost than won. Bishop Bradwardine, for example, imputed the weakness of the French to their service of Venus in his sermon celebrating the English victory at Crécy, while Gower later wrote in *Vox Clamantis* that "feats of arms thrive upon good morals" (p. 207).[63] The competing idea, and the one clearly found in the *Troilus*, is that military feats are not praiseworthy when performed in the hope of carnal result. Chaucer underscores Troilus' intentions very clearly early in the poem, when he comments that he did "ek swich travaille / In armes, that to thynk it was merveille" (I, 475–76). These, and one presumes his subsequent exploits, were performed

> . . . for non hate he to the Grekes hadde,
> Ne also for the rescous of the town,
> Ne made hym thus in armes for to madde,
> But only, lo, for this conclusioun:
> To liken hire the bet for his renoun.   [I, 477–83]

The carnally inspired soldier turns up in a later literary metamorphosis as the Squire in the General Prologue, whose feats in the notorious campaign of Bishop Despenser were similarly performed "In hope to stonden in his lady grace" (88).[64] Gower, too, was familiar with the man who fought, like Troilus "his ladies thank to wynne" (III, 1777), and he asks, rhetorically, in *Vox Clamantis*, "what honor shall a conqueror have if a woman's love can conquer him?" (p. 196). Gower does not suggest that the knight who fights in order to earn a lady's praise will not win on the field; rather he says that a knight earns merit only when he bears arms "for the sake of justice" (p. 196). As we learn in more detail from some of Gower's chapter headings, "the knight who engages in the use of arms when he is burning with lust for a woman's affection certainly does not deserve the honor of praise for it at all. . . . when lustful love for women dominates a knight it veritably extinguishes all chivalrous virtue in him" (pp. 197, 201).[65] It is true that Troilus plays the lion in the field, but in doing so for the sake of a woman he wins one battle only to lose another. As Gower put it, "lest you be conquered like a lion, you must flee like a hare" (p. 200).

The passages we have been examining that assert Troilus' banishment of vice or his military prowess or his lover's manners do not, upon reflection, go very far towards showing that he is ennobled by love. His singing, spending, and changing of clothes are derived from the behavior of a follower of *fol amour* who rejects reason. The claim that he flees vice is ironic, since the love affair he was engaged in was itself a vice, and his affairs on the battlefield, because conducted in the hope of other affairs, win him shame rather than honor. There too, although he is martially successful for a time, he determines to seek death in warfare because of his disappointment in love, prompting the narrator to observe "Swych fyn hath al his grete worthynesse!" (V, 1829).[66]

Perhaps the key to understanding what Chaucer is saying about Troilus comes in a passage at the close of Book III that we have already studied in part. After paying tribute to Troilus' prowess, in which Chaucer says he was second only to Hector, Chaucer notes with disarming casualness that in time of truce Troilus spent his time hawking or would "elles honte boor, beer, or lyoun; / The smale bestes leet he gon biside" (III, 1780–81). Although this is translated directly from the *Filostrato*, it is hard to imagine that Chaucer would not have recognized in it the same humor involving the two hunts that we have already discussed in regard to the *Romance of the Rose*. The hunt for the boar, Adonis' hunt, represents the pursuit of Charity, while the hunt for smaller beasts, usually rabbits, is symbolic of the pursuit of the delights of Venus. In Book III of the *Troilus* the protagonist spends more time in the bedroom than on the battlefield and his real devotion is to Venus rather than Mars.

> By day, he was in Martes heigh servyse,
> This is to seyn, in armes as a knyght;
> And for the more part, the longe nyght
> He lay and thoughte how that he myght serve
> His lady best, hire thonk for to deserve.   [III, 437–41]

It is, therefore, with amusement that Chaucer and Boccaccio *show* Troilus following the commands of Venus, while *saying* that he ignored the little beasts for the boars of the rebellious Adonis.[67]

Action, Imagery, and Proclaimed Virtue

As we noted earlier, intentions were very important for determining moral values in the Middle Ages. What a literary character does must be considered in light of why he does it, while simultaneously the medieval fondness for irony will complicate the problem of evaluation by asserting that a character is virtuous while showing him in the process of doing something that is not virtuous or something that is only nominally virtuous. The narrator's assurance that Troilus' new-found penchant for changing clothes is part and parcel of his new-found virtue inspired by love is in fact a literary or iconographic detail suggesting servitude to the God of Love—something that by definition precludes being virtuous. Moreover, we must be alert not only to the narrator's words and the characters' actions, but to the characters' actions and words as well. For example, Chaucer closes Book III of the poem by blandly saying of Troilus that "moost of love and vertu was his speche" (1786), whereas the "love" depicted by the principals has little to do with virtue. Indeed, Troilus' earlier assertion that he must needs "amenden in som wyse, / Right thorugh the vertu of youre heigh servyse" (III, 1287–88) is somewhat called into question when we reflect that his assurance of moral improvement is founded upon his discovery of himself in Criseyde's bed. Actions themselves may be compared not only with images and speeches, but also with the actions of other characters. K. S. Kiernan has instructively compared the actions of Troilus with those of Hector to the detriment of the former. In his brilliant essay, Kiernan notes Chaucer's expansion of Hector's role from its source, and observes that he has balanced him carefully against Troilus. Hector is forthcoming in the protection of Criseyde, while Troilus is unable to act in any responsible manner, either because he is prostrated by love or because he maintains that he must keep their affair secret. The net effect is to show Troilus' personal failure by contrast with Hector's moral success.[68]

There are far too many of these amusing disparities between action and action, action and statement, statement and fact, or action and imagery, imagery and fact, to permit analysis of more than a fraction. Even so, it is worthwhile to call attention to a few more than we have noted thus far in order to underscore more sharply how often in the poem the proclamations of virtue run counter to the imagery, the actions, or the circumstances of the poem. The disparities on one level direct the reader to see an ironic harmony on another. For example, although love is supposed to lead to virtue in the poem, nevertheless Troilus' first and indeed subsequent action is to try to pretend that he has not fallen in love. Thus, immediately after he is struck by the God of Love's arrow, he sighs *softly* "lest men myghte hym here, / And caught ayeyn his firste pleyinge chere" (I, 279–80). This disinclination to be discovered as a victim of Love's arrow is perhaps understandable in light of Troilus' previously expressed scorn for lovers, but makes us wonder about the assertions that love leads to virtue, since its first result is the deception of one's friends. Whatever verisimilitude Troilus' action might have, its inclusion in the story by both Chaucer and Boccaccio is probably for reasons that are ultimately literary.

In the *Romaunt* the lover is told by the God of Love that he must suffer the pains of love. As he puts it:

"Whanne thou hast yeven thyn herte, as I
Have seid thee heere openly,
Thanne aventures shull thee falle,
Which harde and hevy ben withalle."   [2387–90]

These pains of love, which include the famous castles in Spain of dreamed-of but not enjoyed carnal bliss, are, the God of Love assures the lover, necessary because "'A man loveth more tendirly / The thyng that he hath bought most dere'" (2738–39). This truism, used in the Middle Ages to justify difficult poetry, is probably derived ultimately from God's love for the world being expressed by the sacrifice of his son.[69] The parodically religious nature of the lover's having to suffer prior to the delights of fornication is carefully introduced into this section of the poem by the use of the theological terms "penance" and "repentance." Not surprisingly, in view of the "up-so-doun" nature of this particular love service, penance does not follow repentance but proceeds from concentration upon the rosebud "withoute repentaunce" (2356). One of the so-called penances of love is to have to resort to concealment. "Feyne thee other cause" (2520) than love, the lover is admonished, an arbitrary injunction that is introduced more to alert the reader to the anomalies of the pursuit of the lover's goal than to represent any social truth.

Not all kinds of love, of course, have to be concealed, and the "honest love" of Gower, represented by marriage, was normally a public event. As readers, then, we must remark upon the tension created by the statements in the poem assuring us that love leads to virtue, which are opposed by the statements about Troilus' concern for deception. In addition to his initial concern for secrecy, he soon "gan dissimulen" (I, 322), while in addition to dissimulation his "feigning" being something he is not becomes a characteristic of his subsequent behavior in the poem. He "feyneth" (I, 326) to others that he is happy while he is miserable, and again is shown as an adept at dissimulation in III, 434. That Troilus should have to lie about being in love is never really accounted for in the poem—any more than concealment is in the *Romance of the Rose*—for the necessity for secrecy is obvious enough in moral terms.[70]

Amusingly, deception abounds in this poem in which love is said to ennoble the man described by Pandarus as "That trewe man" (II, 331) and by Criseyde as possessing "grete trouthe" (III, 992). Not only does Troilus deceive his friends about his love for Criseyde, but he shows no scruple when Pandarus suggests that they deceive his favorite brother, Deiphebus, by pretending an illness. Instead, he says that love has so debilitated him that he is "sik in ernest" (II, 1529). Troilus is willing enough to deceive his brother, and indeed he does deceive him, for whether he is truly sick or not we are told that he "held forth ay the wyse / That ye han herd Pandare er this devyse" (II, 1546–47), which suggests he is carrying out Pandarus' deceptive intent. The whole scene in which Deiphebus and Criseyde (who is "al innocent of this" [II, 1562]) are manipulated by Pandarus is introduced by his claim that people rejoice at "a gret empryse / Acheved wel" (II, 1391–92), while later Troilus calls the seduction itself "this grete emprise" (III, 416). The narrator, too, resorts to the phrase, and calls Pandarus' first visit in the campaign to bring about Criseyde's seduction "his grete emprise" (II, 73), and underscores its deceptive nature by asking two-faced Janus to guide him (II, 77).

Deception and seduction, the "great enterprises" of these two books, are not only played off against the idea of Troilus' ennoblement through love, but also against the theme of brotherly love. There are some seventeen instances in which Troilus calls Pandarus "brother" or vice-versa, and these filial addresses are given an added ironic dimension by the promise from each nominal brother to arrange the seduction of his sister! (I, 860; III, 409–13). Thus the proclaimed brothers cooperate in the "grete emprise" of seduction, while deceiving one of Troilus' true brothers. Meanwhile Troilus' blood brother, Hector, stands in tacit contrast as one who does not try to exploit Criseyde. The entire matter of true versus nominal brotherly love is best seen from the perspective afforded at the beginning of the poem when the narrator Chaucer says he will have compassion on lovers "As though I were hire owne brother dere" (I, 51).[71]

Although testimony to Troilus' "truth" is offered by the characters in the poem and by the narrator, Troilus' typical actions are deceitful. Not only does Troilus go along with the deception of Deiphebus, and of Criseyde, but later he deceives Criseyde more directly by falling in with another of Pandarus' Byzantine schemes. In Book II Pandarus invents a person called "Poliphete" (II, 1467, 1616) whom he styles as a foe to Criseyde, and in Book III he creates someone called "Horaste" (III, 797) and tells Criseyde that Troilus is in "peyne and distresse" (III, 792) because he has heard that Criseyde loves the mythical Horaste.[72] Criseyde confronts Troilus with this, and demands to know why he is jealous, since there is no cause, and, note well, she suspects there might be trickery, and accuses him of doing this in malice to "fonden" her; i.e., to persuade her to yield:

> But in effect she wolde wit anon
> Of what man, and ek wheer, and also why
> He jalous was, syn ther was cause non;
> And ek the sygne that he took it by,
> She badde hym that to telle hire bisily;
> Or elles, certeyn, she bar hym on honde
> That this was don of malice, hire to fonde.
>
> [III, 1149–55]

Troilus may or may not have been able to hear Pandarus tell Criseyde about the fabricated Horaste, and he may or may not have been let in on Pandarus' plans. However, since to tell the truth would put him in a very awkward position—it would disclose Pandarus' lie—he chooses the line of least resistance and least ennoblement: "And for the lasse harm, he moste feyne" (III, 1158). Indeed, "feigning" of one sort or another is one of Troilus' characteristics in the poem. Even when Criseyde is to be exchanged for Antenor, it is Hector who tries to keep her while Troilus stands mute "Lest men sholde his affeccioun espye" (IV, 153). There is a fine dramatic irony when the audience, having heard Troilus lie to Criseyde and dissemble about his feelings for her, later hears Criseyde declare that she first loved him because of his "moral vertu, grounded upon trouthe" (IV, 1672). Because "truth" can mean the honesty that the lover in the *Romance of the Rose* is instructed to avoid in favor of feigning, one kind of irony is evident at frequent intervals in the poem. Because "truth" can also mean "fidelity," both Criseyde's ultimate forsaking of Troilus as well as his own fidelity to a questionable relationship are factors that give rise to a related kind of irony when the word is used in the poem. Finally, there are times when both meanings seem to be involved, as, for example, when Chaucer with mock anger castigates those who would call love "a woodnesse or folie" (III, 1382). He remands them to live in woe, "ther God yeve hem meschaunce, / And every lovere in his trouthe avaunce" (III, 1385–86).

The persistent disparities between the assertions of the poem about virtue and the actions of the characters are echoed by the disparities between the statements of the poem and its imagery. For example, whereas the statements of the poem assure us that Troilus is improved in virtue, the various images of birds and animals that accompany him throughout the poem give mainly negative impressions. We have already noted that immediately upon falling in love Troilus is very unflatteringly compared with a fat horse, and shortly thereafter he is compared with a bird caught by the birdlime of Cupid: "For love bigan his fetheres so to lyme" (I, 353). Troilus himself picks up the image of the animal or bird caught by love and a bit further along in the poem sees himself as a fool: "'O fool, now artow in the snare, / That whilom japedest at loves peyne'" (I, 507–08). In the *Romance of the Rose* Cupid sets his "gynnes" or "panters" to catch ladies and gentlemen, for "Love will noon other briddes cacche" (1620–23), and the lover bewails that he has fallen into Cupid's "snare" (1647). Chaucer has added substantially to Boccaccio's passing reference to Troilo's having been caught by Love's snare (I, 50), perhaps to point up the similarities between Troilus and Amant. The function of the images, then, would be to portray Troilus, like Amant, as a follower of "foly love" (5085), and his self-accusation that he is a fool is essentially correct.

The other bird images in the poem also appear not to contribute to the idea of Troilus' ennoblement or indeed to contradict or undercut it. The white eagle of Criseyde's dream, for example, although it has been seen as an image of Troilus who soars up to the heavens, is perhaps better understood in terms of one of the other bird images in the poem.[73] The white eagle changes

Criseyde's heart for its own, and although in the dream she is neither terrified nor hurt, nevertheless the idea of the "longe clawes" which "out hire herte . . . rente" (II, 927–28) present us with an image that may foretell pain outside the world of the dream. A large bird tearing out a vital organ so strongly suggests the vulture that feeds on Tityas' stomach or Prometheus' liver that one has difficulty supposing that Criseyde's dream symbolizes a desirable phenomenon, in spite of the ornithological and anatomical variations. In Book I Pandarus observed that Troilus was suffering pains

> As sharp as doth he Ticius in helle,
> Whos stomak foughles tiren evere moo
> That hightyn volturis, as bokes telle.   [I, 786–88]

Thus in spite of the protestations that Criseyde feels no pain from the eagle, the similarity of the images suggests a darkened future. Whatever Troilus' potential as an eagle may be, his actual physical encounter with Criseyde is portrayed in much less grandiose ornithological terms. When he first embraces Criseyde he is compared to a lark-catching "sperhauk" (III, 1191–92), which bird is a common symbol for simple physical virility—so much so that Harry Bailly uses it somewhat inappropriately to describe the Nun's Priest, and it is one of the birds inciting Thopas in Chaucer's tale.

As the eagle must be thought of in terms of the vulture and the sparrowhawk, so the lion, with which Troilus is so often associated, must be thought of in terms of the wounded bull with which he is compared in IV, 239–45. The bull, already associated with Taurus, the sign of Venus, earlier in the poem (II, 55), is a basic symbol for lechery, so while we might admire the feats of arms that Troilus performs as a lion in the field, we should not forget that he performs them for the sake of Criseyde, and when she is taken from him he is reduced to a frenzied, dying bull.[74]

Another disparity between what the poem says and what the images display is to be found with the image of the mirror. Of course, the disparity exists, as do the others, only on one level, for the statement that the God of Love makes worthy folk worthier of name (I, 251) is doubtless intended to be ironic. Taken either way it compares or contrasts significantly with the scene in which Troilus is shown sitting on his bed—which may have its own significance—and is said to make a "mirour of his mynde" (I, 365). This image, which is added to Boccaccio's version of the story, has the potential for being understood *in bono*, as readers of *Speculum* are well aware. However, in the next line we are told that in this particular mirror "he saugh al holly hire figure," and this imagined vision of the loved one suggests an interpretation along the lines of that found in the *Romance of the Rose*. There, as we have noted, the "mirrour perilous" (1601) costs Narcissus his life and the lover his freedom to reject the carnal impulses that had brought him to the garden in the first place. Since narcissism is central to the idea of self-love in the *Ro-*

mance, the allusion to the mirror in the *Troilus* would not easily be missed, for it is part and parcel of the whole paraphernalia surrounding the God of Love. Thus the text tells us that Troilus should become more worthy, (albeit ironically), while the imagery shows him as becoming less so. Indeed, the mirror of delectable ladies was an image Chaucer was later to use to characterize the scarcely ennobled January in the *Merchant's Tale*, whose elderly lusts create a mirror that, like Troilus', shows "Many fair shap and many a fair visage" (*MerchT*, 1580).

The "Religion" of the God of Love

Troilus' freedom is also a quality that is asserted by the text while being denied by the actions of the poem and its images. The admirable articles by Thomas Van and Stephen A. Barney do an excellent job of describing the imagery of bondage which pervades the poem, but do not, I think, assign the proper cause to the minutely observed effect.[75] The images of bondage are, in fact, a counterpart to the theme of the ennobling power of love, which, in turn, is a parody of some basic Christian ideas and images.

As noted earlier in this chapter, the poem states repeatedly that the service of the God of Love is something that causes one to forsake vice and embrace virtue. It is important to note that the various passages adduced by Dodd and by Utley that speak of vice and virtue, as well as the amusing business in Book III wherein Troilus assures Criseyde that he will "amenden" through her service, are all additions to Chaucer's source. He was, obviously, trying to convey an important theme through irony, for the idea that service of the God of Love will cause one to flee vice and follow virtue is a precise inversion of Christian belief. Chaucer does not, in the *Troilus*, use the imagery of freeing oneself from vice, or releasing oneself from the bondage of vice, but Christianity used this imagery so commonly that it is hard to cite texts selectively. That Christ frees man from the bondage of sin is one of the major themes in the writings of St. Paul, who told Christians to "stand fast in the liberty wherewith Christ has made us free, and be not entangled again with the yoke of bondage."[76] Similarly, the typical Chaucerian image of man's relation to sin is that "Crist is moore strong for to unbynde than synne is strong for to bynde" (*ParsT*, 1072).[77] The importance of this for the *Troilus* is that we have two sets of actions and images played off against one another. Thus the "religion" of the God of Love leads to a putative freedom from the bondage of sin, while paradoxically Troilus himself, caught by the God of Love's birdlime, is shown to be less rather than more free.

Not only is the idea that the service of Cupid frees one from vice a parodic inversion of Christian teaching, it is also diametrically opposed to philosophical beliefs about freedom, vice, and virtue. For example, Lady Philosophy in

Boethius' *Consolation* envisions virtue and vice in terms of freedom and servitude respectively: the souls of men are "more fre" when engaged in divine
speculation, "lasse fre" when embodied, and "yit lasse fre" when they are
"comprehended in erthli membres." But "the laste servage is whan that thei
ben yeven to vices and han ifalle fro the possessioun of hir propre resoun"
(Bk. V, pr. 2). Boethius furthers this idea by the use of chain imagery
throughout the *Consolation*, with the oft-mentioned "hevy cheynes" (Bk. I,
m. 2) of earthly sorrow contrasted with love that binds the "accordaunce of
thynges" and holds the "bridelis" of right order in the world (Bk. II, m. 8).
Indeed, Boethius typically uses images of restraint such as the yoke and
the bridle to indicate both proper service and improper servitude, so that
Boethius is told to "withdrawe thy nekke fro the yok of erthely affeccions"
(Bk. III, m. 1), while Hercules' reward for his labors is paradoxically also a
yoke, but one easy to bear: "and the laste of his labours was that he sus-
teynede the hevene uppon his nekke unbowed" (Bk. IV, m. 7).[78]

Lest there be any misunderstanding about what constitutes the good and
the bad yokes, bridles, or chains, Boethius specifies that the man who would
be mighty should "ne putte nat his nekke . . . undir the foule reynes of leech-
erie" (Bk. III, m. 5), nor will he, if he gains political power, necessarily be
able to control his own lusts: "ne power ne maketh nat a man myghty over
hymselve, which that vicyous lustes holden destreyned with cheynes that ne
mowen nat ben unbownden" (Bk. II, pr. 6). Even kings can be bound by "ful
streyte cheynes" when "lecherye tormenteth hem" (Bk. IV, m. 2). The chain
of lust, the "rosea catena" of the mythographers, is closely akin to the biblical
bondage of sin, and both images must be borne in mind when reading the
Troilus, for the poem's argument that Troilus' carnal infatuation for Criseyde
will lead to virtue is a contradiction in terms. The kind of love that holds the
universe in concord, which Chaucer was later to refer to as the "faire cheyne
of love" (*KnT*, 2988, 2991), is the love that Boethius says "halt togidres peples joyned with an holy boond, and knytteth sacrement of mariages of chaste
loves" (Bk. II, m. 8). Since the *Troilus* is lacking sacramental marriage, the
affair ought to be thought of, as Pandarus puts it, as "but casuel plesaunce"
(IV, 419), and Troilus' relationship to the God of Love is better described as
servitude than service. The good yoke, which Chaucer was to call "that blisful yok / Of soveraynetee, noght of servyse, / Which that men clepe spous-
aille or wedlok" (*ClT*, 113–15), is conspicuously absent from the *Troilus*.
When Troilus sees himself as being a fool, caught in a snare, who must gnaw
his own chain (I, 507–9), he is expressing essentially Boethian ideas about
the bondage of lust. Moreover, when we recall that it was a medieval commonplace to discuss carnal infatuation along with references to the freedom
of the will, Troilus' insight is even more significant, for he has attached the
chain himself. As Boethius puts it, whoever desires unstable things "enlaceth
hym in the cheyne with which he mai ben drawen" (Bk. I, m. 4). When the

poem tells us that Troilus has been freed from vice to follow virtue, we should laugh at the incongruity of the intellectual concepts and the images accompanying them. Indeed, it has been argued by John McCall that the structure of the *Troilus* is an inversion of that of the *Consolation*, in which Troilus becomes increasingly enslaved whereas Boethius gradually became liberated.[79] However, Chaucer's most elaborate treatment of vice, virtue, bondage, and freedom is rendered in a liturgical rather than a philosophical vehicle, and to understand it we must return to the biblical idea of Christ's freeing man from the bondage of sin.

The numerous passages asserting that the service of the God of Love permits one to flee vice for virtue should be examined in light of a crux that Chaucer adds to Boccaccio, namely the mock "confession" to the God of Love that Pandarus leads Troilus through, and which is borrowed from the *Romance of the Rose*.[80] In the *Romance*, the lover performs a hypocritical penance which amusingly precedes rather than follows his confession. "Thus for a long time I performed my penance with such a conscience as God knows, for I did one thing and thought another" (p. 183). Love then asks him "'Have you performed all the commandments?'" (p. 183), to which the lover responds that he has done the best he could. The God of Love acknowledges this, but points out that the lover in fact listened sympathetically to Reason, which leads him to demand "'Weren't you indeed a wicked man?'" (p. 184). The accusation of this nominal sin breaks down the lover's resistance, and he replies "'Mercy, sir, I have confessed it'" (p. 184). The idea of the lover's confession is glanced at again a few lines later, when the God of Love again catechizes him, saying that "in place of the confessional" he wants him to "recall all my commandments" (p. 185), which apparently means that instead of assigning a penance as in the confessional, the God of Love will forgive him if he can recap the commandments which, unsurprisingly, are ten in number.

Chaucer worked the lover's confession into the text of the *Troilus* in a very similar fashion. That is, he used a great deal of religious language and imagery to suggest that Troilus has made a religion of his service to the God of Love. He goes further, though, in playfully linking the religion of love to the release from the bondage of vice. Normally contrition, confession, and penance lead to the forgiveness of sin—that release from the bondage of vice to the freedom of virtue that Christ makes possible in Christianity. Of course, the God of Love cannot effect this, so that the poem asserts that Troilus turns from vice to virtue while showing him mainly turning to Criseyde for carnal solace. Chaucer's scene is inspired by the *Romance of the Rose*, but his religious language is a little different. Even before the confession scene the narrator ironically says of Troilus' sudden subjection to Love "Blissed be Love, that kan thus folk converte!" (I, 308), and the first "prayer" of the "converted" Troilus is to say "'O lord, now youres is / My spirit, which that oughte youres be'" (I, 422–23), a commending of the spirit that in modern liturgical practice is associated with preparation for death rather than for the new life of the "converted." One would not wish to push the analogies too far, but it is a commonplace idea that the way the Christian becomes freed from sin is by a metaphorical "dying" to his former life—as St. Paul writes in Romans 6:3–9 one dies with Christ in order to live with him, "for he that is dead is free from sin." When Troilus first sees Criseyde, "sodeynly hym thoughte he felte dyen" (I, 306).

After Troilus tells Pandarus the name of his lady, Pandarus assures him that he should not ascribe his situation to chance: "'The oughte nat to clepe it hap, but grace'" (I, 896). Troilus, though, whatever grace he may have received, has blasphemed. Specifically, Pandarus says, "'thow were wont to chace / At Love in scorn, and for despit him calle / "Seynt Idyot, lord of thise foles alle"'" (I, 908–10). "Saint Idiot" might seem to the impartial reader a rather good name for the God of Love, but Pandarus harps on Troilus' "japes" at the god, using the word in each of the next three stanzas. Then, instead of merely referring to the confessional as is done in the *Romance of the Rose*, Chaucer has Pandarus and Troilus act out a confessional scene, complete with breast-beating, prayers for the forgiveness of "japes," and advice on the proper "entente" one must have for a confession:

> "Now bet thi brest, and sey to God of Love,
> 'Thy grace, lord, for now I me repente,
> If I mysspak, for now myself I love.'
> Thus sey with al thyn herte in good entente."
> Quod Troilus, "A, lord! I me consente,
> And preye to the my japes thow foryive,
> And I shal nevere more whyle I live."   [I, 932–38]

The wealth of religious language here is marvelous to behold. Grace, repentance, prayer, and forgiveness all figure actively in the text, while the idea of contrition is glanced at in the next stanza when Pandarus hopes that Troilus has appeased the god's wrath since he has "wopen many a drope" (I, 941). Even so, this parody of a confession involves, in a sense, a confession that escapes the notice of both Troilus and Pandarus, for when Troilus says "now myself I love" he not only acknowledges that he is a lover, but, with a little change in emphasis tells us that he loves himself—"for now, *myself* I love!". Of course, since narcissism, self-love, is the real source of this sort of love, the lines invite being read for both meanings.

After contrition and confession we should expect satisfaction, which Chaucer's Parson describes as often managed through "bodily peyne" (*ParsT*, 1029). For followers of the God of Love, though, whether in the *Romance of the Rose* or in the *Troilus*, satisfaction will be more in satisfaction received than given. In the *Romance* the God of Love promises Amant the rose, while in the *Troilus* Pandarus hopes for "comfort" (I, 945) from Criseyde. Amusingly, in terms of what we have seen of Boethian imagery, Pandarus goes on to counsel Troilus to regulate his bridle ("'Now loke that atempre be thi bridel'" [I, 953]), and to "'persevere in thy servyse'" (I, 958). The result of this bridling of himself will be, we are assured by Pandarus, moral improvement from vice to virtue, something that seems unlikely to happen since Pandarus goes on to make use of an earthy joke Chaucer later used with his Friar: that Troilus will be a noble post to the law of love:

> "I thenke, sith that Love, of his goodnesse,
> Hath the converted out of wikkednesse,
> That thow shalt ben the beste post, I leve,
> Of al his lay, and moost his foos to greve." [81]

[I, 998–1001]

Chaucer enjoyed this mock confessional scene so much that he added it to his poem a second time, with a few elegant variations. The occasion for the second scene is Pandarus' visit to Criseyde, when he rehearses what has passed in order to encourage Criseyde to fall in with his schemes. When Criseyde softens to the point of asking "'Kan he wel speke of love?'" (II, 503), Pandarus recounts the confessional. In the telling, Troilus does not beat his breast but rather says "'*mea culpa*, lord, I me repente!'" (II, 525), and his general lack of any sense of proportion is indicated by his attribution to the God of Love the disposition of everyone's lot through just providence, "'juste purveiaunce'" (II, 527).[82] And, in a spirit similar to that he evinced earlier when he had Pandarus assure Troilus that he would be the best post to the law of love, here Chaucer has Troilus ask that in answer to his prayer the God of Love grant him "swich penaunce / As liketh the" (II, 529–30).[83]

Whether we consider the philosophical or the biblical associations of vice with bondage, it is clear that Troilus' capitulation to the God of Love cannot bring about what the poem says it brings about. Although the word "tension" is most often used with reference to Chaucer to describe the equal claims of earthly and heavenly love in his poetry, it is nevertheless a useful word to employ for the relationship between direct and ironic statement. If, however, Chaucer's poetic strategy is to play off ironic against direct statement, we should note that in this poem the ironic utterances prevail for the great majority of the stanzas. Indeed it would be just to say that the *Troilus* is a poem in which a lengthy ironic statement is bracketed by two very short, mostly direct statements that open and close the poem.[84] Small wonder that Chaucer's *indirect* strategies, such as setting up a disparity between the assertions that Troilus flees vice for virtue, played off against a series of images indicating his bondage, are often hard to perceive. Even so, they are undeniably there when we look. When Troilus is confirmed into the religion of the God of Love, a religion with seduction and idolatry for its means and goal, he promptly loses what self-governance he had had. Whereas he was once largely his own man, following his conversion he gives his spirit to the God of Love (I, 422–23), his royal estate to Criseyde (I, 432–33), and his very life into the custody of Pandarus (I, 1053), using the identical words of the lover in the *Romaunt*, who delivers his life into the custody of the God of Love (1955). This self-determined abrogation of self-determination is all for the sake of an illicit passion for Criseyde, and Troilus' self-imposed bondage by sin is accompanied by statements that he is freed from sin. It all leads to one of the most wonderfully ironic lines in the poem when, in the brilliantly contrived consummation scene with its bed as a parodic altar, Criseyde, in order "to deliveren hym fro bittre bondes, / . . . ofte hym kiste" (III, 1116–17).

Upon inspection the arguments for Troilus' ennoblement by love based on external evidence—such as the appeal to courtly love—and the arguments for his moral improvement based on internal evidence—such as the appeals to passages proclaiming his banishment of vice—are all unpersuasive. The more one studies the variation between direct and ironic statement, between what the poem asserts and what the images and actions convey, the more one is led to the conclusion that Chaucer was very much in control of his materials and was trying to present a poem in which superficially perceived contraries lead to more deeply perceived truths. Even Pandarus acknowledges this as a principle of medieval epistemology when he says "By his contrarie is every thyng declared" (I, 637).[85] It is, therefore, not surprising that Chaucer writes a tragedy that includes a great deal of comedy, and that he prepares us for the direct advice to love Christ "syn he best to love is, and most meke" (V, 1847), with the portrait of Troilus, proud not meek, who follows a false religion with its elaborate rules, ceremonies, and language. Although the God of Love has received short shrift, as it were, from critics of the poem, both he and his religion are central to an understanding of it. Thus far we have examined the freedom of the will and the God of Love, as well as the claims that his service is ennobling. Clearly the next step is to study, if not venerate, the Mother of God, who in this instance is Saint Venus.

Chapter IV

Chaucer, Troilus, and "Seint Venus"

Venus and Her Influence on the Principals

For the most part Chaucer's use of Venus in the *Troilus* is straightforward enough. As the planet / goddess associated with carnality, she functions much as does her son Cupid, the God of Love. Thus we find that she is invoked to assist the characters in their carnal pursuits, she is often described with language and actions that provide a parodic religious dimension, and her presence is much more notable in the first three books of the poem than in the final two. As noted in chapter 2, John Gower complained in his *Vox Clamantis* that the inhabitants of London, styled as New Troy, have been mastered by the goad of the flesh and have set up Venus as Mistress of the People. To an extent Chaucer's poem of Old Troy is very similar, and for the most part Venus is a symbol used to show the extent to which Troilus has been mastered by the goad of the flesh. Chaucer, though, is typically more complicated than Gower, and in a few crucial places—notably the Prohemium to Book III and Troilus' hymn to Love and Charity, also in Book III—Chaucer calls attention to a double, or more accurately a multiple Venus, whose function is more elaborate. Let us, though, begin with Venus in her simplest aspect.

Certainly the first and most general point to be made about Venus is that Chaucer significantly increases her involvement in the story when he rewrites the *Filostrato*. In Boccaccio's poem the only passage of any consequence about Venus is Troilo's praise of her after his seduction of Criseida (III, 74–89), which is the series of stanzas that Chaucer transformed into the Prohemium to Book III. The only other references in Boccaccio's poem are VII, 59, where Troilo says that the fear of loss of Criseida makes him useless to either Venus or Mars, and VIII, 16, where Troilo swears by Venus that he will kill Diomede. In Chaucer's poem the emphasis is altogether different. Not only does he move Troilo's hymn to Venus to the Prohemium of Book III, but also substitutes for it a praise of Love that is virtually a paraphrase of Boethius' *Consolation*, Bk. II, m. 8. Since the passage on Venus that Chaucer transfers to the opening of Book III is also based in small part upon the *Consolation*, Bk. II, m. 8, in both Boccaccio and Chaucer, the two passages should be thought of together, even though the latter one does not actually mention Venus. Chaucer also adds a small encomium of Venus to Boccaccio's

text, which becomes the ending of Book III and thus echoes the grand opening of the book. Another addition is the introduction of a hymn to Love just
before the actual seduction, in which Love is addressed as Charity, child of
the Cytherean Venus. Thus, while Venus has some importance in Boccaccio's
poem, she does not have the centrality there that Chaucer assigns her. Indeed, by changing Boccaccio's nine-part poem to one with five books, and by
featuring Venus at the opening, in the middle, and at the close of the central
Book III, Chaucer has signalled that his story of Troilus and Criseyde is very
much a story of Venus.

In addition to making Venus more important structurally in the poem,
Chaucer has also been at pains to involve each of the three principals with the
goddess. Troilus first asks Venus for "helpe" in his affair with Criseyde, lest
he "sterve" (I, 1014). As the plot develops Criseyde falls in love with Troilus
at first sight, a remarkable phenomenon that the narrator explains by noting
that the planet Venus was at that time well-disposed to "helpe" Troilus, and
had also been favorable in his nativity (II, 667–85). Thus, when Pandarus
reports that he has gotten Criseyde to agree to "love of frendshipe," Troilus
praises Venus' "myght" and "grace" (II, 962, 972–73). At the beginning of
the next book the Prohemium to Venus ends rather significantly with the
linking of the praise of Venus with Troilus' "gladnesse" (III, 47–48). The
almost grandiloquent tone of the Prohemium is belied by the tone of the language surrounding the "gladnesse" that Troilus achieves later in this book.
Pandarus has hidden Troilus in an amusingly named "stuwe," and when he
opens the door to let Troilus out, the excited, anticipant, and slightly nervous
Troilus breaks out in a whole congeries of implorations to Venus.[1] He prays
to "seint Venus" for "grace," and hopes that "blisful Venus" will "enspire"
him in the events to come, while concluding with the request to Venus to ask
her father to turn aside by "grace" (III, 705–19) any astrological impediments that may have been present at his birth.[2] Troilus then utters from
Criseyde's bed his encomium of Love as Charity, the supposed child of the
Cytherean Venus. This is a passage that will be discussed in detail below.
Troilus' final speech of Book III, on Love, is not addressed to Venus, but, as
noted already, some of the parallels between the Boethian idea of love that
maintains the order of the universe may be found in the Prohemium to Book
III. It follows that these first and last addresses to Venus and to Love, by the
narrator and by Troilus respectively, should be considered in light of each
other. Indeed, the central speech by Troilus praising Love as a child of Venus
also addresses Love as "'holy bond of thynges'" (III, 1261), and this link between Venus and Love and Boethian harmonic love suggests that this
Boethian idea may inform the whole of Book III. Whether Boethian harmonic love functions as an adjunct to or in opposition to the love inspired by
the carnal Venus, we shall discuss later.

The religious vocabulary used by Troilus in his request to St. Venus for grace functions the same way that religious language does with regard to Cupid: that is, it gives the reader an ironic perspective on the folly of making concupiscence a religion. The effect is much the same with Pandarus, whose involvement with Venus is, like that of Troilus, intense. While Troilus seeks the help, the grace, the inspiration of Venus, Pandarus sees himself as her servant and swears by her, hopes by her, and praises her (II, 234; II, 1524; III, 951). It is, presumably, because Pandarus is Venus' servant that his "hewe" is turned "ful ofte greene" (II, 60) on the third of May—the date on which St. Helena cast down the Temple of Venus and raised up the Cross.[3] The nature of Pandarus' service of Venus may be understood by his hope that Criseyde will fully "conferme" her "grace" (II, 1526) at Deiphebus' house, and from his excited hymn of praise to "'Immortal God'" when the lovers first kiss. This "God" is then specified as Venus' son—"'Cupid I mene'" (III, 185–86). Venus is also praised by name in the same apostrophe, for Pandarus says "'Venus, thow mayst maken melodie!'" (III, 187). What Chaucer means here by the phrase "maken melodie" is made sufficiently clear in the *Miller's Tale*, and the musical affinities of the Venus associated with kissing have not gone unnoticed by scholars.[4] Pandarus utters this apostrophe from an appropriately worshipful posture: he falls on his knees, raises his eyes to heaven, and holds high his hands. Of course, what has aroused his divine praise is a rather earthly kiss (not the kiss of peace)—a kiss that proverbially led to greater intimacy in Chaucer's time.[5] The final association of Pandarus and Venus occurs in the third book, just before Troilus enters Criseyde's bedroom. She has agreed to speak with him, and says that she will get up first, but Pandarus bluntly urges her to "'liggeth stille, and taketh hym right here'" (III, 948). Each of you, he continues, can ease the other's sorrow, and then, with a most equivocal tone he adds:

> "For love of God; and Venus, I the herye;
> For soone hope I we shul ben alle merye." [III, 951–52]

It is the love of the carnal Venus rather than the love of God that will bring the couple into bed with each other, and lines like these are best read with the fact in mind that the punctuation has been added by modern editors. If Troilus appears to be asking for the intercession of Saint Venus, Pandarus takes a more active role, reminiscent (to continue the religious comparison) of the friars who claim to be "Werkeris of Goddes word, nat auditours" (*SumT*, 1937). Insofar as Pandarus hears Troilus' confession, he may be styled a priest in the parodic religion of love. His devotion to Venus is a part of his larger priestly role, and in all of its aspects the religious language and the occasional religious postures—such as kneeling—are to be compared with Pandarus' rather unpriestly modes of speech, action, and locomotion, for he is described as leaping, hopping, joking, and poking.

Criseyde is neither a servant of Venus nor one who approaches her as though she were a saint. Nevertheless, some "veneration" may be found in her portrait. Although Venus largely disappears from the poem after Book III when the love affair is consummated, the two remaining references in the poem are both linked with Criseyde. In the first, when Troilus and Criseyde realize that their parting is inevitable, she asks that Venus preserve her until she can "'quyte hym wel, that so wel kan deserve'" (IV, 1663). She does "quyte" Troilus, of course, but ironically by starting a new affair with Diomede. It is not what Troilus deserves, but it is consistent with the images of Venus that pervade the poem. Finally, when Diomede has taken Criseyde's glove, a possibly sexual as well as social symbol "of which he was ful feyn" (V, 1013), Criseyde retires.[6] To indicate the time of day (evening), and the time of year (the ten days' time for the promised return have been completed), Chaucer introduces a little astronomical periphrasis, and it is hard to think it is accidental that it opens with reference to the planet Venus:

> The brighte Venus folwede and ay taughte
> The wey ther brode Phebus down alighte;
> And Cynthea hire char-hors overraughte
> To whirle out of the Leoun, if she myghte.
>
> [V, 1016–19]

Indeed, in this poem Venus has "taught the way" to more than just where the sun went down.

The Multiple Venus of the Prohemium to Book III

The mock-religious attitudes of Troilus and Pandarus towards Venus are complementary and easily understood. Both men have as their goal the seduction of Criseyde by Troilus, and once that is accomplished in Book III their references to the planet / goddess cease. Insofar as this part of the poem is concerned, therefore, the images, speeches, and actions of the work combine to make it clear that Venus represents concupiscence. Significantly, each of the principal characters calls her "blisful Venus" (I, 1014; II, 234; III, 1661). Thus, Chaucer's displacement of the seduction scene from the first third of the poem—where it occurs in Boccaccio's version—to very nearly the poem's precise center, and Chaucer's bracketing of the seduction scene in Book III with apostrophes to Venus, combine to indicate that he intended the central concern of the poem to be concupiscence. This contrasts with the fickleness of women, which has been suggested as Boccaccio's ultimate preoccupation.[7] The difficulty with this interpretation is that it oversimplifies the Venereal presence in the work, for in addition to her role as goddess of concupiscence she is invoked in the Prohemium to Book III in her roles as goddess of generation, as patron deity of friendship, and as the source of filial and patriotic love.[8] This multiple Venus is closely related to the double Venus discussed in chapter 2, whose manifestations according to Boccaccio's *Chiose* were as a licit Venus having to do with the desire to have children, and an illicit Venus having to do with lasciviousness. The Venuses of generation, of friendship, and of other forms of love than the lascivious may be understood as aspects of the licit Venus. Thus, in Bk. II, m. 8 of the *Consolation*, the passage that inspired both Boccaccio and Chaucer, Love (not Venus, although both the English and the Italian poet used her name when they adapted the apostrophe) is addressed thus:

> . . .—al this accordaunce of thynges is bound with love, that governeth erthe and see, and hath also comandement to the hevene. . . . This love halt togidres peples joyned with an holy boond, and knytteth sacrement of mariages of chaste loves; and love enditeth lawes to trewe felawes.

Boccaccio had Troilo speak of the power of Venus in the heavens, earth, sea, and hell, as did Chaucer when he transferred the speech to the Prohemium to Book III, but in both cases sacramental marriage is absent.

The existence of a double or multiple Venus in medieval mythography and art has been well demonstrated by Robertson and others, and the literary function of a manifold Venus has been fairly well outlined.[9] However, two major, recent studies of Chaucer's *Troilus* have found the two Venuses of the Prohemium to Book III to be ambiguous. Ambiguity as a final effect to be sought is not to be found in medieval literary treatises, but it can be used in a helpful way in discussing medieval texts if we use it to indicate the presence of more than one meaning at a time, rather than in its sense of obscurity or indistinctness. Both Donald Rowe and Ida Gordon employ the idea of ambiguity in a defensible way, and certainly Chaucer's invocation of a multiple Venus in the Prohemium to Book III invites consideration of more than one meaning of Venus. However, I am not persuaded that the ambiguity of the Prohemium, in that multiple sense, is anything more than a device to throw into relief the symbol of the carnal Venus we have been concerned with all along. Rowe, who finds a union of contraries in *Troilus*, uses ambiguity to indicate a continuum of meaning, in which one Venus has both "celestial" and "wanton" effects on man, so that in the Prohemium Chaucer "insists that human sexual love can partake of Venus's 'benignite,' can participate in that love which is the *musica mundana*, for he pictures Venus as potentially ennobling."[10] As with the service of Cupid one could point out that while the text says Venus can ennoble, the text could be ironic. Or, somewhat differently, the text need not refer to the Venus of sexuality when it praises Venus' power to ennoble. Gordon correctly points out that the speeches of the Prohemium can often be construed to apply to either the good or the illicit Venus, depending on just how we interpret the details, so that the claims for Venus' power and benevolence can be made directly for the good Venus or ironically for the personification of sexual desire.[11] However, Gordon leaves this particular ambiguity up in the air—in a sort of Keatsian sense of unresolved contraries—whereas the multiplicity of Venuses in the Prohemium is probably intended to invite us to contrast them with the Venus of sexuality who is the sole subject of the poem. Although St. Augustine said of Scripture that "it is better to be burdened by unknown but useful signs than to interpret signs in a useless way . . . ," he also said that where "two or more meanings are elicited . . . there is no danger if any of the meanings may be seen to be congruous with the truth taught in other passages. . . ."[12]

Chaucer is fond of complexity. With the figure of Cupid, who is commonly just the god of carnal love, Chaucer introduces a variation between direct and ironic statement, not to suggest that serving Cupid and not serving him are the same thing, or that the choice of serving or not serving is of equal moral, intellectual, and personal value, but to give his poem a richer texture. Because Venus is commonly a multifaceted symbol, (Cupid is rarely so), Chaucer has fuller possibilities to begin with, and does not hesitate to exploit all of them. Troilo praises a multiple Venus in Boccaccio's poem, even though the action pertains to only one Venus. In Chaucer's *Troilus* a multiple Venus is invoked in the Prohemium to Book III, but again, since only one Venus is discoverable in the poem, the other Venuses are adduced for contrast. They are in the Prohemium to remind us that they are not present elsewhere. Just as Boccaccio defined the two Venuses in his *Chiose* to the *Teseida* only to go on to assure us that the good Venus was not to be found in the poem proper, so both Boccaccio and Chaucer remind us in their Troy poems of two Venuses, even though only one seems to have any influence. A neat parallel occurs in the *Romance of the Rose*, wherein, as Rosemond Tuve has observed, the poem proclaims itself to be an encyclopedia of love; yet any character who truly loves anyone is notably absent from the poem.[13]

To define a thing, to throw it into relief by defining what it is not as well as what it is, could be called ambiguity, but the end result is precision. If it must be acknowledged that at times the reader is uncertain which Venus is being discussed, it does not necessarily follow that all are the same. Rather, we should conclude that we should be careful in our judgments. As Pandarus, self-servingly echoing a common medieval pedagogical belief stated, "By his contrarie is every thyng declared" (I, 637). Pandarus makes rather a jumble of his own contraries, but the point is that they are commonly used for definition in the Middle Ages. Thus when the Dreamer in *Piers Plowman* cannot understand the explanation of Truth, he is prepared for it by being taught about the false. Similarly, in Dante's *Commedia*, Vergil's central speech on love defines it as the seed of every deed deserving punishment and of every deed deserving reward. Vergil uses the same word for the two impulses, but the purpose of the speech is to fix in the pilgrim Dante's mind—and by extension in the reader's—the urgency of making wise choices. If Chaucer sometimes refers to Venus in a context in which it is difficult or impossible to determine which Venus he means, we should go beyond the ambiguity, or what I would prefer to call the polysemous lines, borrowing a phrase from Dante. Chaucer's goal in writing difficult poetry is to cause speculation beyond the mere identification of his signs and symbols. The pilgrim Dante in hell is moved to pity by the story of Francesca's love and its punishment, but Vergil warns him not to question divine judgment. It is easy to misunderstand love, to confuse serving one Venus with serving another. Thus the poet's task is not only to be monitory but to teach by wrong as well as by right example, and to challenge our responses as his audience. Dante tempts us to react as the pilgrim Dante reacts; Chaucer challenges us to discriminate among the Venuses. In both instances it is not just the identification of the subject but the audience's subsequent judgment about it that is crucial.

Perhaps the best way to approach Chaucer's complex Prohemium on Venus is to look first at its source, for Boccaccio is much more transparent.

The lines that Chaucer adapted for the Prohemium to Book III constitute, in Boccaccio's version, part of a song by Troilo, in the presence of Pandaro, in praise of love. Since Troilo has, at this juncture in Boccaccio's poem, already seduced Criseida, it is clear enough that the Venus he intends to praise is the Venus of concupiscence. That he praises her in terms that are more properly referred to one or more of the other Venuses known to the Middle Ages— such as the goddess of friendship and the goddess who binds kingdoms together—should be understood as an error on Troilo's part and not as an ambiguity inherent in the figure of Venus. Boccaccio signals his intentions fairly clearly, for in two places in the long song Troilo gives the game away: first, he defends his love by comparing himself with Hercules; yet as we noted in chapter 1, Hercules' subordination by Iole was treated by Boccaccio elsewhere as a very undesirable phenomenon. Secondly, Troilo's amusing inability *topos*, the idea that he could not adequately praise his lady even if he had a hundred tongues in his mouth, is a parodic recollection of St. Paul's inability to praise charity even if he had the tongues of men and angels—a reading also examined in chapter 1. Thus, while the only Venus Troilo has had any interest in is the Venus of concupiscence, he is so infatuated after his seduction that he thinks Venus is all in all, and, listing the effects of several Venuses, he unhesitatingly counts his carnal relationship with Criseida among "thy grand effects" ("intra' grandi effeti / Tuoi" [III, 81]). But, for the Middle Ages, it was by the effects that the Venuses were distinguished, and the grand effects of creation, inspiration to worthiness, and universal harmony cannot be imputed to the Venus whose son Troilo now serves. By juxtaposing the goddess who "imposes laws on the universe, whereby it is held together" with the goddess of whom it may be said "nor is anyone opposed to thy son but [he] repenteth of it" (III, 79), Boccaccio makes Troilo's confusion easy enough to see. In the Boethian passage Boccaccio is toying with,

(Bk. II, m. 8), the love that held the universe together was identified with the love that held together people who were joined with a holy bond of marriage, and of course the goddess whose son is Cupid has nothing to do with that. It has long been recognized that Boethius' *Consolation* supplied Boccaccio with many of the images in Troilo's long speech, but the details have needed closer examination.

Because Chaucer does not use this kind of juxtaposition, because he does not use anything quite so obvious as the claim on Hercules to defend the lover or the inability of the lover with a hundred tongues in his mouth to praise his lady, it is true that Chaucer's adaptation of Boccaccio's passage is harder to interpret. However, his removal of it from Troilo and his positioning of it as the Prohemium to Book III do not make an ambiguous passage more ambiguous as Gordon asserts. One can argue that Troilo's confusion of several Venuses is a poetic device by which his confusion is meant to lead to our clarity, and Chaucer's Prohemium works much the same way. Boccaccio's goal was to invite discrimination among the several Venuses by showing Troilo's inability to distinguish among them. Chaucer's goal is to invite discrimination among the several Venuses by invoking them in a neutral tone until the close of the Prohemium, at which juncture he addresses the carnal Venus in the voice of the "clerc" of her servants, and amusingly invokes Calliope, the muse of epic, to help him describe the less-than-epic joys of Troilus' carnal bliss. It is true that as we read the Prohemium, we are not always sure which Venus Chaucer is talking about. However, that does not mean that the several Venuses were causally linked, so that sexual love would lead to ennoblement, nor does it mean that the whole passage could be read as an address to either the good or the bad Venus, depending upon our interpretation. Rather, Chaucer creates suspense by keeping his meaning back for a time, and teases the reader with his apparent unwillingness to make clear his subject or his direction. It is a technique that may best be understood by analogy with art. If we see a medieval psalter with a picture of David playing the harp in the first initial and a contrary figure playing the bagpipe in the margin, there is neither ambiguity about music nor a union of contraries in the concept of the Old Song of the flesh and the New Song of the spirit. Rather, by showing two manifestations of the idea of the song, the artist reminds the viewer of the differences and implicitly endorses a wise choice of which song to sing or play.

A look at the text is now in order. When we remember that the narrator was careful to distance himself from the God of Love, to describe his relationship as that of one who prays for the servants of the God of Love, and to style himself as one who writes of lovers' woe while living himself in charity, we are prepared to think that the poem will concentrate on the mother of the God of Love, the Venus of carnal delight. Moreover, it is this "blisful Venus" who is invoked and prayed to by Troilus and Pandarus as we have noted. However, in the Prohemium to Book III Chaucer suddenly introduces some other Venuses for our consideration, and while all are addressed as "you," as though speaking to one Venus, the different effects of the Venuses require that more than one be involved. Clearly what we should do is consider their relationship to the events of the poem, just as was done by Boccaccio in his *Chiose* when he noted that one Venus was relevant to the poem, and one was not. The first stanza of the Prohemium is quite neutral in tone and invokes the planet Venus somewhat equivocally as "blisful *light*." She can, of course, be the sign of the carnal Venus as she is in the *Complaint of Mars*, or of the Venus of love leading to virtue, as in Dante's *Purgatorio*.

> O blisful light, of which the bemes clere
> Adorneth al the thridde heven faire!
> O sonnes lief, O Joves doughter deere,
> Plesance of love, O goodly debonaire,
> In gentil hertes ay redy to repaire!
> O veray cause of heele and of gladnesse,
> Iheryed be thy myght and thi goodnesse!　　[III, 1–7]

Since the planet Venus has already been used in this poem to describe the Venus who is not a foe to Troilus at his nativity, and who was in good aspect at the time of his first sighting by Criseyde (II, 680–86), one could make a good case that the first stanza of the Prohemium refers to the planetary Venus of carnality—but one could not be *sure*. It is this suspension of judgment, I think, that Chaucer strives for. We may not know which Venus Chaucer is addressing, but we know what the effects of each Venus are. If it is the carnal Venus that is invoked here, the reference to her as "veray cause of heele and of gladnesse" is massively ironic, since the poem is primarily about the double sorrow of Troilus. If, on the other hand, the lines refer to a Venus who is capable of bringing happiness of more than a transitory kind, then her absence from the poem is conspicuous. This, more than the identification of which Venus we are speaking of, is the key to understanding the Prohemium. In every instance any possible Venus other than the carnal one will be found to be significantly absent. If the lines about Venus as bringer of gladness are designed not merely to get us to identify a Venus but to get us thinking about the relationship obtaining between possible Venuses and possible happiness, we have much to ponder. Certainly if the carnal Venus could bring about lasting happiness, she is not responsible for much of it in this poem. The reader has been advised that this is a poem about a "double sorwe," and that Troilus' feelings change "Fro wo to wele, and after out of joie" (I, 4), which vicissitude emphasizes the transitory nature of Venereal weal. In fact, although the point is regularly overlooked by critics of Chaucer, the followers of the carnal Venus are commonly portrayed as sufferers or causers of suffering in the works written prior to the *Troilus*. The hero of the *Complaint of Mars* is left abandoned and in a bad astrological position after his encounter with Venus.

The Temple of Venus in the *Hous of Fame* turns out to be surrounded by a sterile desert, while within we find portrayed the sorrow of Dido in her dealings with Venus' "sone," Aeneas (*HF*, 165).[14] Finally, in the word picture of the Temple of Venus in the *Knight's Tale*, which was probably written at about the same time as the *Troilus*, we find shown on the walls the stories of Venus' servants who "for wo ful ofte seyde 'allas!'" (*KnT*, 1952).[15]

The second stanza of the Prohemium is clearly about the generative effects of one of the good Venuses, for it depends for its wording upon Boethius' idea of ". . . love that governeth erthe and see, and hath also comandement to the hevene" (Bk. II, m. 8):

> In hevene and helle, in erthe and salte see
> Is felt thi myght, if that I wel descerne;
> As man, brid, best, fissh, herbe, and grene tree
> Thee fele in tymes with vapour eterne.
> God loveth, and to love wol nought werne;
> And in this world no lyves creature
> Withouten love is worth, or may endure.[16]   [III, 8–14]

Since, as we noted, Boethius went on to define this particular love as pertaining to marriage, and since neither marriage nor procreation is an issue in the *Troilus*, the stanza conjures up a Venus who has nothing whatsoever to do with the poem.[17]

The subsequent stanza finds Venus as the inspiration for Jove's earthly adventures:

> Ye Joves first to thilk effectes glade,
> Thorugh which that thynges lyven alle and be,
> Comeveden, and amorous him made
> On mortal thyng, and as yow list, ay ye
> Yeve hym in love ese or adversitee;
> And in a thousand formes down hym sente
> For love in erthe, and whom yow liste, he hente.
>   [III, 15–21]

If this stanza opens with the theme of generation, it nevertheless closes with something more like hijinks. If we assume, as has usually been done, that Jove's descents "in a thousand formes" refer to his manifestations as a shower of gold, as a bull, and so forth, then we are dealing with a figure usually treated pejoratively in the Middle Ages. As Hoffman has ably demonstrated, Jove angers Juno *pronuba*, goddess of marriage and fertility, by his earthly amatory exploits, and as a consequence she sends havoc to earth.[18] It is this proclivity that prompts Chaucer to style Jove as "the likerous" in his poem "The Former Age." As Gordon points out, it is possible to think of Jove as Providence in this stanza, but although possible it seems unlikely. When Jove represents Providence, we do not find the Venus of sexual delight awarding him "ese or adversitee" as it pleases her. On the other hand, the themes of lechery and infidelity certainly have a great deal to do with the *Troilus*, and Chaucer may have created this stanza about Jove impelled by Venus in order to convey something of that goddess' power to create mischief—something amply reflected both by the double sorrow of Troilus and by the ultimate destruction of Troy itself as the final consequence of Paris' choice of Venus.[19]

The fourth stanza begins by noting that Venus can "fierse Mars apaisen of his ire" (III, 22). This essentially astrological idea can be found elsewhere in Chaucer. In Hypermnestra's horoscope in the *Legend of Good Women* the planet Venus "Repressed hath" Mars' "crewel craft" (*LGW*, 2591), and similarly in the astrological maneuverings of the *Complaint of Mars* Venus is said to "brydeleth" Mars and to "take him in subjeccioun" (*Mars*, 41, 33). As with generation, though, this aspect of Venus is not to be found in the poem. Troilus is, if anything, more martial after he falls in love with Criseyde than he was before. Prior to seeing her in the temple, Troilus is shown to us only as a young knight admiring ladies, whereas afterwards he does "swich travaille / In armes, that to thynke it was merveille" (I, 475–76) in order to impress Criseyde. In Book II he is compared directly with Mars, "that god is of bataille" (II, 630), and after the seduction in Book III he is, save Hector, "most ydred of any wight" (III, 1775). Mars is invoked in the Prohemium to Book IV, for Wrath will dominate the remainder of the poem. Troilus continues to show the influence of Mars, whether raging like a bull in his own chambers (IV, 239) when he learns of Criseyde's imminent departure, or in the field when his hate for Diomede prompts him to display "his grete myght" (V, 1754). Thus, although Venus *can* mollify Mars, she is not seen to do so in this poem. Rather, the Venus active in the *Troilus* seems modelled on the one of so much concern to John Gower in the *Vox Clamantis*, and she is inimical to true chivalry, as noted in chapter 2.

The following lines concern Venus' ability to "maken hertes digne" (III, 23) and to make those whom she sets "a-fyre" resign vices. Since the fiery Venus is most likely the concupiscent Venus, it would follow that this passage is mildly ironic. People who are concupiscent do not resign vice so much as specialize in concupiscence. Moreover, as Boethius notes in Bk. III, pr. 9, those who concentrate on one earthly pleasure invariably lose both the one they seek and the others as well.

The next stanza features the Venus who is said to "holden regne and hous in unitee; / Ye sothfast cause of frendshipe ben also" (III, 29–30). In spite of the repeated protestations of friendship between Troilus and Pandarus— twice accompanied by offerings of one's sister for the delectation of the other—it has been amply demonstrated in recent years that what the principals of the poem call friendship is almost the precise opposite of what friendship was thought to be in the Middle Ages.[20] One must also remark that while

Troilus and Pandarus invert the ideas of friendship, all the principals are very hypocritical about the use of friendship as a mask for the seduction. From Pandarus' hollow reassurance to Criseyde that should a neighbor see the young prince coming and going from the beautiful widow's house he "Wol deme it love of frendshipe in his mynde" (II, 371), to his later assurance to Troilus that as a first step towards Criseyde's seduction he has won her love of friendship for Troilus (II, 962), to the final, bitter echo of the theme with Diomede, who also wants to be Criseyde's "frend" (V, 128), Chaucer iron- ically uses friendship as a euphemism for seduction. The fact of the matter is that there is a great deal of talking about friendship in the *Troilus*, but not one genuine portrayal of it. To invoke Venus, the goddess of friendship, in the Prohemium to Book III is to throw into relief the absence of friendship from the poem proper.

Of all the guises in which Venus is addressed in this passage, none is more glaringly inappropriate than the Venus who is said to "holden regne and hous in unitee" (III, 29). Were it not for Venus' inspiration of Paris, Troy would not be in the parlous condition discovered in the poem, and of course Troilus' name itself implies that he is a "little Troy." [21] The love between the ruler and the ruled that insures harmony in a kingdom is not to be found in Troy. When Hector declines to exchange Criseyde for Antenor, the "noyse of peple up stirte thanne at ones, / As breme as blase of straw iset on-fire" (IV, 183–84). The fiery people foolishly vote against their ruler in an anachronis- tic parliament, and bring about their own destruction in effecting the ex- change for the treacherous Antenor, "that brought hem to meschaunce" (IV, 203). [22] Thus the inspiration of Paris by the concupiscent Venus brought about the abduction of Helen and ultimately the destruction of Troy, which was incidentally aided and abetted by the absence of the Venus who is sup- posed to hold reigns in unity. In a sort of chiastic analogue, the concupiscent Venus inspires Troilus to love Criseyde, and when the lack of harmony in the kingdom causes her to be exchanged for Antenor, Troilus' betrayal, his de- spair, and ultimate destruction are similarly insured. Thus the presence of one Venus and the absence of another combine to destroy both Troy and Troilus. Looked at that way it is a bitter but not altogether surprising fact that Achilles slays both Hector and Troilus.

Filial love, that which is supposed to hold "hous in unitee," is also conspic- uous by its absence in the poem. [23] The most blatant illustration of this is Pan- darus' cynical exploitation of his niece Criseyde. When Pandarus urges Criseyde, who has lost her natural protectors—her husband and father—to death and desertion respectively, to take a lover before old age catches up with her, he stands as her only male relative and would be expected to advise her accordingly. As the text clearly shows, Criseyde thinks he should counsel her not to love, and wonders what a stranger would advise her when her pre- sumed "frend" and relative counsels her in a way opposite to that of husband or father:

"Allas, for wo! Why nere I deed?
For of this world the feyth is al agoon.
Allas! what sholden straunge to me doon,
When he, that for my beste frend I wende,
Ret me to love, and sholde it me defende?" [24]

[II, 409–413]

Of course, a lack of filial affection was the cause of at least part of Criseyde's troubles, for when her father, Calchas, deserted Troy he did not bother to take his widowed daughter with him. One might also note that Troilus does not object when Pandarus arranges a meeting with Criseyde at Deiphebus' house under false pretences, although Troilus claims to love Deiphebus best of all his brothers. Later, when Troilus complains to Fortune that she took Criseyde from him, he rather unlovingly asks why Fortune did not slay his father or his brothers (or himself) rather than remove Criseyde (IV, 274–78). As a final instance of the lack of filial affection in the poem, there is the episode of Cassandra. When she correctly interprets Troilus' dream of Criseyde and the boar, she is sisterly and sympathetic enough. She smiles and calls him "'brother deere'" (V, 1457) at the outset of her exposition, and brings it to a close by telling him that he can laugh or cry, but his place has been usurped by Diomede: "'Wep if thow wolt, or lef! For, out of doute, / This Diomede is inne, and thow art oute'" (V, 1518–19). Troilus, not displaying any noticeable brotherly affection, lashes out at the messenger (not the instrument) of his unhappiness by calling her a liar ("'Thow seyst nat soth'") and a sorceress. He commands her to go away and says Jove will give her sorrow (V, 1520–25).

Perhaps the only positive display of brotherly affection in the poem occurs not many lines later, when Hector has been killed. Having spent most of his filial emotional force addressing Pandarus as "friend" and "brother" throughout the poem, now at the end Troilus grieves for Hector, his slain blood brother. However, rather than assuming military leadership as his prowess in arms (second only to that of Hector) and duties to his father and brothers as prince of the realm might suggest, his concurrent love for the faithless Criseyde paralyzes him:

And namely, the sorwe of Troilus,
That next hym [Hector] was of worthynesse welle.
And in this wo gan Troilus to dwelle,
That, what for sorwe, and love, and for unreste,
Ful ofte a day he bad his herte breste.   [V, 1564–68]

Following the apostrophe to Venus the keeper of friendship, filial love, and patriotism, there is a curious reference to a Venus who knows "al thilke covered qualitee / Of thynges" (III, 31–32). The particular *invisiblia* known to this Venus, though, have to do with why people fall in love with one person rather than another; why "this fissh, and naught that, comth to were" (III, 35). Since fishing imagery is used elsewhere in the *Troilus* to indicate sexual attraction and even seduction, we must assume that we are here dealing with an aspect of the concupiscent Venus, whose doings pervade the poem.[25]

Before concluding his Prohemium with a sort of prayer, the narrator has one last aspect of Venus to mention. She has, he says, set a law in the universe, and he knows from those who are lovers that "whoso stryveth with yow hath the werse" (III, 38). The point to be made here is exactly the same as observed in chapter 2 with reference to the God of Love's powers listed earlier in the *Troilus*: insofar as universal laws of nature, or procreation or sexuality are concerned we are dealing with forces that are neither good nor bad in themselves, but which can be followed for better or for worse by humankind. However, when we speak of "lovers" who strive with Venus, we are presumably speaking of those who try to resist Venereal or concupiscent promptings by force of will and who, like Troilus in the temple and Criseyde at her home, are unsuccessful. As Reason points out in the *Romance of the Rose*, the only way to conquer this kind of love is to flee it. Neither Troilus nor Criseyde flees temptation, and both lose the struggle with Venus; Troilus in an instant and Criseyde after some inner debating and exterior urging.

The remainder of the stanza has the narrator remind us again that his role is that of a servant of the servants of the God of Love—a duty he undertakes in Book I by writing of the woe of the servants while living in charity himself. Although the lines have often been taken to indicate that Chaucer styles himself as a clerk of Venus, the meaning in fact is that he is the clerk, for which understand learned advisor, of those who themselves serve Venus:

> Now, lady bryght, for thi benignite,
> At reverence of hem that serven the,
> Whos clerc I am, so techeth me devyse
> Som joye of that is felt in thi servyse.[26]   [III, 39–42]

At the opening of Book I Chaucer proposed to write of woe; now he will write of the joy of the servants of the carnal Venus. There is "som joye" in the service of Venus, of course, but the early warning about woe and the invocation of so many beneficent Venuses combine to make us cautious about the quality and quantity of the joy that is to be described.

In the opening of Book I the narrator used a modesty *topos* for humorous effect—painting a picture of himself as one who was so far from any real knowledge of the God of Love that he did not dare to ask for the help he needed to describe the service of the god. In the Prohemium to Book III a somewhat similar inability *topos* is offered when the poet asks Venus to teach him how to describe the joy of her service, and then invokes Calliope, the muse of epic poetry, to assist him. This invocation is part and parcel of the general series of inappropriate apostrophes that make up the Prohemium.

Chaucer repeatedly invites the reader to compare and contrast the Venuses invoked with the actions of the poem, while with Calliope, as I have suggested elsewhere, the effect is one of contrast. The substance of the action of Book III is to show a nervous, fainting, young prince bodily thrown into bed with a compliant widow while her uncle reads at the fireside. Whatever this is, it is not epic.[27] Surely Chaucer meant this to be something of a running joke in the poem, for in Book II he twice refers to the widow's seduction as a "grete emprise" (73, 1391), while in Book III this undistinguished event is called a "grete emprise" (416) as well as a "grete effect" (505). The joke here is something like that in the *Merchant's Tale*. There the teller says that Martianus Capella, who wrote a treatise on the seven liberal arts in the form of an allegorical marriage of Mercury and Philology, is not a great enough poet to describe the marriage of January and May, "Whan tendre youthe hath wedded stoupyng age" (*MerchT*, 1738). Of course, Martianus is too great rather than insufficiently great to describe this bathetic "myrthe" (*MerchT*, 1739). When Chaucer invokes Calliope, elsewhere described as "the myghty Muse" who sings songs of "hevenysshe melodye . . . ful of armonye" (*HF*, 1395–1400), to help him praise the evanescent and comic seduction scene that occurs in the *Troilus*, the incongruity creates humor.

Chaucer closes the Prohemium with his declaration of his need for Calliope in order to express the "gladnesse" of Troilus which constitutes a praise of Venus.

> Caliope, thi vois be now present,
> For now is nede; sestow nought my destresse,
> How I mot telle anonright the gladnesse
> Of Troilus, to Venus heryinge?   [III, 45–48]

Thus the poet speaks of the "joye," the "swetnesse" (III, 42–44), and the "gladnesse" that may be found under Venus' auspices, but any potential for ambiguity, any confusion as to which Venus it is that the Prohemium is finally concerned with, is obviated when Chaucer declares that he must somewhat loudly sweep the string when he describes the "gladnesse" of Troilus, who serves the carnal Venus.

There is less "ambiguity" in this Prohemium than one might imagine, but there are, to be sure, some lines that could refer to the Venus of carnality or to one of the other Venuses. However, the pattern of the whole is not ambiguous either in the sense of being obscure or in the sense of having a plurality of meanings. Through skillful positioning and structuring of the Prohemium, (Chaucer departs from Boccaccio's version for his final direction of the whole towards Troilus' tutelary Venus), Chaucer manages to throw the several aspects of Venus into stark relief. We pay homage to Venus genetrix, ultimately the source of life in the universe, to love of friend, family, and country, but ironically the muse of epic poetry is invoked only for the Venus who gets

Troilus into bed with Criseyde. The rest, or the other Venuses, are, by implication, not worthy of epic; they are only so much small beer. As we have seen, many of the aspects of Venus praised here have no counterpart in the poem. They serve as reminders of what is absent rather than as guides to what we may find. Chaucer forces us to remember what Venus can represent in order better to understand what she does represent in this poem and more particularly in this book of the poem. By beginning the Prohemium with the praise of Venus as "veray cause of heele and of gladnesse," Chaucer prepares us for the later specification of Troilus' "gladnesse," which is evanescent and fugitive. The very last line of the Prohemium particularizes Troilus' gladness in contrast to the other possible gladnesses presented, as Chaucer very ironically says, "To *which* gladnesse, who nede hath, God hym brynge!" (III, 49).

The Ascent to Heaven

When the different elements of the Prohemium to Book III have been weighed and evaluated, the other addresses and apostrophes to Venus in the same book may be more readily understood. As we might expect from our examination of Troilus' earlier prayers to Venus to bring about the seduction of Criseyde, his two major addresses in this book, to Venus and to Love, are in a sense hymns of thanksgiving. However, while the narrator was able to address Venus in her several aspects simultaneously because of his and the Prohemium's detachment from the action, Troilus' praises are necessarily to the Venus of concupiscence. They are delivered, nevertheless, in language more suitable to something else. The net result is therefore a comedy rather than an epic. Or perhaps it would be even closer to the mark to see the addresses as having elements of mock epic.[28] When Troilus praises Venus in Boethian and even quasi-liturgical language, while having nothing more exalted than the Venus of fleshly delight on his mind, it seems quite clumsy to suppose that Chaucer is trying to tell us that the concupiscent Venus is the same as or closely analogous to the others. Yet this critical reversal of what I take to be Troilus' confusion into what is claimed as Chaucer's wisdom may commonly be encountered.[29] When Chaucer transferred a modified version of Troilo's hymn to Venus in Boccaccio to a Prohemium, surely his intention was to show all the possibilities, categories, and powers of Venus in a fairly detached way, both structurally and narratively, so that the actions of the book might be referred back to the schema that introduced it. What the narrator does in the Prohemium is to show that Venus can be this and this and this, but there is no suggestion that the force of creation and generation is indistinguishable from the love of friends or the friendship of lovers. If the function of the Prohemium is to show the panoply of Venus' aspects, the function of Troilus' apostrophes is just the opposite: to conflate the Many into the One, and the one that he knows about is the sexual Venus. The whole may indeed be the same as the sum of the parts, but surely it is never—either mathematically or literally—equal to one of its parts.

The medieval fondness for distinction lends itself well to comedy, but the humor is sometimes hard for us to see because we no longer maintain the same distinctions. Because of the usual allegorizations of Canticles in terms of a spiritual union, it is easy enough to see that when the language of Canticles is addressed to Alisoun in the *Miller's Tale* and May in the *Merchant's Tale* its unsuitability is meant to be funny. It is less easy to see that when Chaucer puts St. Bernard's hymn to the Virgin into Troilus' mouth, when the last thing on Troilus' mind is virginity, a very similar comic effect is sought. However, the difficulty arises from a difference in modern reaction, for there is no difference in Chaucer's technique. We are much more apt to see the humor in earthy tales involving cuckoldry than we are in a tragedy of love, because the professed sincerity of the principals in the *Troilus* corresponds with contemporary ideas of highmindedness rather than with a potential for comedy. Similarly, when Reason expounds the several kinds of love to the sexually inflamed lover in the *Romance of the Rose*, we should laugh at the lover's inability to discriminate between the loves described by Reason and at his assumption that if he cannot lust he must needs hate:

> "Dame, and is it youre wille algate
> That I not love, but that I hate
> Alle men, as ye me teche?"   [*RR*, 5157–59]

Troilus, too, has difficulty in making distinctions, but since he is not involved in a running dialogue with a character like Reason, it is much harder for us to judge the tone. As is typical of Chaucer's best art, there is a greater burden of interpretation on the audience than there is with some other medieval poets. This burden is heavier still on our shoulders, since our ideas about extramarital sexuality do not depend solely upon the teachings of St. Paul, or, for that matter, Lady Reason, who advised the lover that "Fleshly delit" had made him so "mat and wood," that he desired "noon other good" (*RR*, 5095–5100). Even allowing for cultural differences, though, Troilus' precoital prayer of thanks for "grace," expressed in the language used by St. Bernard to the Virgin, seems to reflect more on the indelicacy of Troilus than on the philosophical intentions of Chaucer.

Indeed, some of the most humorous passages in Book III are Troilus' repeated calls upon Venus (and every other deity) for help in what turns out to be a fairly simple conquest. The function of timorousness and delay is in part to permit a contrast between the procrastinating Troilus and "sodeyn" Diomede (V, 1024), but even by itself Troilus' hesitation makes the seduction very funny. Chaucer was later to exploit the humorous laboriousness of some love affairs by contrasting the years and years that pass in the *Knight's Tale* with the immediacy of desire and event in the *Miller's Tale*, and even some staunch defenders of the nobility of love have found Troilus' hesitancy in Book III rather amusing.[30] Chaucer sets the whole thing up by playfully defining Troilus' sexual accommodation with Criseyde as an entrance into Heaven. This, of course, like any entry into Heaven, must be accompanied by prayer.

Pandarus, whose role as mock "priest" in the love affair has been commented upon,[31] starts the final ascent, so to speak, by summoning Troilus from the "stuwe" (an unlikely starting place for this sort of journey) where he has been hidden. Pandarus bids him to prepare for what is to be his earthly apotheosis:

> "Make the redy right anon,
> For thow shalt into hevene blisse wende."
>
> [III, 703–4]

Lest we think Chaucer is serious, just a few lines earlier the text asserts that Pandarus, like the Wife of Bath, "wel koude ech a deel / The olde daunce" (III, 694–95)—a dance not designed for getting to Heaven.

Troilus, who wants to enter Heaven, immediately prays to the patron saint of that particular region for the necessary grace. "'Now, seint Venus, thow me grace sende!'" (705). He is right, of course, St. Venus is just the goddess to pray to under the circumstances, but Troilus lacks confidence that he really is going to enter Heaven's bliss, so prays again to Venus, to her father, to Jove, to Mars, Phoebus, Mercury, Diana, and the three Fates! While it seems doubtful that the chaste Diana will be of much help, the main function of this outburst is to associate prayer to the pagan gods with entrance into an earthly heaven, while simultaneously portraying the prince, fearless in battle, as fearful in love. This timorousness exasperates Pandarus, who accuses him of being a "wrecched mouses herte" (736) and leads him into Criseyde's bedroom by means of a "secre trappe-dore" (759). A trap door might not seem the normal mode of entrance into Heaven, but in light of the idea of the entry through a door as a euphemism for the sexual act, the door is in fact more appropriate to this Heaven than would be a set of pearly gates.[32]

In keeping with the quasi-religious imagery that accompanies prayers for the entrance into Heaven, there is a good deal of kneeling in the following scenes. Troilus kneels by Criseyde's bed (III, 953), an attitude remarkable both for the prince's humility and for the bed as "altar" to which he kneels. Lest anyone overlook the significance of the action Pandarus points it out— "'se how this lord kan knele!'" (962)—and runs to get a cushion for Troilus' knees. The cushion will of course serve as a kind of priedieu in the circumstances. Troilus kneels again somewhat later in the action (1080), and it is at

this juncture that he faints and must be heaved bodily into bed with the heroine. As the penultimate step in the ascent to Heaven it is not an altogether
holy or epic action, but it serves.[33]

Once in bed with Criseyde Troilus is within reach of the Heaven he has
sought so long. Continuing the religious imagery of the occasion Chaucer
portrays him as putting the matter "in Goddes hand" (1185), and then taking
matters into his own hands as he grasps Criseyde. As soon as he has her he
begins to thank "the blisful goddes sevene" (1203),[34] and Chaucer remarks of
this rather untidy series of events by which Troilus has been brought to
the Heaven of Criseyde's person, "Thus sondry peynes bryngen folk to
hevene" (1204).

Once arrived in Heaven, Troilus loses little time in exploring the topogra-
phy of the place:

> Hire armes smale, hire streghte bak and softe,
> Hire sydes longe, flesshly, smothe, and white
> He gan to stroke, and good thrift bad ful ofte
> Hire snowisshe throte, hire brestes rounde and lite:
> Thus in this *hevene* he gan hym to delite.   [1247–51]

Prayer, of course, is not out of place in Heaven, and now Troilus renders up a
prayer of thanksgiving. To be sure, there are aspects of this Heaven still to be
enjoyed—the lovers have not consummated the affair—but Troilus inter-
rupts his fondling of Criseyde to thank Venus and others for the "grace" that
he has received. As the narrator remarks, immediately before this astonishing
intrusion, which perhaps is but one more manifestation of Troilus' proclivity
for procrastination, "what to don, for joie unnethe he wiste" (1253).

The prayer itself is a gallimaufry. In one breath Troilus thanks Love,
Charity, the Cytherean Venus, and Hymen, god of marriage, for bringing
him in from the cold:

> Than seyde he thus, "O Love, O Charite!
> Thi moder ek, Citherea the swete,
> After thiself next heried be she,
> Venus mene I, the wel-willy planete!
> And next that, Imeneus, I the grete;
> For nevere man was to yow goddes holde
> As I, which ye han brought fro cares colde.   [1254–60]

The joke is much the same here as in Boccaccio. In the *Filostrato* Troilo uttered an extended praise of Venus after the seduction in which his confusion
about which Venus pertained to his own situation was manifest. This passage
was discussed earlier in this chapter, and we remember that it is the speech
that Chaucer removed, with changes, and transformed into the Prohemium

of Book III. At this juncture, albeit the affair has not yet been consummated, Chaucer makes up a brand-new jumble for his own figure of Troilus. Inaccurate definition is one of Chaucer's characteristic devices for humor, and as he had Pandarus define immortal God as Cupid earlier in the same book, now he has Troilus define the love which is charity as the child of the Cytherean Venus!

Because Chaucer styles the Cytherean Venus in the *Parlement of Foules* as the Venus characterized by a "fyrbrond" (113–14), then she could be appropriately thanked for the amusing deliverance from "cold" to heat.[35] This Venus, however, is not properly related to Hymen and marriage.[36] Even if she were, we remember that Troilus has never concerned himself with marriage, and Criseyde consciously rejected it. Those critics who, following the lead of C. S. Lewis, find a kind of unofficial marriage in Book III because of the noble, legal, or sacramental language Chaucer uses are victims of severe cases of wishful thinking.[37] The whole purpose of marriage, from St. Paul onwards, was to avoid Venus' firebrand, not exploit it. Delighting in fleshly "heavens," however sincere one may be about one's delight, did not constitute marriage in the Middle Ages, and indeed even in marriage one had to beware of the "perilous fyr, that in the bedstraw bredeth" (*MerchT*, 1783). Sin can result even when Venus throws her firebrand into a marriage bed; as Chaucer's Parson puts it, a man can slay himself with his own knife. The only remedy is "chastitee and continence," and this does not apply to what transpires between Troilus and Criseyde, even if we pretend that they are married. Venus is not necessarily at odds with Hymen, but the Cytherean Venus invoked after the "thousand" kisses has everything to do with the situation of the lovers, while Hymen does not impinge upon their past, present, or future.

Troilus has all along had *hope* that he would enter the Heaven he so yearned for, his prayers to the seven gods have indicated a kind of *faith*, and to these virtues we are asked to add the third and greatest, *charity*. Whether or not Troilus has much to *do* with charity there in the widow's bed, he undeniably *talks* about charity, and in an astounding genealogy he styles the Cytherean Venus as mother of Charity. To be sure, true charity comes from love, but Chaucer has put this genealogy in Troilus' mouth to show that Troilus has in mind a different kind of love. Were we to define charity as beginning at home, Troilus' suggested maternity might make more sense. Throughout the poem Troilus has invoked a Venus who will enable him to seduce Criseyde. Now that he is in her bed, he thanks Charity, Venus' daughter, for getting him there. Obviously, if he has any idea at all about charity, he assumes that it has to do with getting rather than giving, or else he is calling Criseyde's compliance charity. After all, Troilus was able to call Pandarus' dubious activities "'gentilesse, / Compassioun, and felawship, and trist'" (III, 402–3), so that a penchant for assigning wrong names is part of the character Chaucer is building up.[38] Finally, though, we must bear in mind that Troilus' fulsome praise of charity as somehow responsible for the success of the love affair runs exactly counter to the narrator's ideas about charity. When Chaucer began the poem he was careful to set himself apart from the principals and their activities, and to do so in terms of charity:

> For so hope I my sowle best avaunce,
> To prey for hem that Loves servauntz be,
> And write hire wo, and lyve in charite.   [I, 47–50]

If the narrator, who does not love because of his "unlikeliness," describes his own life as one of charity, it is surely ironic that Troilus, the likeliest of lovers in his position in Book III, thanks Charity for his success.

It has been known for a long time that the next stanza of Troilus' thanksgiving is modeled upon Dante's *Paradiso* 33:13–18.[39] However, that Dante's words are addressed by St. Bernard to the Blessed Virgin while Troilus' are addressed to "'Benigne Love, thow holy bond of thynges,'" (III, 1261) has been noted without sufficient comment. To begin with, there is the yawning chasm between Troilus, whose concern throughout the poem has been for sexual gratification, and St. Bernard, the great contemplative, whose mystical vision of Mary qualified him to be the pilgrim's final guide to God. St. Bernard prayed that Dante be vouchsafed the vision of God; Troilus thanks Love for carnal love. St. Bernard addressed his prayer to the woman who so ennobled human nature that God was born a human, whereas Troilus, often said to have been ennobled, here addresses his prayer first to the imagined figure of Cupid-Charity, son of the Cytherean Venus, then to Boethian Love as Holy Bond of Things. This latter image of love cannot accurately be thanked for bringing about the union of the two lovers. As Ida Gordon has succinctly put it, "an illicit relationship cannot, by its very nature, belong to the divine order of harmony."[40] Or, to cite Boethius directly, "This love halt togidres peples joyned with an holy boond, and knytteth sacrement of mariages of chaste loves" (Bk. II, m. 8). What are missing from the relationship obtaining in Criseyde's bed are the holy bond, the sacrament of marriage, and the chaste love. But the irony does not stop with the inappropriateness of the Boethian holy bond to what is going on between Troilus and Criseyde. The substitution of a holy bond for the Virgin is less jarring than, say, the substitution of Venus, but makes the same impossible demands on the logic of the prayer. The prayer in both versions asks for grace and succor—essentially active qualities—that the Virgin, in her role as intercessor and in her role as helper, can provide, but which cannot be performed by what amounts to a universal law. When the stanza is seen this way, the drift of the whole would clearly have been better directed to the Virgin, although in the last analysis neither the holy bond nor the blessed Virgin is likely to have helped Troilus into the "hevene" of throat, breasts, and sides.

"Benigne Love, thow holy bond of thynges,
Whoso wol grace, and list the nought honouren,
Lo, his desir wol fle withouten wynges.
For noldestow of bownte hem socouren
That serven best and most alwey labouren,
Yet were al lost, that dar I wel seyn certes,
But if thi grace passed oure desertes."   [III, 1261–67]

Troilus, of course, has not served either the Virgin or the Holy Bond of Things, but the greatest irony comes in the next stanza, when he thanks the holy bond for having bestowed him in so high a place.[41]

"And for thow me, that leest koude disserve
Of hem that noumbred ben unto thi grace,
Hast holpen, ther I likly was to sterve,
And me bistowed in so heigh a place
That thilke boundes may no blisse pace,
I kan namore; but laude and reverence
Be to thy bounte and thyn excellence!"   [1268–74]

And, with this plangent hymn of thanksgiving to Benign Love ringing in our ears, the next line is, "And therwithal Criseyde anon he kiste."

Venus, the Holy Bond of Thynges, and Fortune

There are two more apostrophes in Book III with which we must concern ourselves. One is Troilus' praise of Love, borrowed at length from Boethius' Book II, m. 8, which he sings to Pandarus in the garden towards the end of the book. While not addressed to Venus, this song replaces the hymn to Venus sung by Troilo in the *Filostrato*, and continues Troilus' confusion over the relationship of Boethius' Holy Bond of Things and his own illicit relationship with Criseyde. Gordon has already dealt with this passage at length, suggesting that Chaucer inserted it while revising (it does not appear in all manuscripts of the poem) in order to balance the ambiguities inherent in the Prohemium. Although some of the aspects of Venus recounted in the Prohemium could apply either to a sexual Venus or a Venus of a less physical love, Troilus' praise of his affair with Criseyde in terms of Boethian Harmony "is to reveal how misdirected is his love, since the very terms of the hymn make clear that the 'holy bond of love' must exclude a love that had become an end in itself."[42] To this cogent analysis I can add only that the theme of Troilus' entry into Heaven that has occupied us for some time is here picked up again, for now that Troilus has arrived in his heaven it is (ironically, of course) heavenly to hear him speak of it. As the narrator laconically puts it:

> And by the hond ful ofte he wolde take
> This Pandarus, and into gardyn lede,
> And swich a feste and swich a proces make
> Hym of Criseyde, and of hire womanhede,
> And of hire beaute, that, withouten drede,
> It was an hevene his wordes for to here.   [III, 1737–43]

The curious image of the two men, walking almost like lovers hand in hand in a garden, tells us much about the "progress"—perhaps "retrogression" would be the better word—of Troilus. Upon his first sight of Criseyde he resigned his royal estate into her hand (I, 433–34), and when Pandarus offered to advance his suit, he knelt to him, embraced him (I, 1044–45) and said "'my lif, my deth, hol in thyn hond I leye'" (I, 1053). He again knelt to Pandarus after the seduction to thank him for bringing him to "hevene" from "helle" (III, 1592, 1599–1600). Having resigned his claims on life and position, he is wholly dependent upon Criseyde and Pandarus. His holding hands with Pandarus is perhaps meant to underscore the extent to which he is cut off from everyone else by his secret passion. The lover in the *Romance of the Rose* similarly gives up his life ("'My lyf, my deth is in youre hond'" [*RR*, 1955]) to the God of Love in another garden, compounding his humility by offering to kiss the god's feet. Criseyde walks arm in arm in a garden with the lying and dissimulating Pandarus (II, 1116–17), holds hands with the unfaithful Helen (II, 1604), and is led arm in arm by Pandarus from a garden to a meeting with Troilus (II, 1725). Pandarus, the professed servant of Venus, links most of the garden imagery in this poem. In joining with Pandarus' manipulations (so to speak) both principals, like the lover in the *Romance of the Rose*, give themselves up to the pleasures and pains of fleshly love. Thus to hear Troilus sing of his joy is not "an hevene to here." The only greater irony is Troilus' final specification in his prayer—"'kepe hem that ben trewe!'" (1771).

It is seldom noticed that Chaucer not only opens Book III with an address to Venus but also closes it in the same way. Thus while Troilus calls upon Venus (and Boethian love) throughout the book, the book itself is bracketed by addresses to a Venus of more than just sexual love. Chaucer opens Book III with an invocation of Venus in all conceivable aspects, then as "clerc" of the servants of Love asks the carnal Venus to teach him how to tell the "joye" that is "felt in thi servyse" (III, 42), adding an invocation of Calliope for this humorously epic task. He now closes the book by thanking Venus, mother of blind Cupid, and all the Muses, not just Calliope, for helping him to write his account thus far. While there is some parallel to be seen between Troilus and the narrator, both first praising and then thanking Venus, the differences are more striking. Troilus asks Venus and the other planetary deities for aid in reaching his carnal heaven, and is so transported once there that he thanks

Venus, Hymen, Charity, and the Boethian Holy Bond of Things. He knows what he wants, but seems to misunderstand what he gets. At the opening of the book he is singleminded, at the middle and end he is profoundly confused. The narrator, on the other hand, opens the book with a complicated apostrophe to Venus in which he first sketches the multitude of loves that Venus can represent, then ironically calls upon Calliope for help in showing the "gladnesse" of Troilus to the praise of Venus. The narrator has already announced that the poem will concern a double sorrow, but in this book he shows us that the brief moment of happiness in the "Heaven" of the lovers is itself difficult to enjoy.

The ironic note of invoking an epic muse to describe the happiness of Troilus is underscored at several junctures in Book III. For example, after the meeting of the lovers at Deiphebus' house, where they first kiss, Troilus is described with exaggerated phrases as being joyful. After Pandarus extracts a promise of secrecy about his role as go-between and tells Troilus that he is already in "blysse" (342) Chaucer says that Troilus is supremely happy:

> Who myghte tellen half the joie or feste
> Which that the soule of Troilus tho felte,
> Heryng th'effect of Pandarus byheste?
> His olde wo, that made his herte swelte,
> Gan tho for joie wasten and tomelte.
> . . . .
> Right in that selve wise, soth to seye.
> Wax sodeynliche his herte ful of joie,
> That gladder was ther nevere man in Troie.
>
> [III, 344–57]

However, the "joie" that Troilus feels is bought at a price. He swears to keep Pandarus' activities secret with one of his characteristic negations of his own free will: "'I wol the serve / Right as thi sclave, whider so thow wende'" (III, 390–91), sounding like some latter-day Ruth. His success in keeping the secret is wryly commented on by Chaucer, who observes that no one "sholde han wist, by word or by manere, / What that he mente, as touchyng this matere" (431–32). Troilus is as far removed from others as is a cloud, "so wel dissimulen he koude" (434). Thus the poem's language moves rapidly up and down the rhetorical scale.

Continuing his mock-epic effect, Chaucer has Troilus refer to the proposed seduction of Criseyde as "this grete emprise" (416), and then the narrator proposes to tell "the grete effect" (505). This greatness, though, is qualified by the lack of time the lovers have together, which is the necessary result of their secrecy.

> But to the grete effect. Than sey I thus,
> That stondyng in concord and in quiete,
> Thise ilke two, Criseyde and Troilus,
> As I have told, and in this tyme swete,—
> Save only often myghte they nought mete,
> Ne leiser have hire speches to fulfelle.   [III, 505–10]

The "grete effect" is qualified by "save only." The sweet time is sweet enough, but there is not time enough. The problem with secrecy is the fear of discovery, and Chaucer does not let us forget this. Even at the height of the lovers' bliss, when Troilus is rejoicing in the heaven of Criseyde and she is calling him "'My ground of ese'" (III, 1304), Chaucer reminds us that the outside world impinges. "That nyght, bitwixen drede and sikernesse, / Felten in love the grete worthynesse" (1315–16). The fear of discovery and necessary departure make the night of love unreal, so that the lovers wonder whether it actually happened, or whether "al this thyng but nyce dremes were" (III, 1342). This uneasiness leads both of them to curse the day and the shortness of the night. Criseyde says to the night "'Thow doost, allas, to shortly thyn office'" (1436), while Troilus complains to the "'cruel day'" (III, 1450), and both are later seen to hate the day:

> And day they gonnen to despise al newe,
> Callyng it traitour, envyous, and worse,
> And bitterly the dayes light thei corse.
>
> [III, 1699–1701]

The unhappiness of the lovers in the midst of the "Heaven" of Book III is noticed as the narrator quietly closes the book with his "praise" of Venus, her blind son Cupid, and the nine Muses.

> Thorugh yow have I seyd fully in my song
> Th'effect and joie of Troilus servise,
> Al be that ther was som disese among.   [III, 1814–17]

The "disese" goes far to counter the narrator's breathless comments on the wonders of sexual love, which seem more ironic than anything else. The many references to the lovers' uneasiness, the narrator's portrayal of other, better forms of love in the Prohemium, and Troilus' confused paeans to Charity and the Boethian Holy Bond of Things combine to give us a scale of values against which we can measure the rhapsodically described sexual transports of the two principals. They do not measure up well if objectively studied. When Chaucer closes his book by saying "Troilus in lust and in quiete / Is with Criseyde" (1819–20), Troilus is only quiet in the sense of being inactive, for his "disese" reminds us that he is not at peace. There are three references in Book III to the lovers' supposed tranquility. They are said to be "in concord and in quiete" (III, 506), to be "in quyete and in rest" (III, 1680), and "in lust and in quiete" (III, 1819) in the penultimate line of the book. We have noted that Chaucer specifically undercuts these statements in two instances, but in a larger sense they are inevitably ironic. As Chaucer is careful to point out, the union of the lovers represents a submission, on their part, to Fortune:

> And many a nyght they wroughte in this manere,
> And thus Fortune a tyme ledde in joie
> Criseyde, and ek this kynges sone of Troie.   [III, 1713–15]

In the same book, then, we are told that the lovers are led by Fortune and that they are at rest, in quiet, but it is not in the nature of Fortune to let her servants be at rest. As even Pandarus knows, borrowing from Boethius, "'if hire whiel stynte any thyng to torne, / Then cessed she Fortune anon to be'" (I, 848–49). The assertions about the lovers' tranquillity ring hollow even in Book III, and the final lines of the book are best read without a pause between their testimony to the "quiete" of Troilus and Criseyde, and the opening lines of Book IV: "But al to litel, weylaway the whyle, / Lasteth swich joie, ythonked be Fortune." This is the best that the Venus of sexuality can bring Troilus to. Whereas Book III opened with an invocation of Venus and Calliope, Book IV invokes Mars and the Furies. By Book V Troilus no longer prays to Venus but rather curses her (V, 208).

The "Triomphe de Vénus"

When Lady Philosophy, in prose 12 of Book III of Boethius' *Consolation* has proven to Boethius that evil is nothing, Boethius says that her reasoning is like the "hous of Dedalus," that is, "so entrelaced that it is unable to ben unlaced." Moreover, her arguments are based on internal proofs, or as Boethius puts it: "thise thinges ne schewedest thou naught with noone resouns ytaken fro withouten, but by proeves in cercles and homliche knowen, the whiche proeves drawen to hemself heer feyth and here accord everich of hem of othir" (Bk. III, pr. 12). This affirmation of the usefulness of the hermeneutic circle is adduced here because thus far the attempt has been to examine the significance of Venus in the *Troilus* primarily by reference to the actions and images of the text itself, and if I have not made a House of Dedalus, I hope I have made a stronger argument about the mood created by the references to Venus than I could have done by reference to Venus as portrayed by medieval mythographers and in other medieval literary contexts. The problem with the approach via the mythographers is that when the several possible meanings of Venus have duly been collected, scholars and critics can still disagree about which aspect is functioning in any particular literary situation. For example, the Temple of Venus in the *Hous of Fame* has within it a portrait of Venus, naked, floating in the sea, with a white and red rose garland, a comb, doves, Cupid, and Vulcan. B. G. Koonce, drawing upon Boccaccio's notes to the *Teseida* and on the mythographies of Fulgentius, Bernard Silvestris, and the third Vatican mythographer, argues that the details selected are "traditionally identified with the carnal Venus." J. A. W. Bennett, on the other hand, while also drawing upon medieval mythographers (although not always the same ones) is concerned to show that the Venus portrayed in the *Hous of Fame* is not necessarily the meretrix or harlot of the moralizers. And, finally, Meg Twycross has argued that because Venus in this passage is shown with a comb, which probably is derived from Oiseuse's comb in the *Romance of the Rose*, Chaucer's selection of this detail "tends to neutralize any 'moral' condemnatory associations which the mythographical Venus may have collected in her dealings with the clergy."[43] That Oiseuse's comb, which is derived iconographically from Luxuria's comb, can be assumed not to have condemnatory moral associations is rather too broad-minded.[44] However, Twycross' argument—almost diametrically opposed to Koonce's—does show that an appeal to mythography and iconography does not invariably settle questions of tone.

Of course, the Venus invoked in *Troilus and Criseyde* is not specifically iconographic: that is, she is not described in terms of dress, attitude, and accompanying paraphernalia in such a way that we might be inclined to look to the descriptions in medieval mythographers for an explanation of the significance of these details. However, the only remaining approach—to examine who she is and what she does—which has been followed so far, should not be construed to exist in a vacuum. There is an obvious literary source for a Venus who brings together in sexual union two people who are not married to each other: the *Romance of the Rose*. Moreover, the *Romance*'s final scene, in which the lover imagines the sex act as a liturgical phenomenon, could well have been the source for Chaucer's amusing images of Venus as a saint in the religion of love, the great bulk of which are additions to the *Filostrato*.[45] If the *Romance* is Chaucer's source for the figure of Venus in the *Troilus*, then the question of whether or not he intends us to understand the moralizations of the mythographers when he employs only their descriptions and not their moralizations is done away with. If Chaucer was inspired by the *Romance*, then the lover's acquiescence to the God of Love and his exploitation of the opportunity afforded by Venus are actions clearly opposed to the counsel of Reason. Thus, whether or not the religion of sexuality appears to moderns to be moral or immoral, it was undoubtedly thought to be unreasonable by our medieval ancestors, and so probably sinful.[46]

One of the difficulties in assessing the tone of medieval works of art having to do with Venus is that it is incumbent upon the artist, whether painting a picture or a word picture, to show the Venus of fleshly delight as attractive.

An ugly Venus is a contradiction in terms. Consequently, it is all too easy, in the absence of an explicit condemnation, to deduce that because Venus is attractive therefore the love she represents is attractive, but this deduction confuses what Venus looks like with the conduct she inspires. Moreover, the conduct itself is sometimes misinterpreted when portrayed artistically, for it is a part of contemporary habits of mind to assume that a picture of a couple in a passionate transport carries with it at least a tacit approval. No better instance of this mistaking of form for meaning in a medieval picture could be found than in an interpretation of the so-called "Triomphe de Vénus" that is the frontispiece of this work.

This particular portrait of Venus is of special interest in these discussions because one of her devotees is Troilus. The depiction of Venus is on a lying-in tray, a *plateau d'accouchement*, which was used in northern Italy for serving meals to women in childbed. The significance of Venus and her devotees has been explicated by Roger Sherman Loomis and Laura Hibbard Loomis as "frankly sensual." The details are analyzed as follows:

> A nude, winged Venus hovers above in a mandorla, attended by two cupids with clawed feet. Golden rays stream from her body toward a group of knights kneeling in adoration in a flowery mead. The devotees of Venus (and of Mars as well, for all were famed in battle) are identified by the inscriptions on their very contemporary costumes as, from left to right, Achilles, "Tristan, Lancelot, Sanson," Paris, Troilus. . . . Parodies on sacred things and a bold adoration of Venus were far from unknown to the Goliards and other wayward spirits of the twelfth and thirteenth centuries. But here we have in art a clear prognostic of the paganism of the Renaissance, the idolization of the flesh set up in opposition to the idealization of the spirit.[47]

The basic fallacy in this interpretation is the assumption that it is religion that is parodied by the artist's placing Venus in a mandorla. I should prefer to say that the satire is aimed at those who worship Venus as though she were a sacred deity. The mandorla is placed in the picture not because it belongs there (no such thing is ever described by the mythographers) but because it does not. The incongruity between a sacred form and a pagan, indeed sensual, subject can cut either way: the artist could be satirizing religion and exalting Venus, or satirizing people who themselves exalt Venus. However, a major incongruity between form and subject should signal at least the possibility of some species of mock-heroic artistic endeavor.

When Alexander Pope uses epic machinery to describe the trivial incident that is the central concern of "Rape of the Lock," it is not Homer's techniques but rather contemporary social superficiality that is the object of Pope's mock-heroic verse. By the same token, when the Nun's Priest employs dream lore, alludes to philosophical analyses of simple and conditional necessity, and invokes Judas Iscariot, Ganelon, and Synon to characterize the treachery of the fox, it is not these three or "Augustyn, / Or Boece, or the Bisshop Bradwardyn" (*NPT*, 3241–42), or even Macrobius who is satirized. Rather, all of this incongruous machinery is employed in what has been called the first mock-epic in English in order to underscore the triviality of barnyard affairs. It is Chauntecleer's pretension, not Augustine's, that is the butt of the humor. If Chaucer's ultimate goal is to satirize foolish pride in humans, he nevertheless arrives at the goal by creating a distorted perspective. He heightens the style on the one hand and debases the subject (the affairs of a man and woman are treated like the affairs of two chickens) on the other. The resulting incongruity is both humorous and instructive, and amusingly manipulates both "fruyt" and "chaf."

One of the techniques of the mock epic is to describe a commonplace, trivial event, in religious imagery. In "Rape of the Lock," for example, Belinda's dressing table is described as an altar, and the tension between the subject and the imagery is designed to disparage those who make altars of dressing tables, not to suggest that Pope believes that self-adornment is a proper religion.[48] In the *Romance of the Rose*, as has been noted, Amant's fevered imagining of his genitalia as a pilgrim's staff and scrip (worth £50,000,000) and his lady's private parts as a sanctum sanctorum, is not intended to satirize pilgrims or shrines but rather the astonishing pride of Amant on the one hand and his unreasonableness on the other. Amant, as Rosemond Tuve has observed, is pliant in everyone's hands but Reason's, and his determined unreasonableness results in his making a religion out of sexuality, from his catechism in the "commandments" of love to his final lifting of the veil that covers the holy of holies.[49]

When Chaucer associates religious imagery with sexuality, it is usually for broad comic effect. When January and Absolon employ the language of Canticles for non-spiritual purposes, it is their carnality that is satirized and not the mystical love of the biblical book or the habit of spiritual exegesis. Similarly, when Palamon in the *Knight's Tale*, as well as Troilus in the poem presently considered, wonder whether the lady they see is a woman or a goddess, the humor is directed at their unreasonableness and pride, much as it is in the *Miller's Tale* when John the carpenter complacently imagines himself a second Noah, third father of the world.[50] When Pandarus defines Immortal God as Cupid, and Troilus imagines Venus as the mother of Charity, one does not find in the actions of the characters an illustration of Chaucer's devotion to the cult of Venus.

To return to our painting, then, we may have more reason to find the adoration of Venus to be satirized in the picture than to find a "parody" of religious art. The attendant deities are helpful in determining the tone of the whole. As the Loomises noted, they have clawed feet, but it was not made clear that this is an almost invariable device for indicating a devil.[51] Furthermore, the cupid on the right is holding a chain as well as an arrow, and the chain in association with Venus is interpreted by the mythographers as symbolic of the enchaining power of lust.[52] The picture, therefore, in showing a Venus attended by devils ready with chains and arrows, displays a Venus that prudence could counsel a man to flee; yet the lovers are kneeling in devotion rather than taking to their heels. What keeps them there, presumably, are the rays streaming from precisely that part of Venus' anatomy that can best be depended upon to overcome prudence. These lovers have not just made Venus a saint, they are depicted in a kind of mystical vision of what the Wife of Bath calls the "chambre of Venus."[53]

Although Chaucer did not know of this particular artistic rendering of Troilus as a devotée of Venus, the analysis of either the poem or the picture is helpful for an examination of the other. A good case can be made that both the lying-in tray and *Troilus and Criseyde* are contrived to show an unreasonable adoration of Venus by Troilus. The precise kind of unreasonableness that Troilus indulges in is condemned in both artistic renditions by virtue of its very absurdity. Even without recourse to the moralizations of the mythographers, it is possible to see that neither Chaucer nor the painter of the Louvre tray has taken the trouble to show Troilus as a foolish disciple of the religion of Venus in order to praise him, or, as some critics would have it, in order to reserve judgment. Implicit condemnations are as telling as explicit ones, but they require us to be alert for tonal shadings. A poem that begins with the invocation of "cruwel" Tisiphone and continues with the activities of the concupiscent Venus is bound to show the unhappiness that concupiscence brings about, for according to the author of the gloss on the *Echecs Amoureux*, the fierce Tisiphone may herself be defined as concupiscence.[54] To argue, as Meech has done, that Venus is presumed benevolent by the narrator as well as by the hero, heroine, and confidant, is to overlook the nature of the passages in which Venus is named.[55]

Thus far we have examined Chaucer's primary source and the nature of several key images in the poem. Let us now look more closely at the major characters in the work, for it is only after we have dealt generally with the figures of Cupid and Venus that we can analyze with any specificity the protagonists of the action.

Chapter V

Persons and Images

Criseyde and the Eyes of Prudence

The vast quantity of critical energy expended in efforts to analyze the character of Criseyde is ample evidence that if *Troilus and Criseyde* was not written as a "psychological novel" it has nevertheless been read as a poem with psychological dimensions. In many respects this has been a fruitful endeavor, for while Robertson has pointed out that Chaucer's goal is not to "delineate character in a psychological sense but to call attention to abstractions which may manifest themselves in human thought and action," the abstractions must nevertheless be identified and their relationships clarified.[1] If Chaucer's characters are not three-dimensional psychological entities responding to situations like the characters in a novel by Henry James, that is not to say that they are one-dimensional personifications either. Chaucer frequently creates "new and striking combinations and elaborations" of what are "conventional and derivative" descriptive materials, and critics would be remiss if they did not examine Chaucer's manipulation of his materials, for in the significance of the "attributes" of his characters will lie the significance of much of his poetry.[2] Thus the more restrained of the psychological criticisms give us valuable clues about the meaning of the poem, although the authors are best read with reservations about the extent to which these attributes constitute a personality that can be understood psychologically. On the other hand, the oft-reiterated claim that Chaucer fell in love with his heroine typifies a criticism that has transcended the psychological analysis of character in favor of the psychological analysis of the author.[3]

Thus, while we might better speak of the configuration than the character of Criseyde, these elements of abstraction rather than personality nevertheless invite analysis. And we must remember that while Chaucer is not concerned with creating a consistent psychological entity whose character traits will "explain" her behavior, still the customary medieval respect for Ciceronian decorum will result in something very similar. Chaucer can be relied upon to make a Placebo a flatterer, and while he will on occasion turn a literary or artistic convention upside down, his literary creations can usually be expected to act in accordance with their données. Custance will be constant, Saint Cecelia will be saintly, and foolish January will have his eyes opened only to remain foolish.[4] So, if we can identify the elements that Chaucer draws upon for his portrait of Criseyde, perhaps we can also account for her behavior in the poem without recourse to imagining some inconsistency between the description of the character and her actions that we would have to account for by supposing that Chaucer fell in love with her.[5]

Certainly the major element in Chaucer's portrait of Criseyde is her fearfulness. As C. S. Lewis brilliantly argued, fear is Criseyde's "ruling passion." She fears loneliness, old age, death, hostility, and love itself, Lewis observes, and indeed if such an academic exercise were desirable, it would be possible to cite dozens of additional references to reinforce Lewis' case. It suffices to note, however, that in addition to the key line cited by Lewis, "she was the ferfulleste wight / That myghte be" (II, 450–51), she is also described as "Tendre-herted, slydynge of corage" (V, 825).[6] Criseyde's fearfulness goes a long way towards accounting for her actions in the poem. Her fear of enmity because of her father's treachery causes her to seek Hector's protection and to seek Troilus' too. Her fear of separation from him causes her to devise schemes to return, and when she is in the Greek camp, her fear for her wellbeing causes her to seek another protector, Diomede. Thus, while fear is not the only element of Criseyde's literary character, it is certainly a prominent feature. Her fearfulness is not meant to indicate a neurotic personality, both because Chaucer did not know about personalities (neurotic or otherwise), and because some of Criseyde's fears are real enough. In spite of Hector's protection, we must remember, the stormy people shout him down and send her off against her will to the Greeks. The security of a widow was seldom absolute in the Middle Ages, even when she had powerful and disinterested champions.[7] On the other hand, even when we allow for a certain amount of reasonable fear in Criseyde, we are left with a great deal of irrational anxiety. When Pandarus tells her of an "aventure" that is to befall her, she fears to hear it (II, 314–15), and later she fears to accept a letter from Troilus (II, 1128). Indeed, she even seems to fear that Pandarus' ludicrous avowal to starve himself to death if she "kills" Troilus with unkindness will come true unless she acts (II, 439–62).

This may not exhibit a neurosis, but C. S. Lewis has sensibly declared it a "flaw" in Criseyde. Significantly, Gordon notes that Chaucer's indication that a deliberate decision has been made by Criseyde—typically following an internal debate—is meant to demonstrate that problems of love are ultimately moral problems.[8] To put the matter into a more specific medieval frame of reference, we might say that Criseyde's fearfulness represents a moral characteristic insofar as she exhibits a notable absence of the virtue of *fortitudo*. This virtue, recommended by Chaucer's Parson as a cure for "the angwissh of troubled herte" (*ParsT*, 678), is not a psychological but a moral phenomenon; yet it accounts for a literary character's actions in much the same way.[9] Criseyde acts and reacts throughout the poem in accordance with the deficiency in *fortitudo* with which Chaucer has supplied her. Nor is this her only lack.

Criseyde herself, late in the poem, comments upon her own "character," and observes that she could not foretell the future, lacking one of the three eyes of Prudence:

> "Prudence, allas, oon of thyne eyen thre
> Me lakked alwey, er that I come here!
> On tyme ypassed wel remembred me,
> And present tyme ek koud ich wel ise,
> But future tyme, er I was in the snare,
> Koude I nat sen; that causeth now my care."
>
> [V, 744–49]

Like many exercises in self-analysis, whether by real people or literary characters, Criseyde's portrayal of herself as lacking in foresight is only partly correct. More accurately one might simply say that she is lacking in prudence generally, for the essential nature of prudence is not merely to judge the past and view the present but to use this knowledge in order to exercise caution about one's choices for the future. Indeed, *cautio* is one of the eight-fold divisions of prudence outlined by Thomas Aquinas. The three eyes notwithstanding then, the failure of prudence in foresight is really the failure of prudence altogether.[10]

This deficiency in Criseyde would make a substantially greater impact on a medieval rather than a modern audience because of its theological and moral significance. Chaucer himself thought very highly of prudence. In *The Canterbury Tales* the "moral tale vertuous" (*Thop Endlink*, 940), the *Tale of Melibee*, which he assigns to himself, is about prudence, and he includes prudence as a characteristic of two of his apparently virtuous heroines, Griselda and Virginia.[11] Griselda and Virginia, of course, not only in their prudence but in several other ways, are everything that Criseyde is not. We may note too that though Prudence helps Melibee cope with the onslaughts of the world, the flesh, and the devil, Criseyde, lacking prudence, has some difficulty with the temptations of the flesh.

High regard for prudence is almost inevitable in a Christian author, for Prudence is the chief of the four moral or cardinal virtues. Her appearance with three eyes Chaucer probably took from her description in Dante's *Purgatorio*, wherein the pageant at the top of the mountain features the cart of the church with Faith, Hope, and Charity circling one wheel, while Prudence, Temperance, Justice, and Fortitude circle the other.[12] Criseyde's lack of prudence symmetrically balances her lack of fortitude, and her behavior throughout the poem is consonant with her deficiencies.[13] It should be added that in addition to these two moral deficiencies, Criseyde, like Troilus, also suffers from pride.[14] Thus Chaucer has given us a fairly substantial amount of information about the moral posture of his heroine. Unlike Boccaccio's Criseida, in whom *luxuria* is the major ingredient, Chaucer's Criseyde behaves in accordance with deficiencies more than in accordance with excess.[15]

While C. S. Lewis has demonstrated the relationship between Criseyde's actions and her fear, it is of almost equal importance to see her lack of prudence, even though this dimension of her portrait is not called by name until late in the poem. For example, the seemingly gratuitous reference to Amphiorax in Book II may make a good deal more sense when we understand that Criseyde is imprudent. Pandarus comes to Criseyde's residence, filled with the news of Troilus' passion for her, and finds Criseyde and some other ladies reading a romance about Thebes. They have just stopped reading, they tell him, where Amphiorax falls through the ground to hell. Amphiorax or Amphiaraus, unlike Criseyde, had a great deal of foresight. Knowing that the struggle against Thebes would result in disaster, he tried to dissuade the Greeks from fighting. However, the Greeks disregard his sage advice, and in Lydgate's version of the story their decision represents the lack of "wisdam" and "discrecioun," "wher prudence can fyndë no socour."[16] Those who act against good sense, then, are types of imprudence, but, as Robertson remarks, Criseyde does not seem to learn very much from her reading.[17] Her own better judgment tells her to reject Pandarus' advice to put down her book, rise up, and dance; yet before long she has fallen in with his schemes. While her first reaction to Pandarus' suggestion is "'God forbede!'" (II, 113), her lack of prudence causes her to reject before long what she considers proper for a widow. This is not only a question of foresight but of good judgment in general, for while Criseyde indignantly tells Pandarus that as a widow she should live "'ay in a cave'" and "'rede on holy seyntes lyves'" (II, 117–18), the fact of the matter is that she is doing neither. Rather, we encounter her in a garden reading a romance.

Criseyde's lengthy debate with herself over whether or not to love Troilus is another part of the poem that is best understood with reference to the heroine's lack of prudence. A medieval debate typically leads to an answer, and this is true of poetic debates as well, in spite of the often heard comment that the debate is left up to the reader to resolve.[18] Chaucer quite characteristically takes this convention and employs it for humorous effect, as, for example, in the *Nun's Priest's Tale*, where Chauntecleer and Pertelote debate the significance of dreams. Chauntecleer wins the debate, but allows himself to ignore his own good sense because of his infatuation with his opponent, Pertelote, and comes to grief with the fox for his folly. An even closer analogue with the situation in *Troilus* is provided by the *Romance of the Rose* in which the protagonist is determined to serve the God of Love and seek the rosebud in spite of the excellent arguments advanced by Reason against such an action. The reader is expected to understand that Reason's arguments against an extra-marital amatory exploit are very sound, and the lover's rejection of her and her philosophy is not only irrational and unreasonable, but slightly ridiculous as well. In the *Troilus* Criseyde's internal debate is not ridiculous, but it is unreasonable. To join in the dance, as Criseyde correctly observes, is more suitable for maidens and young wives than for a widow like herself (II, 119). Her argument, however, is long and complex in Chaucer's poem, and we may better understand its weaknesses by first considering Boccaccio's much more transparent (but equally amusing) version of the same inner debate.

In response to Pandaro's suggestion that Criseida should be joined with an as yet unnamed lover, she asks the obvious question: "who hath any right to have perfect pleasure of me, if he should not first become my husband?" (II, 45). On learning Troilo's name she turns the tables on Pandaro and says that if she had "fallen into such folly" as to desire Troilo, she would have thought that "thou wouldst have beaten me, not merely restrained me, as one who should seek my honor" (II, 48). She then remarks on the transitory nature of love ("love changing as thought changeth" [II, 50]), and says again "it is meet for me to remain virtuous" (II, 51). There is however, a rather abrupt change in her attitude when Pandaro observes that age will take away her beauty. She agrees, and straightaway asks if she may "still have solace and joy of love" (II, 55). Pandaro then relates to her the tale of Troilo's love-sick grief, and she is moved to "pity" by "reason of what thou hast said" (II, 65). She adds, however, that in order to avoid "shame" and "perhaps worse," Troilo should be discreet (II, 66). After Pandaro leaves, Criseida thinks over what he has said in a "joyful mood" while picturing Troilo in her mind (II, 68). She then goes into some specific pros and cons about the proposed affair. Her first thought, considering her youth, beauty, widowed and childless state is, why not? However, she immediately remembers why not. All her previous concern for her virtue and honor and her indignant response to the idea that someone should have perfect pleasure of her without benefit of clergy, however, are now easily waved aside. If "onestà" forbids what she wants to do she will simply keep her desire hidden (II, 69). This point is crucial, for of course it is choplogic. Concealing the loss of virtue does not meliorate the loss but rather compounds one mistake with a little convenient hypocrisy.

The arguments that follow from this point are also either sophistical, irrelevant, or otherwise contrived to encourage Criseida to do what she has already decided to do. Virtue and honesty are forgotten, and only practical impediments are considered. First she thinks again upon her vanishing youth, then considers that everyone else in Troy has a lover, concluding that "to do as others do is no sin" (II, 70), a comforting if morally dubious idea. She then considers that it is a good idea to "make provision in season" (II, 71), a sensible idea for one's garden, perhaps, but not very wise when applied to the abandonment of virtue before it becomes difficult to abandon. Whereas shortly before she was much against the idea of sex outside of marriage, now she feels that for unexplained reasons the time is not right for a husband, and, even if it were, "water aquired by stealth is sweeter far than wine had in abundance" (II, 74). Whether or not a little guilt improves the taste of water is not really the issue, though, for as she herself pointed out previously, honesty and virtue militate against love outside of marriage. Moreover, as noted in chapter 1, Criseida's ideas on stolen water are taken from the speeches of the harlot who opposes Wisdom in Proverbs, and so undercut rather than support her decision to love Troilo.

When Criseida "turned her thoughts in the opposite direction" (II, 75), it was not to go back to the moral arguments against an illicit affair with which she had begun, but rather to worry about abandonment by Troilo (rather ironically in view of what happens), the chance of discovery, and what might happen to her "reputation" (II, 77), which seems subtly to have replaced virtue as the subject of her concern. Thus she vacillates now because of practical rather than moral hesitation, but once she actually sees Troilo, "that indifference which was holding Criseida at cross-purposes with herself vanished . . ." (II, 83). While Boccaccio does not stress his heroine's lack of prudence, she certainly does not display much of it in these scenes, and Chaucer apparently saw the chance to point up the particular failing that lies behind this kind of reasoning. Typically, though, Chaucer is a little more subtle and a little less transparent than his literary models, and what he chooses to suppress in the *Troilus* is Boccaccio's unambiguous opening statement about the immorality of an illicit relationship.[19]

As we have already noted, the internal debate in the *Troilus* begins with Pandarus' invitation to Criseyde to join in the dance, which, although it serves as a metaphor for sexuality in the poem, is not so overtly a moral issue as is Criseida's straightforward indignation at the idea that anyone should enjoy her outside of marriage.[20] After Criseyde's refusal, Pandarus manages to work Troilus' name into the conversation and to compare him favorably with Criseyde's protector, Hector. Then, pretending to leave without telling her the "'thyng to doon yow pleye'" (II, 121) he had promised, he again urges her to dance and "'cast youre widewes habit to mischaunce'" (II, 222). The emphasis on Criseyde's widowhood is surely designed to remind the reader of the usual medieval expectations about widowhood—what Chaucer's Parson calls "chastitee of widwehod" (*ParsT*, 916), which is endorsed because it was believed desirable that a widow should neither be licentious nor cheapen the sacrament of marriage like the Wife of Bath by multiple marriages. Rather, she should be "a clene wydewe, and eschue the embracynges of man, and desiren the embracynge of Jhesu Crist" (*ParsT*, 944).[21] Thus, while Pandarus' invitations would be much more pointed to a medieval audience than to a modern one, nevertheless Chaucer begins the action more obliquely than does Boccaccio. Boccaccio has his heroine speak of virtue and marriage; Chaucer has his heroine speak of widowhood and the dance.

Following the second invitation to dance, Pandarus accedes to Criseyde's curiosity about the news he brings, and launches into a long speech in which he not only announces that Troilus loves her, but also tries to forestall any adverse reaction she might have to this information by quieting what he imagines would be her "worste" fear, that "'Men wolde wondren sen hym come or goon'" (II, 368). This, he triumphantly announces, is really nothing to fear, because everyone, "'but he be fool of kynde, / Wol deme it love of frendshipe in his mynde'" (II, 370–71). This insidiously suggests, of course, that the issue is not a moral but a social one and that the issue is not what she should do but what people might think. Pandarus quickly follows this up with more of the same: "'Swych love of frendes regneth al this town; / And wry yow in that mantel evere moo'" (II, 379–80). This is much more subtle than Boccaccio's having Criseida say that what everyone does cannot be a sin, but the effect is ultimately the same. Pandarus suggests that she can hide herself with the mantle of others' activities; that is, that her similar behavior would create a sort of protective coloration, and this avoids confronting the moral question that might damage Pandarus' case.

Criseyde decides that she had better determine exactly what Pandarus is talking about, so asks him to explain just what he has in mind: "'What is youre reed I sholde don of this?'" (II, 389). Pandarus replies that she should grant her love for Troilus' love, and adds the warning that she had better hurry, since age is hourly wasting her and once old, "'there wol no wight of the'" (II, 396). Again, Pandarus typically puts the matter forth as a practical rather than moral one, but Criseyde understands well enough what his intentions are, and bursts into tears at the idea that the man who should prohibit her from loving is instead counseling it. Whether her tears are manufactured to counterbalance those of Pandarus, or whether they are the result of her fearfulness, is less important than their narrative function, which is to underscore the moral nature of the request. Her weeping leads Pandarus into an outpouring of self-vindication. He feigns indignation at being "'mystrusted thus'" (II, 431), and, swearing oddly and proleptically by Mars and the three Furies of hell, who will reappear in the Prohemium to Book IV, he barefacedly maintains that he did not mean "'harm or any vilenye'" (II, 438). He then claims Criseyde's actions will "wikkedly" cause both him and Troilus to die, so that he might as well get on with it by starving to death, which Criseyde rather imprudently takes as a real threat. She determines to play "sleighly" (II, 462) lest Pandarus' demise create some embarrassment for her.

This is an important crux in the dialogue, for by taking Pandarus at his word while trying to be sly, she is not being clever enough by half. She knows from his first invitation to dance and from his urging her to love Troilus that his intention is to exploit her; yet even though she determines to play slyly, she has consented here to play Pandarus' game. Late in the poem Chaucer says that as well as being tenderhearted and "slydynge of corage" she was "symple, and wys withal" (V, 820), which is a sufficient modification of the "wisdom" she possesses to account for her imprudence. Criseyde is not stupid, but she is not sufficiently wise either. The Bible enjoins men to be as wise as serpents, as simple as doves (Matt. 10:16), and these precepts were cited in more than one discussion of prudence, since the Vulgate text reads "estote vos ergo prudentes sicut serpentes."

Criseyde, however, although she had been "astoned" (II, 427) at Pandarus' urging that she love Troilus, now decides that in the knight's request she "saugh noon unryght" (II, 453), and determines to eat her cake and have it too: "'I shal so doon, myn honour shal I kepe, / And ek his lif'" (II, 468–69). This is much more subtle on Chaucer's part than the use of honor by Boccaccio. In the Italian work the terms were first defined, and then Criseida dismissed their importance by invoking secrecy. In the English poem Pandarus first suggests a new name for affairs: "swych love of frendes" (II, 379). Criseyde picks up this cue and pretends—perhaps to herself as well as to Pandarus—that she can enter into this relationship while keeping her honor. Three times within the space of thirteen lines she speaks of her honor, but if she has not actually joined the dance, she has not declined the invitation. A few lines further on she asks if Troilus can "'wel speke of love'" (II, 503).

Chaucer's heroine, then, like Boccaccio's before her, makes her most important choice in an undramatic fashion. She shifts gradually but discernibly from a refusal to participate in an action she considers morally improper to a qualified acceptance of Pandarus' invitation. From this point forward in the narrative Criseyde will argue with herself a great deal, but the arguments will more often be about practical than ethical considerations. It will be the qualifications that will slowly be eroded, for the basic moral scruple that initially caused her caution has been forgotten.

Criseyde determines to play slyly. She asks if Troilus can speak well of love, and when Pandarus assures her that he can and that if she is as smart as she is pretty, the two of them will be as well suited as the ruby set in the ring, Criseyde's only reaction to the obvious sexual innuendo is an unwidowlike laugh: "'Nay, therof spak I nought, ha, ha!' quod she" (II, 589).[22] We hear no more of the cave, of the reading of hagiography. We do hear about her honor, but the next time it is mentioned it has undergone a subtle transformation and no longer stands alone—rather it is mentioned in the same breath as her "name" (II, 762). Chaucer is like Boccaccio in having his heroine reject real for putative virtue, and in Chaucer's hands the substitution is perhaps even subtler and slower than in Boccaccio's. However, where Boccaccio chose to let the sight of Troilus operate dramatically on his frankly concupiscent heroine, Chaucer's Criseyde debates the practicality (and to a much lesser extent the morality) of the affair long after she has seen Troilus. In this regard, Chaucer's Criseyde adheres a little more closely to a standard literary pattern for enamorment: *visio, cogitatio,* and *passio.*[23]

A detailed perusal of Criseyde's *cogitatio* would really not serve any useful purpose. Insofar as her prudence is concerned, her key decision is her falling in with Pandarus' general proposal even when she knows he is not a good counsellor and indeed has just told him so. However, some of her thoughts are worth considering as part of the aftermath of her acquiescence in Pandarus' schemes. For example, we should note that her vision of Troilus is intoxicating, leading her to ask rhetorically, "'Who yaf me drynke?'" (II, 651). However, intoxication is held in check. Immediately after her *visio* there is *cogitatio*:

> And gan to caste and rollen up and down
> Withinne hire thought his excellent prowesse,
> And his estat, and also his renown,
> His wit, his shap, and ek his gentilesse;
> But moost hir favour was, for his distresse
> Was al for hire. . . .   [II, 659–64]

This curious combination of thoughts shows sexual attraction, Criseyde's desire for a powerful protector, and a little bit of pride. Criseyde is strongly impressed by the sight of Troilus, as was Boccaccio's heroine, but Chaucer is not concerned to show only the power of concupiscence.

Indeed, Chaucer here calls attention to what he is doing by interjecting into the narrative a little "explanation" of what is happening. Some people might say, the narrator remarks, that this was a sudden love, but as a matter of fact everything has to have a beginning, and what we have just heard is the beginning. "For I sey nought that she so sodeynly / Yaf hym hire love, but that she gan enclyne / To like hym first" (II, 673–75). Precisely. This is not the story of a character swept along by passion but of a character lacking prudence and fortitude. She starts by refusing to play the game, then tries to play by her own rules, and at last she just plays. Even after she has seen Troilus and begun to "like hym," she looks back toward her earlier reluctance to get involved in this sort of thing, but now it is qualified:

> And thus she seyde, "Al were it nat to doone,
> To graunte hym love, ye, for his worthynesse,
> It were honour, with pley and with gladnesse,
> In honestee with swich a lord to deele."   [II, 703–6]

Yes, it would be an honor to deal honestly with such a lord even while it would not do to grant him love. The juxtaposition of the words "honour" and "pley" mark a semantic decline in Criseyde's concept of her honor.[24] Somewhat like Troilus in the temple when he laughed at lovers, Criseyde thinks that she can play with fire and not get burned. She will find out that it is difficult to reconcile play and gladness with a refusal to grant love.

A similar weak rationalization occurs a few lines further along when

Criseyde takes up the proverbial idea of "mesure" in all things. Her logic is faultless as she develops her argument, but her application of her conclusion is very dangerous.

> "In every thyng, I woot, there lith mesure.
> For though a man forbede dronkenesse,
> He naught forbet that every creature
> Be drynkeles for alwey, as I gesse." [II, 715–18]

Like so many of the intellectual adornments of this poem, Criseyde's logic is a little piece of the *Romance of the Rose*, but in this instance uprooted and made to serve the opposite of its original intention. When Amant hears Reason excoriate love, he naively asks if she expects him to hate people?[25] After a lengthy discourse on other matters Reason returns to this idea and points out that he is foolish to think that the counsel to avoid harmful love is the same as counselling him to hate.

> I do not wish to forbid love which one ought to understand as good, only that which is harmful to men. If I forbid drunkenness, I do not wish to forbid drinking. . . . you are not a good logician. I do not explain love in that way. Never, out of my mouth, has come the counsel that one ought to hate anything. One must find the right mean. It is the love which I love and esteem so much that I have taught you to love.[26]

Criseyde, like Amant, is not a very good logician. She takes Reason's argument about drink and drunkenness, which leads Reason to recommend good love, and uses it to rationalize her progression in an affair that will end in what Reason calls "*fole amour*."[27]

Criseyde continues:

> "Ek sith I woot for me is his destresse,
> I ne aughte nat for that thing hym despise,
> Sith it is so, he meneth in good wyse." [II, 719–21]

It is small wonder that this kind of reasoning leaves Criseyde "Now hoot, now cold" (II, 811), up until Antigone's song. It would seem that the most prudent thing a widow with a traitorous father might do in the circumstances is to get married, but Criseyde consciously rejects the possibility:

> "Shal noon housbonde seyn to me 'chek mat!'
> For either they ben ful of jalousie,
> Or maisterfull, or loven novelrie."[28] [II, 754–56]

Antigone's song seems ideally designed to remove any lingering doubts that Criseyde might have about continuing on her course. Has she lingering moral scruples? Antigone's song says that love is not a vice (II, 855). Does she still fear that love will "thrallen libertee" (II, 773)? Antigone's song reassures

her that love is not "thraldom" (II, 856). Does she still think that love might
be the "mooste stormy lyf" (II, 778)? The song assures her that rather it is
"blisse" (II, 849). Can she really combine an extramarital affair and honor,
honesty, and the like? Antigone claims that in fact love is a positive virtue:

> "This is the righte lif that I am inne,
> To flemen alle manere vice and synne:
> This dooth me so to vertu for t'entende,
> That day by day I in my wille amende."   [II, 851–54]

Every day, in every way, improving in virtue through love—something
Criseyde thought should be off limits for a widow. Since Antigone appears in
the poem as one of a group of unmarried ladies, and since no lover is named
or alluded to, the audience may wonder where she comes by her knowledge
of love and belief in its goodness. Such speculation does not, however, bother
Criseyde, who overlooks these incongruities. The question is, why does
Criseyde follow her niece's advice rather than her own self-counsel? To some
extent it could be argued that she is by nature a follower. Lacking fortitude
she follows the advice of her uncle, Pandarus—even while doubting its morality—and of her niece, Antigone, just as later she will follow the strong lead
of Diomede. Rosemond Tuve once remarked of Amant in the *Romance of the
Rose* that he was "pliant in all hands save those of Reason" and Criseyde,
deficient in prudence and fortitude, is a very similar character.[29] Abandoned
by her father, widowed, she follows now her uncle, now her niece.

Perhaps the crowning irony of this passage is that the song is not really
Antigone's at all. Rather, she learned it from "'the goodlieste mayde / Of gret
estat in al the town of Troye'" (II, 880–81). In the poem's own terms, the
high-ranking lady who is an authority on love would likely be Helen, which
should suggest to Criseyde that the song's conclusions are something less
than impartial. Earlier, when Pandarus was urging an affair upon Criseyde,
one of his arguments was that such affairs were the rule rather than the exception in Troy: "'Swych love of frendes regneth al this town'" (II, 379). And,
later, when Troilus is debating what to do about Criseyde's imminent departure for the Greek camp, Pandarus again reminds us that "taking" women is
a Trojan characteristic:

> "Artow in Troie, and hast non hardyment
> To take a womman which that loveth the,
> And wolde hireselven ben of thyn assent?"   [IV, 533–35]

Paris and Helen presumably set the pace for Trojan society, if Pandarus can
be trusted, and as he puts it to Troilus, "'Thenk ek how Paris hath, that is thi
brother, / A love; and whi shaltow nat have another?'" (IV, 608–9). Thus,
when Criseyde lets herself be swayed by an essentially "Trojan" outlook on
love affairs, she is letting the apologetics of another Trojan woman outweigh

her own good sense. It is powerfully symbolic that her acceptance of Antigone's song is followed by the onrushing dark. The sun "Gan westren faste, and downward for to wrye" (II, 906).

Antigone's song, in spite of what should be to Criseyde its suspect origin, does tip the balance in Criseyde's judgment even more in the direction of participating in the affair. She has already made the decision to go forward, but now she confirms that decision and goes forward less fearfully and with no more looking back:

> And ay gan love hire lasse for t'agaste
> Than it dide erst, and synken in hire herte,
> That she wex somwhat able to converte.   [II, 901–3]

The last line is important, for it indicates Criseyde's complete acquiescence in the affairs of love. Earlier, when Troilus was struck with the arrow by the God of Love, the narrator somewhat ironically noted his different behavior, and remarked, "Blissed be Love, that kan thus folk converte!" (I, 308). Criseyde too is now "converted." Yet there is a great difference. For Troilus the sight of Criseyde overwhelmed him, and his scorn for love vanished instantaneously. For Criseyde the sight of Troilus was only part of a gradual abandonment of reluctance. For Criseyde the process of entering into the affair includes *visio* and *cogitatio*, as we have remarked, and finally a *passio*. In many ways the process culminating in a *passio* is the most interesting difference between Criseyde and Troilus and between Criseyde and her Italian literary predecessor. *Passio* is in fact a motion of the reason against the reason—a kind of willing suspension not of disbelief but of belief.[30] Criseyde's trust in Pandarus and in Antigone ultimately countervails against her trust in her own knowledge and common sense. The explanation for her decision to reason against her own reason may be found in her pride, her concupiscence, her lack of fortitude, and her lack of prudence.

We cannot terminate a discussion of Criseyde's interesting depiction without at least glancing at her "infidelity" to Troilus, which has caused a good deal of critical agony. Interestingly, Criseyde's carryings-on with Diomede are often regarded as a "sin," although the critics who so regard them at the same time make of her similar affair with Troilus something very much more virtuous.[31] This curious attitude results from a refusal to consider the very real medieval phenomenon of Christianity, in which extramarital affairs were regarded as sinful, and to substitute for Christianity the fanciful rules of courtly love. Even if one were to do this, it is difficult to see how Criseyde's violation of her oath to be true to Troilus constitutes a "sin" against courtly love. Andreas Capellanus, who is often (if improperly) cited as an authority for courtly love, makes it a "rule" that a new love puts to flight an old one.[32] To go further and to argue that "in Christian ethics it [Criseyde's infidelity] is as far below her original unchastity as Brutus and Iscariot, in Dante's hell, lie lower than Paolo and Francesca," is simply to compound confusion.[33] Francesca is as much a betrayer of her marriage vow as Brutus and Judas are betrayers of secular and religious leaders. The difference in their positions in hell has much more to do with the degree to which their sins are calculated and premeditated than with the extent to which they are involved with infidelity.

We must, I think, take a hard look at just what kind of vow it is that Criseyde breaks. It is certainly not a vow like a marriage vow, where two people exchange sacramental vows of fidelity. Nor is it like the vow of chastity taken by an entrant into a religious order. Rather, two people who are engaged in an illicit affair agree to be "true" to each other. Now if it is granted that the relationship is illicit in the first place, then the most fundamental ethical canons would indicate that breaking the vow in favor of a return to continence would be a good thing. As Robert Mannyng puts it in *Handlyng Synne*, "Bettere ys a foly w[o]rde be wyþdrawe / þan wyþ euyl dede to fulfyl þat sawe."[34] Of course, Criseyde does not break her vow this way. Rather she breaks off an illicit relationship with one man to start a similar relationship with another. While breaking the vow is not a good thing, it is certainly not a sin, whether considered by the standards of courtly love or Christianity. Indeed, it isn't much of anything at all. Vows of fidelity and truth in illicit matters are not very meaningful to start with, and departure from them is, as Tatlock put it thirty-five years ago, "trivial."[35]

If there is no shocking infidelity, we need not seek for any change in Criseyde's character, or for some curious psychological quirk, that would cause her to switch abruptly from being perfect to committing an unpardonable sin. More simply, again to quote Tatlock, it is "the nature of the first *amour* which led so quickly to the second."[36] Although Chaucer emphasizes Criseyde's lack of fortitude throughout while mentioning her deficiency in prudence only in Book V, neither characteristic is especially emphasized in her yielding to Diomede. They do not have to be, for they have already been amply demonstrated in Criseyde's yielding to Troilus, and, just as they combine to move her from chaste widowhood to a love affair in the first instance, they may be presumed to be at work in moving her from one affair to another.

At an early stage in Criseyde's role in the poem, Pandarus urged her to cast her "'widewes habit to mischaunce'" (II, 222), which is figuratively just what she did. It is noteworthy that when Diomede is pressing her for a reply, she retreats to her widowhood as an excuse to avoid loving:

> "But as to speke of love, ywis," she seyde,
> "I hadde a lord, to whom I wedded was,
> The whos myn herte al was, til that he deyde;
> And other love, as help me now Pallas,
> Ther in myn herte nys, ne nevere was."   [V, 974–78]

Troilus seems conveniently forgotten in this little lying speech, but what is more striking is her recognition—once again—of her widowhood. Both Troilus and Diomede assault that fortress, both prevail, and we can assume that her acquiescence is for similar reasons in both cases.

The language of the poem suggests that Criseyde changes very little. In Book I, after the departure of Calkas, Criseyde is depicted as "both a widewe . . . and allone / Of any frend to whom she dorste hir mone" (I, 97–98). In Book V, in the Greek camp, she once more suffers from an inability to talk to anyone: "And this was yet the werste of al hire peyne, / Ther was no wight to whom she dorste hire pleyne" (V, 727–28). Her widowhood is alluded to in the passage already discussed, and a few hundred lines further along she reminds herself that she is "allone" (V, 1026) as she was in Book I. Before seeking Hector as a protector she is "of hire lif . . . ful sore in drede" (I, 95), while before deciding to go ahead with the affair with Troilus she considers that her "'estat lith now in jupartie'" (II, 465). Similarly in Book V she fears that she might fall into the hands of "'som wrecche'" (V, 705), and notes that she "hadde nede / Of frendes help" (V, 1026–27). Finally, in both affairs Criseyde is susceptible to verbal argument. Throughout the progress of the affair with Troilus, his spokesman Pandarus talks Criseyde into seeing things his way, while in Book V Diomede is significantly described as being "of tonge large" (V, 804).

The similarities between the two affairs are emphasized by Chaucer. There is, however, a significant difference between her love affair with Troilus and her love affair with Diomede. That difference, which has perhaps caused the sense of her "sin" in some critics (although it is seldom mentioned), is that she is described as loving Troilus but never Diomede. The narrative difference is precise. Of the affair with Troilus the audience is told that it was no sudden love, but rather "she gan enclyne / To like hym first, and I have told yow whi" (II, 674–75). The narrator again brings up the "why" of things in Book V, but there it is not love but the words of sudden Diomede, the peril of Troy, and Criseyde's friendlessness that "bygan to brede / The cause whi . . ." (V, 1027–28). Finally, the narrator underscores the difference in his own feelings or beliefs about the two affairs—if not the facts—when he says of the affair with Diomede, "Men seyn—I not—that she yaf hym hire herte" (V, 1050).

Criseyde promises to be true to Troilus and is later "sory . . . for hire untrouthe" (V, 1098). Sorry or not, she does not hesitate long, and begins her second, presumably loveless affair, by giving Diomede a brooch given to her by Troilus. It is this apparent callousness towards her first lover that disturbs us; yet, upon examination her affair with Troilus appears to have been motivated as much by solitude, fear, and self-interest as by love. Criseyde's father, Calkas, is vilified for his falseness in the poem (e. g., I, 89, 93, 107), and Criseyde, in her self-interest, is very much her father's daughter. Any truth she professes, whether to Troilus or, as she says later, "'To Diomede algate I wol be trewe'" (V, 1071), are vows of truth to herself. If she must be false to others to be true to her interests, she will be, just as Calkas was. Her double rejection of chaste widowhood is founded upon weakness and self-interest. That one affair is based in part upon love and the other is not does not serve to distinguish them much. Criseyde loves Troy, as well as Troilus, and tells Diomede "'I love that ilke place / Ther I was born'" (V, 956–57), but her love for Troy does not prevent her from following her father's example and staying with the Greeks when she becomes convinced of the "perel of the town" (V, 1025). Criseyde, au fond, does not love anything strongly enough to overcome her own self-love. She is unfaithful to Troilus, whom she loves after a fashion, but if her infidelity to Troilus is deplorable, it is nevertheless characteristic of her more general lack of allegiance. As the narrator puts it, "bothe Troilus and Troie town / Shal knotteles thoroughout hire herte slide" (V, 768–69).

Pandarus: "'Werk al by conseil, and thou shalt nat rewe'"

Pandarus is, in modern psychological terms, a highly manipulative person. While in the Middle Ages he would have been called by other names, his astonishing degree of involvement in the forwarding of the love affair between Troilus and Criseyde would scarcely have gone unnoticed. Although Pandarus himself observes that in love "'I hoppe alwey byhynde'" (II, 1107), he is nevertheless eager to "quike alwey the fir" (III, 484) in others. Whether his eagerness and inability represent a Chaucerian insight into deviant psychology or merely a change rung on some familiar literary *topos*, they are important for any study of the poem. Pandarus uses everything from sarcasm and deceit to the arrangement of scenarios for the meetings of the lovers; he not only prods, pokes, and leads the pair, but actually lifts the fainting Troilus into Criseyde's bed. All this verbal and physical coercion, exertion, and manipulation is accompanied by a continuous stream of sententious chatter that is nothing short of remarkable under the circumstances.

That Pandarus laces his speech with proverbs, maxims, and sententious advice has been remarked upon frequently enough. However, most critics dissociate his proverbial speech from his goal of arranging a love affair. Thus B. J. Whiting argues that the use of proverbs by Pandarus (and by Criseyde) "add *ton* and a touch of sophistication to the characters who use them," while Robert Lumiansky contends that Pandarus is more sophisticated than Troilus because Troilus tends to be overly impressed by proverbial wisdom, whereas Pandarus knows that proverbs express half-truths.[37] Actually, the issue is not sophistication but hypocrisy, and the reader should respond not to evaluations of relative belief in proverbial wisdom but to the amusing yet unattractive picture of a man who spouts proverbial wisdom while arranging for carnal knowledge. That Pandarus is no true friend to Troilus has been demonstrated by Gaylord, Cook, and Freiwald, and that he is a liar has been noted by Robertson, McCall, Bolton, and Farnham.[38] That he is reprehensible as an uncle is obvious unless we invent some system of courtly love to circumvent Criseyde's view of his avuncular shortcomings. As Beryl Rowland has aptly put it, "to know him further would be to like him less."[39] When we consider that this lying, deceitful character offers his own niece to Troilus out of what it pleases him to call "friendship," all the while strewing his persuasive speeches with homely proverbs, philosophical reflections, and moral sentences, we have displayed for us the darker side of Chaucer's comic genius.

If the most sententious character in Chaucer's works is Prudence, in Chaucer's tale of *Melibee*, whose advice brings peace out of discord and who restores to health the man who had suffered from the world, the flesh, and the devil, then surely the sententious Pandarus is a kind of opposite. His advice leads to fornication, betrayal, and death; yet when he talks, the *form* of his speech is much like that of Prudence. The *content* of his advice, however, is another matter. What, after all, does he tell his "friend" and his niece? His counsel to Troilus is to do what he wants to do, best summed up in Book IV when Pandarus advises him to "'Devyne not in resoun ay so depe / Ne corteisly, but help thiself anon'" (589–90). His advice to Criseyde is essentially the same, but phrased in terms of gathering roses while one may:

> "Thenk ek how elde wasteth every houre
> In ech of yow a partie of beautee;
> And therfore, er that age the devoure,
> Go love; for old, ther wol no wight of the."   [II, 393–96]

The advice is neither profound nor attractive, and Pandarus is best understood when the intention of his advice is as clearly understood as the sententious manner in which it is delivered.

In the unfolding of events in the poem, it is noteworthy that both Troilus and Criseyde at first reject Pandarus' counsel and advice. Troilus specifically tells him "'thi proverbes may me naught availle'" (I, 756); yet such are Pandarus' powers of persuasion that within the space of a few hundred lines Troilus throws himself on his knees in front of Pandarus (I, 1044) and completely delivers himself to the other's tutelage: "'My lif, my deth, hol in thyn hond I leye'" (I, 1053). Similarly Criseyde is moved to tears when Pandarus suggests that she should have a love affair; yet as we have noted Pandarus threatens to make a scene, and Criseyde's resolve quickly melts away. Thus, as the reader is expected to judge Melibee for at first declining and then accepting the wise counsel of Prudence, so are we invited to consider the wisdom of Troilus and Criseyde in first rejecting and then accepting the counsels of self-indulgence proposed by Pandarus.

Of course, just as the lovers are to be judged for accepting Pandarus' advice, so is he to be judged for offering it. When we once note Pandarus' insistence on advising and manipulating the lovers and contrast his sententious speech with his amoral promptings, he emerges as a recognizable medieval moral figure: the Evil Counselor. Pandarus may be as proverbial as Solomon (although the book of Proverbs has much to say against fornication and adultery) but his actions nevertheless put him in the category of those who are like Achitophel in proffering evil counsel. Closer to home one can encounter evil counsel in the figure of Placebo in the *Merchant's Tale*, and it is treated in the abstract in the *Parson's Tale*. There it comes under the genus Ire, species spiritual manslaughter, subspecies "yevynge of wikked conseil by fraude" (*ParsT*, 567). In the medieval evaluation of sin, evil counsel is a serious matter—vastly more serious than the affair of the flesh of Troilus and Criseyde. Dante puts the overreaching Ulysses and the unrepentant papal advisor Guido da Montefeltro in the eighth *bolgia* of the eighth circle of hell, while the adulterous Paolo and Francesca are on a much higher level.

It is only coincidental that Guido was known in life as "the Fox," but it is no accident that after her seduction Criseyde addresses Pandarus as "'Fox that ye ben'" (III, 1565), while blaming her compromised condition on Pandarus, much like Francesca before her. Chaucer would not have known Guido's nickname, but he would certainly have known that the archetype of evil counselors in the *Romance of the Rose*, Fals Semblant, exercises what he calls his "foxerie" (6795). And it is also pertinent that the deceitful "counselor" in the *Nun's Priest's Tale* (and its innumerable sources and analogues) is a fox. Finally, since evil counsel is a form of wrath, it is not altogether surprising that for all Pandarus' outward high spirits, his leaping, hopping, joking, and poking, his last speech in the poem begins, "'I hate, ywys, Cryseyde'" (V, 1732).

Under scrutiny, then, the superficially amusing Pandarus is unattractive. Moreover, Alan Gaylord has demonstrated that Pandarus is a parody of Boethius' Lady Philosophy, which is analogous to his misplaced sententiousness. Lady Philosophy, a type of the good counselor, is parodied by Pandarus, a type of the evil counselor.[40] Boethius was fortunate in that Lady Philosophy drove off the evil Muses who were advising him, but more typically the individual must choose his counselors. Thus when Prudence tells Melibee "'Werk alle thy thynges by conseil, and thou shalt never repente'" (*Mel*, 1003), she goes on to give him a long discourse on how to choose his counselors. Chaucer uses the same phrase for comic effect in the *Miller's Tale* when Nicholas mendaciously assures old John that he should work all by his (Nicholas') counsel. In the *Troilus* the phrase is not used, but the lovers' acquiescence in Pandarus' schemes is more serious in moral terms, for they perform the acts whereas old John is merely duped. The kind of elementary caution about selecting one's counselors that is stressed in the *Melibee* and the

Parson's Tale must have been an ingredient in the audience's responses to the _Troilus_. The Parson warns us against counselors who are "to muche worldly folk" (641), while Melibee cautions us against those who speak "plesante wordes, enclynynge to the lordes lust" (_Mel_, 1152). Surely Troilus' abasement before the man who tells him that Love has "converted" him out of "wikkednesse" (I, 998–99) and Criseyde's quick reversal of her outraged morality would have been understood by the audience as lapses in both morality and judgment.

Although Pandarus has been proven to be no friend to Troilus (and an improper uncle to Criseyde), and his lying has been pointed out by several critics of the poem, his overall reputation is not so tarnished as one might expect. P. M. Kean, for example, finds that "his business, the zeal with which he drives his niece like a deer to Troilus' net, may at times appal us, but we cannot deny that the total effect is of a figure for whom we feel liking and that his charm and tact reflect a pleasant light on the other two main figures—to have provoked such zeal and such devotion is an added worthiness."[41] Those who "like" Pandarus perhaps should not, for his charm and tact are in fact hypocritical. Any positive feelings we may have about Pandarus are more likely our responses to Chaucer's lively portrayal of him than to the negative moral valences that Chaucer also provides him with. As with the counselors of Amant in the _Romance of the Rose_, on whom to some extent Pandarus is modelled, glibness cannot be divorced from counsel. Besides which, Pandarus mixes charm with bullying, tact with sarcasm. Like the _vetulae_ described by Guilielmus Peraldus in his _Summa seu tractatus de viciis_, Pandarus is one of the _consiliatrices turpitudinis_ whose exhortations constitute one of the seven incitements to lechery.[42] If we see Pandarus for what he is and look closely at the text of the poem, his proverbial speech is accompanied by a counterpoint of unattractive images, words, and actions.

For example, shortly after Pandarus' entry on the scene he addresses his supposed friend Troilus as "'thow fol,'" (I, 618), a harsh term that follows on his attempts to learn the cause of Troilus' discomfiture by making him angry (I, 561–63).[43] Immediately after he calls Troilus a fool, Troilus demands to know how Pandarus, who has been unsuccessful in love himself, can presume to bring Troilus to bliss. This brings forth such a flood of proverbs, examples, and self-vindication from Pandarus that we may justifiably think he protests too much. There is another dimension to his situation, however. As one who advises on love in spite of a lack of success in its practice, Pandarus is not altogether dissimilar to the narrator of the poem. The narrator, though, is not an unsuccessful lover but rather one who does not love for "unliklynesse" (I, 16), and instead of advising lovers to indulge themselves, he says he will pray for them and write their woe (I, 47–50). By structuring his materials this way Chaucer shows two different kinds of "counselors," and sets off Pandarus' counsel by contrast.

Pandarus' vigorous response to Troilus' logical question about his abilities as a counselor should be examined at length as an example of Chaucer's use of verbal barrage to cover up inadequacy. In *Troilus and Criseyde* we may well ask with Troilus how a man who is unsuccessful in love can successfully advise in that pursuit, and we shall find, as does Troilus, that Pandarus' arguments are not very convincing. The basis for Pandarus' series of arguments is that the unlikely is nevertheless true. Thus one who goes wrong himself can still give good counsel, the blind man can lead the sighted, the fool can advise the wise, and the whetstone, while it cannot cut, can make a sharp knife, which leads him again to the fool who can alert the wise man. While many if not all of these ideas can be related to some bit of proverbial wisdom, the accumulation of a series of proverbs has the potential for the creation of a structure so top-heavy it will collapse of its own weight. The sententiousness of Prudence is not funny because she is, after all, Prudence, while the sententiousness of Pandarus *is* funny because he is, after all, Pandarus.[44]

Some insight into how we may read this passage is afforded by Pandarus' proclamation of the doctrine of contraries—a doctrine that can be used seriously or humorously depending upon the circumstances in which it is uttered.

"If thow do so, thi wit is wel bewared;
By his contrarie is every thyng declared.

For how myghte evere swetnesse han ben knowe
To him that nevere tasted bitternesse?
Ne no man may ben inly glad, I trowe,
That nevere was in sorwe or som destresse.
Eke whit by blak, by shame ek worthinesse,
Ech set by other, more for other semeth,
As men may se, and so the wyse it demeth.

Sith thus of two contraries is o lore,
I, that have in love so ofte assayed
Grevances, oughte konne, and wel the more,
Counseillen the of that thow art amayed."   [I, 636–48]

Like most doctrines, the doctrine of contraries can be employed by the sensible sensibly and by the foolish foolishly. Thus Lady Philosophy first teaches Boethius about false goods on the grounds that "hony is the more swete, if mouthes han first tasted savours that ben wykke" (Bk. III, m. 1), while a close parallel to Pandarus' theoretical statement may be found in the *Romance of the Rose*. There Amant declares, "thus things go by contraries; one is the gloss of the other. If one wants to define one of the pair, he must remember the other . . ." (p. 351).

The difference between Lady Philosophy and Amant is easy enough to perceive, for while Lady Philosophy is teaching Boethius about false goods, Amant employs the theory of contraries and an excursus on the sweet and the bitter in order to justify the seduction of both young girls and old women. Indeed, he goes so far as to conclude blithely that "he who has not tried evil will hardly ever know anything of the good" (p. 351), an idea that seems more than a bit self-serving considering that he is preparing to make his final assault on the rose. Amant continues with the proposition that one must know honor to know shame, which closely parallels Pandarus' contrast between shame and worthiness. The doctrine of contraries is, in itself, neither good nor bad, foolish nor wise. But Pandarus' employment of it is clearly self-serving, for he tries to convince Troilus that a loser can offer good advice. The whole passage is best judged in retrospect, when we learn that with Pandarus' scheming Troilus indeed seduces his lady but ends up sorrowing from love. It is doubtful that Chaucer intended this to be the proof of good as opposed to bad counsel.

Pandarus' next ploy is to recount to Troilus the text of Oenone's letter to Paris, arguing that there is a parallel between himself—one who is unsuccessful in love but who can give good advice—and Oenone. The analogy is fair enough as Pandarus tells it for Oenone says "'yet, peraunter, kan I reden the, / And nat myself'" (I, 668–69). What is remarkable is that Pandarus would use this story to attempt to convince Troilus of anything, for Paris' desertion of Oenone for Helen was the cause of the war that surrounds all the characters in the poem. Curiously, then, Oenone's story of the miseries brought on by an unfaithful lover is used to pry from Troilus the name of his own beloved so that Pandarus can advance his suit. In the edition of the *Heroides* that Chaucer used, this particular letter has an introductory gloss stating that Ovid's "intenzione" is to reprove lying husbands who leave their wives.[45] Pandarus' employment of the letter to encourage Troilus to accept him as a counselor in bringing Troilus to bliss is a neat reversal. That which reproves Troilus' brother Paris will nevertheless provide good advice for Troilus![46] The story of the betrayed lover is ominously proleptic for the reader, who already knows about the double sorrow of Troilus who is also to be betrayed; yet this nine-stanza passage is almost completely neglected critically.

Pandarus' subsequent relations with Troilus proceed along the general lines established by his calling Troilus a fool. He treats Troilus, who is, after all, a prince of the realm, with a kind of indulgent contempt. When Troilus is, in his suffering, about to disclose the name of his beloved, Pandarus' coolly detached thought is "'A ha! . . . here bygynneth game'" (I, 868), an image of hunter and prey that he will later use with reference to Criseyde.[47] His insistence that Troilus "confess" to the God of Love, accompanied by a recapitulation of Troilus' "sins" against that deity, establishes him in the role of confessor and "moral" advisor, which is an aspect of his function as evil counselor. In spite of his own failures in love and Troilus' superior social station, Pandarus leads him in "confession" and when Troilus grovels at his feet accepts it without comment or embarrassment.

In the second book Pandarus arranges under false pretenses for the lovers to meet. Typically, the man he deceives in the affair is chosen because he is the brother Troilus loves best (II, 1396–1400), indicating a disregard for any of Troilus' personal relationships other than the one Pandarus himself is fostering. Troilus himself is prompted to a remarkable degree. Pandarus not only tells him to write a letter to Criseyde, but also instructs him on the form ("'Ne scryvenyssh or craftily'" [II, 1026]) and on the usefulness of dribbling some tears on it ("'Biblotte it with thi teris ek a lite'" [II, 1027]). With a little flattery ("'I woot wel that thow wiser art than I / A thousand fold'" [II, 1002–3]), Pandarus manages to have Troilus agree to write the letter to Criseyde according to instruction, and he also arranges for Troilus to ride by Criseyde's house as and when advised. As Pandarus increasingly manipulates him, it is no wonder that Troilus "hym bisoughte of reed and som socours" (II, 1354). His capitulation to Pandarus of Book I is underscored in Book III when he says "'I wol the serve / Right as thi sclave'" (III, 390–91), an avowal Pandarus does not find it necessary to rebuff.

As Pandarus increasingly dominates him, Troilus begins to think like him. Thus after Pandarus' long discourse on his pandering, which he says he does "'Bitwixen game and ernest'" (III, 254), Troilus begins to call things by inappropriate names in the fashion of his mentor. Since Pandarus says of his manipulations that he has "'bigonne a gamen pleye'" (III, 250), Troilus goes further and says that what Pandarus does should be called "'gentilesse, / Compassioun, and felawship, and trist'" (III, 402–3). In the same manner he picks up Pandarus' language. Just as Pandarus had referred to the love affair as "'a gret empryse'" (II, 1391), now Troilus calls it "'this grete emprise'" (III, 416). Furthermore, just as Pandarus had earlier sworn that he would help Troilus in love even to the extent of pandering for his sister (I, 860–61), now Troilus offers as a token of his high esteem of Pandarus' "servise" "'my faire suster Polixene, / Cassandre, Eleyne, or any of the frape'" (III, 408–10). Small wonder that "held hym ech of other wel apayed" (III, 421), although the real lesson is that Troilus has learned all of Pandarus' less attractive qualities. Not only has he picked up his inappropriate language and his free way in offering of sisters, he has also learned how to dissimulate. "From every wight as fer as is the cloude / He was, so wel dissimulen he koude" (III, 433–34).[48]

Pandarus arranges for Troilus to conceal himself in a "stuwe" within his house in anticipation of Criseyde's arrival, but when it is time for him to join her, Troilus evinces some shyness. Pandarus is contemptuous of this, and after calling him a "'wrecched mouses herte'" (III, 736), he literally drags him forward "by the lappe" (III, 742). This is only a prelude, though, to the subsequent necessity Pandarus encounters, which is to lift Troilus bodily into Criseyde's bed (III, 1097). Troilus never sees any indignity in thus being physically manipulated by Pandarus, and indeed continues his seemingly habitual self-abasement by again kneeling to Pandarus (III, 1592), and again avowing that his life is dependent on Pandarus—"'For thorugh thyn help I lyve'" (III, 1613).

In some ways the degree of Troilus' acquiescence to Pandarus' will in seducing Criseyde is underscored by his very different relationship to Pandarus after he learns that Criseyde will depart. He rejects Pandarus' inducements to seek another lady, and to take Criseyde forcefully, causing Pandarus finally to despair of cheering him up since Troilus will no longer be counseled by him. "'Whoso wil nought trowen reed ne loore, / I kan nat sen in hym no remedie'" (V, 327–28). About the only "reed" (V, 428) he requests from Pandarus is the location of some place to try to cheer himself up while waiting for Criseyde's return. Pandarus, who has dissimulated to everyone else, now pretends a confidence about Criseyde's return that he does not in fact feel:

> "Ye, haselwode!" thoughte this Pandare,
> And to hymself ful softeliche he seyde,
> "God woot, refreyden may this hote fare,
> Er Calkas sende Troilus Criseyde!"
> But natheles, he japed thus, and pleyde,
> And swor, ywys, his herte hym wel bihighte,
> She wolde come as soone as evere she myghte.   [V, 505–11]

Pandarus is a realist, for all his hypocrisy, and he suspects that Troilus may as well say "'fare wel al the snow of ferne yere'" (V, 1176). This does not stop him from expounding Troilus' dream of the boar who kisses Criseyde in the manner he thinks Troilus would like to hear it. "'It may so be that it may signifie, / Hire fader'" (V, 1283–84). However, his heart is not in the deception. For the last time in the poem he offers advice "'My red is this . . .'" (V, 1292), suggesting again that Troilus write to his lady. This time, though, the deceitful Pandarus surprisingly hits on a plan to ascertain the truth: "'Now writ hire thanne, and thow shalt feele sone / A soth of al'" (V, 1308–9). Troilus and Pandarus do find out the truth from Criseyde's response, but the truth moves Troilus to seek his own death in arms (V, 1718) and Pandarus to wish the death of Criseyde. It is a bitter ending to Pandarus' role as Troilus' counselor.

Pandarus' treatment of Criseyde is much like his treatment of Troilus: a little flattery, a little mockery, a little physical prodding, and a great deal of manipulation and coercion through threats, promises, and lies. The man who will advise Troilus to blot a letter with his tears here sheds some presumably manufactured tears himself (II, 326). He alternately threatens her that if she denies Troilus' suit both he and Troilus will die (II, 323), and smoothly forecasts that any visits between the two will be thought of merely as "'love of frendshipe'" (II, 371). When Criseyde evinces her disillusioned incredulity at his advice, Pandarus counters with another threat of death, again casting her (not Troilus or himself) as somehow the guilty party:

> "But sith it liketh yow that I be ded,
> By Neptunus, that god is of the see,
> Fro this forth shal I nevere eten bred."   [II, 442–44]

Criseyde, seeing what she believes to be "the sorwful ernest" (II, 452) of Pandarus, begins to fall in with his plans. She thinks she can control the love affair if once she embarks upon it, and, determining "'ful sleighly for to pleie'" (II, 462), she insists on preserving her honor in the affair—an insistence that Pandarus does not overtly protest.

Pandarus, though, has other ideas. When, for example, she coyly declines to accept Troilus' letter, Pandarus refuses to take no for an answer: "'Refuse it naught,' quod he, and hente hire faste, / And in hire bosom the lettre down he thraste" (II, 1154–55). The narrative underscores his insistent pressure on Criseyde shortly after she takes the letter, when, following her sight of Troilus himself, Pandarus "Felte iren hoot, and he bygan to smyte" (II, 1276). The blow he delivers is another threat of Troilus' death if she fails to have "routhe." Criseyde again tries to delimit the affair, this time by suggesting she grant him only her sight, and again Pandarus makes no overt protestation. What he thinks, though, is very different, for while he hypocritically assents to her plan, he inwardly determines to undermine it:

> But Pandarus thought, "It shal nought be so,
> Yif that I may; this nyce opynyoun
> Shal nought be holden fully yeres two."
> What sholde I make of this a long sermoun?
> He moste assente on that conclusioun,
> As for the tyme . . .   [II, 1296–1301]

We have already noted that in his manipulative attitude towards Troilus Pandarus employed a hunting metaphor to describe Troilus' uttering of Criseyde's identity—"'here bygynneth game'" (I, 868). The image of the hunter and his prey is used even more callously with regard to Criseyde herself when Pandarus describes his bringing her to Troilus as driving the "'deer unto thi bowe'" (II, 1535). Since the deer is driven to the bow to be slain, it is hard to assume that Pandarus thinks he is doing an admirable thing in arranging for the seduction of his niece. His own words suggest otherwise. Moreover, while Troilus was an accomplice in Pandarus' scheme for the couple to meet at Deiphebus' house and at Pandarus', Criseyde is "al innocent" (II, 1562) of the first meeting and Pandarus "swor hire nay" (III, 570) when she asked if Troilus would be at the proposed dinner party.

When he is not smiting hot iron, driving the deer, or deceiving the innocent, Pandarus uses other means of applying pressure on Criseyde. As with Troilus he leads her "by the lappe" (III, 59), but also prods her a bit when he is eager for an answer: "Pandare wep as he to water wolde, / And poked evere his nece new and newe" (III, 115–16). Then, when her response indicates bewilderment (whether feigned or not is a matter for surmise), he sarcastically mimics her to elicit the answer he wants to hear:

> "I! what?" quod she, "by God and by my trouthe,
> I not nat what ye wilne that I seye."
> "I! what?" quod he, "that ye han on hym routhe,
> For Goddes love, and doth hym nought to deye."
>
> [III, 120–23]

This belittling approach is used again by Pandarus when Criseyde is told that Troilus has been hidden in Pandarus' house awaiting her. She suggests that Pandarus take him a ring as a token of her good faith, and Pandarus comments acerbically on her reasoning powers:

> "A ryng?" quod he, "ye, haselwodes shaken!
> Ye, nece myn, that ryng moste han a stoon
> That myhte dede men alyve maken;
> And swich a ryng trowe I that ye have non.
> Discrecioun out of youre hed is gon." [III, 890–94]

Criseyde must be judged for accepting Pandarus' advice when her own good sense impelled her to behave differently, but his natural authority as the uncle of a widowed woman perhaps mitigates her error. As the narrator observes "as his nece, [she] obeyed as hire oughte" (III, 581). Moreover, there is no doubt that at least to some extent she is deceived by Pandarus as well as bullied. While we might think that she could have learned a little sooner of Pandarus' unreliability, certainly there is greater fault with him for deceiving her than with her for being deceived. As she puts it, "'for al youre wordes white, / O, whoso seeth yow, knoweth yow ful lite'" (III, 1567–68). Pandarus' response to this is a strangely ambivalent kiss—surely not one of peace, perhaps one of lust, or perhaps like Judas', one of betrayal, offered after the fact rather than before.[49]

According to the données of the poem Pandarus has an obligation to give moral counsel to Criseyde, and this obligation he inverts as a type of Evil Counselor. At the end of the poem his professed hatred of Criseyde for her "treachery" is not too different from his earlier contempt for her while he exploited her. For all his proverbs, jokes, and positive thinking, Pandarus is no true friend to Troilus and is irresponsible, callous, and sexually harassing in his role as Criseyde's uncle. If we are to understand the character of Pandarus, we must discriminate between what he says and what he does, between his oft-admired good humor and his regularly neglected penchant for bullying. And, finally, we must not mistake Pandarus' enthusiasm for Chaucer's and so think, with Tatlock, that Chaucer "evidently tolerates and even rather likes him." [50] Meech has tried to excuse the many faults he finds in Pandarus by saying "censure on all counts is mollified by an affection more engagingly evidenced in him than in Pandaro toward friend and relative. . . ." [51] Rather, it is the *lack* of anything like true affection for his friend and his relative that permits Pandarus to play his role as Evil Counselor.

Blind Fortune, Blind Cupid, Blind Troilus

Insofar as Criseyde lacks one of the eyes of Prudence, she may be said to have a metaphorical impairment of her moral and intellectual vision; insofar as Pandarus comfortably remarks that he has "'ek seyn a blynd man goo / Ther as he fel that couthe loken wide'" (I, 628–29), he may be said to be a metaphorically blind guide; insofar as Troilus is "'Cupides sone'" (V, 1590), he may be said to be the major vehicle for the imagery of blindness that pervades the poem. He is the figure who serves both the "blynde and wynged sone" of Venus, "daun Cupide" (III, 1808), and succumbs to the goddess styled in the translation of Boethius as "thilke blynde goddesse Fortune" (Bk. II, pr. 1). With Chaucer's characteristic fondness for indirection, Troilus is never *said* to be either literally or figuratively blind, but rather is *shown* to be metaphorically blind by his impressment into the ranks of the lovers he has himself called "'veray fooles'" who are "'nyce and blynde'" (I, 202).

This passage in Book I on the blindness of lovers leads into a discussion of the God of Love rather than Cupid, but as we earlier noted that for literary purposes Venus and the God of Love could often be considered as functioning in much the same way, so too Cupid and the God of Love can to a considerable degree be identified in the works of Chaucer. Cupid is called the "god of love" in *LGW*, 1140, and also in the ME *Romaunt* we find "Cupide, / The God of Love, blynde as stoon" (3702–3). Although no explicit statement is made in the *Troilus* that Cupid and the God of Love are the same, the God of Love's arrow, shot at Troilus, suggests Cupid's arrow, while Troilus' service of the "'blisful lord Cupide'" (V, 582) echoes his address to the God of Love as "'lord'" (I, 936). Similarly, no explicit statement is made in the poem that Fortune is blind, but Chaucer does note that she blinds her followers (IV, 5), while the general idea of blind Fortune was a commonplace in the Middle Ages. [52] Chaucer himself calls Fortune the "blind goddesse" (50) in his poem "Fortune," and it is worth noting that there as in Boethius' *Consolation* blindness is associated both with Fortune herself and with ignorance—of those who do not understand the philosophical distinctions between Fortune and Providence in "Fortune," and of those who cannot perceive the true good in the *Consolation*. Thus the "blinde bestes" (68) of "Fortune," the folk who "suffren hemselve to ben so blynde" (Bk. III, m. 8) of the *Consolation*, and the "blynde world" and "blynde entencioun" (I, 211) invoked by the narrator to describe Troilus' foolish provocation of the God of Love, can all be instructively compared.[53]

Chaucer's concern to align Troilus with both blind Cupid and blind Fortune is significant, for he develops his material very far beyond the few hints in Boccaccio's *Filostrato*. There, although blindness in love is mentioned a few times, as is Fortune, Cupid is not referred to at all. Moreover, neither the development of the ideas of blindness nor of the service of Fortune is present. Because of the numerous connections already noted in this study, it is my contention that Chaucer was inspired to develop Troilus' subjection to the two blind deities by certain passages in the *Romance of the Rose*—passages that may also have influenced Gower's *Vox Clamantis* if indeed Gower was not directly influenced by Chaucer himself. At any rate, the prominence of Fortune and Cupid in the *Troilus* is unlikely to be accidental, and indeed one can argue that the service of blind Cupid would inevitably lead a medieval audience to expect servitude to blind Fortune. Perhaps more than any other motif in the poem, the idea of blindness is the key to unlocking the tone of the work.[54]

The causal relationship between the service of the God of Love and the service of Fortune is implied rather than directly stated in the *Romance of the Rose*, but on the other hand it would be difficult to overestimate the extent to which the lover's unhappy situation is perceived as a specific manifestation of the general dangers of serving the goddess Fortune, who was represented by the ancients "with her eyes bandaged" (p. 122). In Jean de Meun's section of the poem we have what amounts to a Boethian commentary on the nature of love. As we noted in chapter 2, the lover's failure, causing him to be in the garden seeking the rose, is with his "wit," and so it is Reason rather than someone like Chastity or Humility who must come to his aid. Reason arrives from her tower and, like Philosophy, upon whom she is clearly modelled, talks to the lover at some length about love. In order that the lover may understand why the love he follows has made him unhappy, she first defines it, then contrasts it with good love, and then talks about the wheel of Fortune. As in the *Consolation* a discussion of Fortune leads into a consideration of those things that can bring true happiness, and all external goods are rejected as potential bearers of it. In fact, Reason points out to the lover's discomfiture, his desire to have the rose, which he wants as a "possession" (p. 99) is parallel to the desire for the more tangible gifts of Fortune, and so along with renouncing the love of wealth, along with renouncing the so-called love of friends for their wealth or for worldly esteem, the lover is also abjured to renounce "loving *par amour*" (p. 110). For the lover, who had earlier proclaimed that not to love *par amour* left him only the alternative of hating, Reason now lays open some more positive alternatives: he can love everyone unselfishly, which is to say he can be charitable, or he can love her. If, she assures him, he will leave the god who has put him in this plight, he will not "value at one prune the whole wheel of Fortune" (p. 117). She then bluntly makes three requests of the lover:

> They are that you will love me, that you despise the God of Love, and that you put no value on Fortune. If you are too weak to sustain this triple feat, I am ready to lighten it so that it may be more lightly carried. Take the first alone; and if you understand me sensibly you will be relieved of the others, for if you are not crazy or drunk, you should know . . . that whoever accords with Reason will never love *par amour* nor value Fortune.   [p. 132]

To which the lover illogically and absurdly replies that he cannot abandon his master Love, who will make him a hundred thousand times richer when he pleases, and besides Reason was discourteous in using the word "testicles."

If indeed Chaucer received a general idea from the *Romance* for his *Troilus*, he nevertheless presented the relationship between love *par amour* and Fortune in terms of imagery and action rather than dialogue and dialectic. That Cupid and Fortune were both blind did not escape the notice of the mythographers, and indeed Panofsky has noted that Blind Cupid was, in the later Middle Ages, especially associated with Fortune and Death.[55] The precise sources are not important. What matters is that Chaucer saw an opportunity to add to Boccaccio's *Filostrato* the themes of Troilus' subjection to both Fortune and Cupid, by which addition he would to a degree imitate the Boethian elements of the *Romance of the Rose*. But he decided merely to suggest rather than delineate their interrelatedness. This he effects by introducing into the key scene of Troilus' submission to the wheel and the arrow in Book I some very general imagery of blindness, which the reader must determine is pertinent to Troilus insofar as he becomes a follower of the two blind deities. Gower has much to say in the *Vox Clamantis* about Fortune, about the freedom of the will, and about the knight who "goes blindly mad because of his blind love" (p. 199), but Chaucer's subtlety is beyond him. In Book I Chaucer has Troilus call lovers blind fools, which arouses the traditionally blind God of Love—although he is not so specified here—then Chaucer notes that because of Troilus' "blynde entencioun" he has had to climb on the "staire" of the conventionally blind Fortune—although she is not so specified here— and then he compares Troilus with the conventionally blind Bayard—although he is not so specified here. Chaucer merely brings together the horse, the lover, blindness, and the two deities, and lets the reader make the connections.

The same indirect associations are found throughout the poem. In the Prohemium to Book IV Fortune is said to have the power to blind fools. Since "on hire whiel she sette up Diomede" (IV, 11), we understand that any blind, foolish love is, like that of Troilus and Diomede, in Fortune's domain, and conversely. This is confirmed directly when Troilus complains to Fortune (IV, 260) and to the God of Love (IV, 288) about his loss of Criseyde, and then displays his envy of those lovers who are "'heigh upon the whiel / . . . set of Fortune, in good aventure'" (IV, 323–24). The twin complaints to Fortune and to the God of Love in Book IV are echoed in Book V, where Troilus complains to Cupid (V, 582 ff.); yet later the narrator observes that it is Fortune who "japes" Troilus (V, 1134).

This, then, is the outline of the relationship that obtains among Troilus, Cupid, and Fortune—a relationship that depends more upon traditional associations than upon actual descriptions. Let us look now in more detail at the particulars of the several kinds of real and metaphorical blindness expressed and implied. On the simplest level, Troilus is just another lover made "blind" by passion much like January in the *Merchant's Tale* or like the knights mentioned by Gower in the *Vox Clamantis*. For this reason Troilus is firmly linked with Cupid in the poem, both by himself and by another. Criseyde addresses him as "'Cupides sone'" (V, 1590) in her letter to him from the Greek camp, and Troilus avers to Cupid "'I am thyn, and holly at thi wille'" (V, 587). If Troilus is the son and servant of Cupid—and therefore metaphorically the grandson of Venus—it behooves us to inquire more deeply into Cupid's significance. Not surprisingly, Cupid turns up several times in Book III in contexts associated with sexual success. When the lovers first kiss, Pandarus falls on his knees and utters a hymn of thanks to "'Immortal god'" who turns out to be "'Cupid I mene,'" who can be happy at the sight (III, 185–86). In a similar vein when the two lovers wish to progress from speaking to a closer relationship, it is Cupid they hope will send them "grace" to put an end to this phase of their affair so that the next can begin:

> . . . al this world so leef to hem ne were
> As that Cupide wolde hem grace sende
> To maken of hire speche aright an ende.   [III, 460–62]

And, finally, in the closing stanza of Book III, the narrator observes that his guiding deities thus far in the poem have been the nine Muses, Venus, and her "blynde and wynged sone ek, daun Cupide" (III, 1808).

Troilus the lover, then, is not surprisingly described as Cupid's son and servant, but it is important to note that while Cupid in Book III is related to the stages of success in the love affair, nevertheless when he is invoked by Troilus in Book V, it is to be blamed for Troilus' unhappiness. Thus in his "throwes frenetik and madde" he curses "Jove, Appollo, and ek Cupide" (V, 206–7), and later he asks at length why Cupid has been so unkind to him. The passage is important, for it shows that Troilus' inability to understand the inherent vicissitude of the service of Cupid is parallel to his inability to understand the same unevenness of Fortune.

Thanne thoughte he thus, "O blisful lord Cupide,
Whan I the proces have in my memorie,
How thow me hast wereyed on every syde,
Men myght a book make of it, lik a storie.
What nede is the to seke on me victorie,
Syn I am thyn, and holly at thi wille?
What joie hastow thyn owen folk to spille?

"Wel hastow, lord, ywroke on me thyn ire,
Thow myghty god, and dredefull for to greve!
Now mercy, lord! thow woost wel I desire
Thi grace moost of alle lustes leeve,
And lyve and dye I wol in thy byleve;
For which I n'axe in guerdoun but o bone,
That thow Criseyde ayein me sende sone.

"Distreyne hire herte as faste to retorne,
As thow doost myn to longen hire to see,
Than woot I wel that she nyl naught sojorne.
Now blisful lord, so cruel thow ne be
Unto the blood of Troie, I preye the,
As Juno was unto the blood Thebane,
For which the folk of Thebes caughte hire bane."

                                    [V, 582–602]

This remarkable prayer to Troilus' ruling deity, Cupid, rather too neglected by critics, underscores emphatically Chaucer's concern to show
Troilus' dependence upon the god. The corresponding passage in Boccaccio
is addressed to Love, not to Cupid.[56] The final request that Cupid not be as
cruel to the Trojan Troilus as Juno was to the Thebans raises a number of
ironies, for it was Jove's extramarital exploits that aroused Juno's ire, and it is
Paris' choice of Venus and of someone else's wife that lies behind the Trojan
difficulties.[57] Hence Troilus' prayer to Cupid, Venus' son, that Criseyde continue faithful to him in their extramarital relationship is a bit misdirected.
Neither Cupid nor Venus is concerned with constancy. It is not for nothing
that Cupid is styled as "the rechcheles" in the *Hous of Fame* (668). In medieval allegorizations of Cupid's iconographic appearance, his wings were commonly associated with love's mutability.[58] This long and significant passage,
then, simultaneously emphasizes Troilus' service of Cupid and his misunderstanding of Cupid's essential nature.

Troilus does not understand Cupid because he follows him. This seeming
paradox depends upon Cupid's blindness—a blindness that is taken on by his
followers and becomes not only the blindness of love specifically, but the
blindness of ignorance more generally. We have already noted that Chaucer

calls Cupid the blind and winged son of Venus at the end of Book III, and we must now ask what Cupid's blindness means. The classical Cupid was not blind or blindfolded, and the widespread development of this characteristic in the Middle Ages may be traced to the influence of various iconographers, who emphasized that his blindness signified the blindness of lovers. As Boccaccio more specifically put it, the blindfold of Cupid causes us to understand that lovers do not know where they are going, they lack judgment, cannot make distinctions, and are led solely by passion.[59] By the very nature of the service of Cupid, then, the servant will find it difficult to understand what it is that he is doing.

Cupid's wings, indicating mutability, and his blindness, indicating a kind of ignorance, are significantly like the characteristics of Fortune. Chaucer, we have noted, styles that lady as "blind goddesse" in his short poem "Fortune," the same words describe her in Chaucer's translation of Boethius' *Consolation* (Bk. II, pr. 1), and she was said to be blind as early as the time of Pliny.[60] Of course, her mutability needs no special evidence, for as Lady Philosophy puts it, "yif Fortune bygan to duelle stable, she cessede thanne to ben Fortune" (II, pr. 1, l. 114). As noted already, in Chaucer's poem "Fortune," not only is the goddess styled as blind, but she protests that those who complain about good and bad Fortune do not understand what they are talking about, and are in fact "blinde bestes" (68). The impeding of vision by blind Fortune is also made explicit throughout the imagery of Boethius' *Consolation*, for Lady Philosophy begins her treatment of the man suffering from Fortune by wiping "a litil his eien that ben dirked by the cloude of mortel thynges" (Bk. I, pr. 2). She continues by noting that "blisful is that man that may seen the clere welle of good!" (Bk. III, m. 12), she condemns the "blyndnesse of ignorance" (Bk. IV, pr. 2), and towards the end of the *Consolation* describes man's freedom in terms of sight:

> But the soules of men moten nedes be more fre whan thei loken hem in the speculacioun or lokynge of the devyne thought; and lasse fre whan thei slyden into the bodyes; and yit lasse fre whan thei ben gadrid togidre and comprehended in erthli membres. But the laste servage is whan that thei ben yeven to vices and han ifalle fro the possessioun of hir propre resoun. For aftir that thei han cast awey hir eyghen fro the lyght of the sovereyn sothfastnesse to lowe thingis and derke, anon thei derken by the cloude of ignoraunce. . . .   [Bk. V, pr. 2]

Figuratively speaking, then, the blindness of submission to Fortune is very much like the blindness of submission to Cupid, and in the *Troilus* we find both kinds. Troilus' submission to Fortune has been amply demonstrated by Robertson and needs no systematic redaction here.[61] It does, however, enhance our understanding of what is going on in the poem to recognize that Troilus' protestation against Cupid in Book V, which was discussed above, is parallel to his remarks on fate and free will in Book IV. Just as his submission to Fortune led to his inability to recognize the existence of free will, so his submission to Cupid blinded him to understanding Cupid's essentially fickle nature. The parallel nature of the two themes is alluded to, albeit somewhat obliquely, early on in the poem in a passage it will be profitable to reconsider.

When Troilus is satirizing lovers as "fooles" who are "blynde" (I, 202) he is already, in his pride, more than a little bit "blind" himself. It is this caustic remark about lovers that irks the God of Love, who, since he is virtually the same as Cupid, shoots an arrow at Troilus, and "hitte hym atte fulle" (I, 209). The very next stanza, as if to underscore the similarity of following Cupid and Fortune, abruptly shifts from Love to Fortune, and observes that in his pride (remember that Troilus was "Byholding ay the ladies of the town" [I, 186] while thinking himself immune to Love), Troilus has in fact submitted himself to Fortune:

> O blynde world, O blynde entencioun!
> How often falleth al the effect contraire
> Of surquidrie and foul presumpcioun;
> For kaught is proud, and kaught is debonaire.
> This Troilus is clomben on the staire,
> And litel weneth that he moot descenden;
> But alday faileth thing that fooles wenden.   [I, 211–17]

The imagery of the stanza is arresting. Blindness applies equally well to Fortune, to blind Cupid, and to Troilus himself. The "fooles" of the last line are fools of Fortune in one sense, but remind us inevitably of the blind fools of Love scorned by Troilus a few lines earlier, and proleptically tell us what Troilus is destined to become himself. Finally, we should note that the image of the stair that Troilus now ascends and later will descend applies equally well to his progress in love and to his fortune generally.

The images of blindness that follow in the poem present—not surprisingly—a measure of progression of intensity. The gentlest, and funniest, is Pandarus' confident if ridiculous contention that the blind can lead the blind—an assertion that by implication is unflattering to both the leader and the led, although Troilus seems incapable of seeing, as it were, the implication.

> "I have myself ek seyn a blynd man goo
> Ther as he fel that couthe loken wide;
> A fool may ek a wis-man ofte gide." [62]   [I, 628–30]

When the blind lead the blind, of course, both fall into the ditch. Amusingly enough, Chaucer stands this proverb on its head in order to make a little joke at his own expense. In the Prohemium to Book II, the narrator apologizes if he should speak of love unfeelingly:

> Ek though I speeke of love unfelyngly,
> No wondre is, for it nothyng of newe is;
> A blynd man kan nat juggen wel in hewis.   [II, 19–21]

The "blind" narrator, then, will nevertheless tell the story of those blind ones who follow the blind boy Cupid, becoming by extension a sort of blind leader of the blind. Without entering the disputed issue of the relationship between the narrator of the poem and Chaucer the man, it is still possible to see in the "blind" teller of the tale of love one of Chaucer's many jokes at his own expense in which he portrays himself as unlikely, ignorant, or unable in amatory matters. It is, ultimately, a very amusing variation on the modesty *topos*, used in this Prohemium to ring the changes on the theme of blindness in the poem.[63]

Book III has numerous oblique references to impairment of vision if not actual blindness, compounded by repeated references to darkness. That darkness would be important we are forwarned by the opening invocation of Tisiphone, who is later specified as one of "Nyghtes doughtren thre" (IV, 22). When Criseyde first visits Troilus in his sickroom in Deiphebus' house he looks up and asks "'Who is al ther? I se nought trewely'" (III, 67). Significantly, the time for the meeting of the lovers is set at the changing of the moon (a common symbol of the mutability of blind Fortune) "Whan lightles is the world a nvyght or tweyne" (III, 550). Further instances of this sort of imagery occur in the actual bedroom scene when Pandarus moves the candle away from the lovers, on the grounds that "'Light is nought good for sike folkes yën!'" (III, 1137). The lovers enjoy the dark, and when dawn comes Criseyde wishes that the night could last three days "'As longe as whan Almena lay by Jove'" (III, 1428). Troilus joins in with this theme, condemning the sun and averring that "'us nedeth no day have'" (III, 1463). And, later, "bitterly the dayes light thei corse" (III, 1701).

The fourth book opens significantly with imagery of folly and blindness repeated from the passages in Book I already examined.

> But al to litel, weylaway the whyle,
> Lasteth swich joie, ythonked be Fortune,
> That semeth trewest whan she wol bygyle,
> And kan to fooles so hire song entune,
> That she hem hent and blent, traitour comune!   [IV, 1–5]

Blind Fortune blinds her foolish followers, and Troilus, who is metaphorically already blind, will, in this book, wish for physical blindness. Whereas in Book III Troilus loved the darkness of night and cursed the day, now in his first knowledge of Criseyde's imminent departure he creates an artificial night of sorrow by closing every door and every window of his house (IV, 225–35). In this darkness he first rails against the inconstancy of Fortune, then against the fickleness of Cupid (invoked as "'O Love! O god, allas!'" [IV, 288]), indicating a kind of mental blindness. Then he vows to "'ende . . . as Edippe, in derknesse / My sorwful lif, and dyen in distresse'" (IV, 300–301).

Troilus' determination to blind himself as did Oedipus marks the most extreme use of the image of blindness in the poem. Chaucer adds this remark to his source, and in every way it underscores the thematic significance of blindness. To modern and classic sensibilities Oedipus' flaw was pride, something of which Troilus has a generous measure, but in addition to this Oedipus was thought to represent licentiousness by Fulgentius.[64] Thus the son of blind Cupid is consistent in wishing to blind himself physically like the licentious Oedipus. It is a threat uttered in a kind of bombast, though, for just a stanza later Troilus reverts to a promise of a more metaphorical blindness, based upon his loved one's absence:

> "O woful eyen two, syn youre disport
> Was al to sen Criseydes eyen brighte,
> What shal ye don but, for my discomfort,
> Stonden for naught, and wepen out youre sighte,
> Syn she is queynt, that wont was yow to lighte?
> In vayn fro this forth have ich eyen tweye
> Ifourmed, syn youre vertu is aweye."   [IV, 309–15]

At any rate, in his suffering his physical vision is certainly impaired, for after his muddled soliloquy on predestination, Pandarus observes that "'in thyn hed thyne eyen semen dede'" (IV, 1092).

There is some further mention of Troilus' visual impairment in the poem, and in contrast with Troilus' grandiose metaphors about his useless eyes, the emphasis is pathetically literal. When Troilus and Pandarus stand on the wall, looking for Criseyde who has promised to return, Troilus excitedly says "'I se hire! yond she is! / Heve up thyn eyen, man! maistow nat se?'" (V, 1158–59). But, when Pandarus looks, all that he sees is a "'fare-carte'" (V, 1162). Troilus' spiritual blindness has now become a physical inability. After this point in Book V we hear that hope always blinded Troilus (V, 1195), and Troilus tells us in his letter to Criseyde that his tearful eyes see only in vain (V, 1373–74). Now, at the very end of the poem, we are ready for all the reversals that come about after Troilus' death, when his soul is liberated from his body. As in T. S. Eliot's "Burnt Norton," earthly concerns are reconciled among the stars.

If Troilus was blind both metaphorically and to an extent literally while alive, after death his spirit is characterized by vision and understanding, which replace his ignorance and blindness. Expectably he sees, and what he both sees and understands is the motion of the erratic stars: "And ther he saugh, with ful avysement, / The erratik sterres" (V, 1811–12). Beyond that what he sees is, paradoxically, blindness, for he understands and condemns "blynde lust" (V, 1824). The man who, in spite of his protestations, became one of the blind fools he held in contempt is now changed utterly. The man who protested to Pandarus that he was not deaf (I, 753), in spite of a certain metaphorical deafness of a piece with his blindness, now hears as well as sees, for the stars make harmony "With sownes ful of hevenyssh melodie" (V, 1813).[65] And, although Chaucer does not allude to the idea overtly, one wonders if the imagery of "loves daunce" (II, 1106), the "olde daunce" (III, 695), and "th'amorouse daunce" (IV, 1431) that typified carnality on earth is not here replaced by the "dance" of the stars, which was a common medieval term used to describe the motion that accompanied their heavenly harmony.[66]

We do not know what power frees Troilus to see and to hear and to understand, what power raises him from the earthly dance, but we do know who can help us and how. For our lust, a manifestation of our erring natures generally, there is the "moral Gower" (V, 1856), and for our ignorance the "philosophical Strode" (V, 1857). That Gower, who said he was blind in the Dedicatory Epistle to *Vox Clamantis*, is here made the dedicatee of Chaucer's poem with its abundant imagery of metaphorical blindness is probably not coincidental.

More generally, the enemies we can recognize are not as dangerous as those we cannot see. We must be on guard against both "visible and invisible foon" (V, 1866) the poet acknowledges, but it is those that are invisible to us against whom we need the most help. And so, the imagery progresses from Tisiphone, the daughter of Night who opened the poem, to Mary, the mother of Christ the light of the world. The poem opens with an invocation of the cruel Fury, and closes with an invocation of the "mayde and moder . . . benigne" (V, 1869). Thus there is a movement from woe to joy as well as from darkness to light. If Fortune and Cupid bring blindness and darkness, nevertheless the means for redress are available to Chaucer's readers even if they were not to Troilus himself. After Chaucer dedicates his poem to the moral Gower and the philosophical Strode, he then invokes the Trinity to protect us from the foes we can and cannot see, significantly using language from Dante's *Paradiso* XIV—the canto of the prudent in the sphere of the light-giving sun, the canto which gave Chaucer the idea of three-eyed Prudence to characterize something lacking in Criseyde.

> Thow oon, and two, and thre, eterne on lyve,
> That regnest ay in thre, and two, and oon,
> Uncircumscript, and al maist circumscrive,
> Us from visible and invisible foon
> Defende, and to thy mercy, everichon,
> So make us, Jesus, for thi mercy digne,
> For love of mayde and moder thyn benigne.
>
> [V, 1863–69]

We need prudence, we need light, and we need Christ and Mary, both of whom cure blindness. As we observed earlier, Christ is regularly a healer of the blind, and in his "ABC" Chaucer calls Mary "verrey light of eyen that ben blynde" (105).[67] Thus the poem that began with sorrow, the cruel Fury Tisiphone, daughter of Night, the blind God of Love, and a narrator who ironically claimed to be in "derknesse" (I, 18), now ends with the joyous images of a loving God (not a God of Love), light, and the benign Mary, cure for blindness.

Epilogue

A book that treats the elements of the *Troilus* is perforce somewhat elementary, and a work that is elementary and introductory cannot really have a conclusion. Nevertheless, this study, like the poem it addresses, has an epilogue.

Chapter 1 of this study, on the principal source of Chaucer's *Troilus*, presents a tentative reading of the *Filostrato* and a plea for more and better work on this curiously neglected and challenging poem. Before we can know with any precision what Chaucer did to the *Filostrato*, we had better have a clearer idea of what the Italian poem is and says. Too many studies of the *Troilus* have neglected the *Filostrato* (and the other versions of the Troy story), and those that have adduced Boccaccio's poem for comparison have not infrequently looked at changes from the source without much concern for the tone and meaning of the original. Throughout this study the neglected influence of the *Romance of the Rose* on the *Troilus* has been noted, and it is a subject large and important enough to demand a book-length treatment in its own right. I have only glanced at the story of Thebes, but its significance in the *Troilus* also deserves more study. Finally, the tone of the *Troilus* cannot be fully appreciated without a consideration of the Ovidian elements in the poem—an issue not even raised in the present inquiry.

Chapter 2, on love and will, attempts to refute the commonplace critical assumption that Troilus is not free to choose with regard to love. I have moreover tried to show that the issues of love, freedom, marriage, and loyalty in Old Troy are essentially the same as those treated by John Gower in his poem *Vox Clamantis* about New Troy. In an as yet unpublished essay, D. W. Robertson, Jr., has sharpened the parallels between Chaucer's London of the mid-1380s and Old Troy. It is very thought-provoking to reflect that Chaucer's poem about Troy and Troilus, with its intrinsic and unavoidable parallels with the New Troy of London, might have been read before the court during the difficult times when John of Gaunt was mounting his "crusade" against Spain, and England feared invasion from France. If the *Troilus* were indeed, as some would have it, a great poem in praise of love, it would have been received as something very irrelevant to the times—having all solas and no sentence. If, however, it was perceived as a poem about love and duty, about the claims of the libido and the claims of reason, about chivalry and survival, about service of country as well as service of ladies, then it would have been received as Gower's poem undoubtedly was: as a poem offering both delight and instruction.

Chapters 3 and 4 of this study are both, in one way or another, about love. Although not so many critics today as formerly try to justify their readings of the *Troilus* with appeals to courtly love, I have nevertheless thought it instructive to look at the history of that subject as it relates to analyses of the *Troilus*. Whether one appeals to courtly love or to the text of the poem, it is hard to maintain that Troilus is ennobled by his love for Criseyde or that any love ruled by Venus and Cupid could, in medieval times, lead to positive values. Whatever we moderns may think of the value of Troilus' love or his faithfulness, our medieval ancestors found greater contrast between kinds of love—heavenly and earthly, wedded and unwedded—than we do. Troilus' fidelity to the unfaithful Criseyde strikes a strong responsive chord in modern estimates of the poem, yet Criseyde's fickleness is an emblem of the mutable Fortune Troilus also embraces. As every reader of Boethius knows, it is not through the mutable that one finds happiness. Truth, as Chaucer makes clear in his little poem of that title, is opposed to Fortune. Thus Troilus' allegiance to the unfaithful, mutable Criseyde, cannot possibly bring him happiness, either immediate or ultimate. In the last analysis, one cannot be true to the false.[1]

The last chapter, on the imagery accompanying the three principals of the poem, focuses on images that carry with them strong negative, judgmental connotations. Although many critics are uncomfortable with the idea that a great poet might make judgments—especially judgments with which his critics might not agree—medieval poets seem more regularly to praise or blame than to remain in some sort of Keatsian state of unresolved contraries. Happily, critical uneasiness about judgmental tonalities may be disappearing. In very recent times Stephanie Yearwood has argued from a rhetorical analysis of the *Troilus* that its tone is "detached and judgmental." In a similar vein Thomas H. Bestul has likened the narrator's tears to the rhetorical weeping of St. Augustine for Dido, while Michael Olmert has concluded from a line in *Piers Plowman* that in the fourteenth century the *Troilus* was understood as a story of "treachery, betrayal, and trust misplaced in the transitory nature of human life." Thomas E. Maresca, by demonstrating that Troilus is the antithesis of an epic hero—indeed that he prefigures the heroes of mock epic—implicitly inclines toward a reading of the poem in which judgments play a part.[2] These various readings of the judgmental nature of the poem are, I believe, warranted on the grounds their authors advance, and also in light of the somewhat broader background examined here. Although many find it hard to believe that the "blynde lust" Troilus condemns from the spheres is the same love for Criseyde described earlier, the evidence presented here suggests that it must be. Thus if this love is shown to be attractive, it is only so in the sense that all false or lesser goods must be attractive or no one would follow them,

while if this love is praised, it is to be understood ironically. As John Steadman has shown, the *Troilus*, like Boethius' *Consolation*, uses error to proceed
to knowledge. Charles Dahlberg has similarly argued that it is from the use of
unlike signs to show celestial things that later medieval vernacular literatures
derived their characteristic use of irony and contrast.[3] To cite Steadman
again, the *Troilus*, like other tragedies, ". . . might be a *carmen reprehensivum
viciorum*, even though the vices it portrays are more amiable than those of the
conventional tragic protagonist and spring rather from concupiscence than
from violence or fraud."[4] Those critics who do not respond positively to the
love affair in the *Troilus* are sometimes declared to be "reductive" by those
who do. Of course, in one sense all criticism is reductive, but the criticism
that finds Chaucer condemning the love of Troilus sees the poem as different
from, not as less complicated than (for that is what I think is meant by this
use of reductive), the reading of it as praising both loves in their different
spheres or trying but failing to condemn earthly love. The complexity I find
in the poem is not in the subject matter but in the treatment of it, which
alternates between direct and ironic statement. St. Augustine did not mean to
reduce the Bible when he argued that it preached charity and condemned
cupidity, nor did Boccaccio mean to disparage his idol, Dante, when he said
that the allegorical subject of the *Commedia* had to do with God's rewarding
and punishing justice. Yet many modern critics feel almost instinctively that
greatness must arise from or depend on some sort of nonjudgmental con-
trariety or indecision.[5] Statements about the "simultaneous rejection and
affirmation of the world," are characteristic not only of essays on Chaucer but
also of twentieth-century responses to Dante's *Commedia*. However, the early
commentaries by Pietro, Benevenuto, Jacopo, and Boccaccio simply do not
use this sort of vocabulary.[6] When we do find a yoking together of opposites
in medieval literature or criticism, as when Walter Map opens his letter to
Ruffinus by saying that he is forbidden to speak yet cannot keep silent, the
effect is intended to be rhetorical rather than to display a genuine intellectual
ambivalence.

If we insist on placing our own views about romantic love on top of medieval ones, we may write criticism that is more palatable to us, but not always
faithful to its subject. One recent critic, having discovered a fifteenth-century
text in which a verse of the *Troilus* is used as part of a condemnation of romantic love outside of marriage, prefers his own interpretation to the earlier
one and writes of it: "our reader begins his condemnation of love by quoting
one of the most beautiful stanzas of love poetry in the language, and despite
its new context the stanza remains to an important degree what it is in *Troilus
and Criseyde*—a celebration and submission to the god of love."[7] What I have
tried to do in this study is to draw attention to images that require us to respond negatively rather than positively to the love affair in the poem. If we do
so respond, we do not lose anything. The poem is still a poem, albeit one with

moral judgments, and it is demonstrably sad, funny, cautionary, yet ultimately optimistic. Indeed, I would submit that the moralistic, judgmental
reading of the poem adds to its literary complexity and does not reduce but
enhances it as a literary document.

Chaucer's Parson says, much too bluntly for modern taste, ". . . fornica-
cioun, that is bitwixe man and womman that been nat maried . . . is deedly
synne, and agayns nature" (*ParsT*, 865). It is uncomfortable to hear lovemak-
ing described as fornication, perhaps irritating to be reminded of the medieval concern for sin, and the idea that sex outside of marriage is unnatural
would meet with outright rejection by most contemporary thinkers. And yet,
whatever medieval people did in their private lives, when they wrote about
love and marriage they regularly wrote about it in terms of this sort. The
anonymous commentary on *The Chess of Love*, for example, asserts that although Venus inclines the heart towards concupiscence, nevertheless it is important for man to follow the rule of reason in matters of concupiscence, "or
he disnatures himself. . . ." [8] What is natural to us could be "disnaturing" to
Chaucer, and in the Middle Ages the libido was not something opposed to the
id but rather to reason; hence it is called "fallax libido" by Pseudo-Aristotle
in his *Commentary on Boethius*. [9]

Gower closes his *Confessio Amantis* with a contrast between wedded, honest love and other, lesser kinds. It is hard to imagine that Chaucer would
write a poem praising unmarried love and dedicate it to Gower. As Paul
Strohm has nicely put it, Gower ". . . treats the behavior of lovers as a metaphor for social behavior in general, with the amorous promptings of lovers
offered as examples of the failure of self-regulation which has undermined
personal and worldly order. . . ." [10] It is this medieval sense of the role of the
individual's free actions in the historical past, present, and future of a state
that most sharply differentiates the appearance of the Trojan love affair to a
medieval as opposed to a modern audience. In a brilliant essay approaching
the *Troilus* semiotically, Eugene Vance has written:

> . . . we know . . . that this war . . . has been initiated by an erotic trans-
> gression, by that breaking of "trouthe" (troth + truth) which occurred
> when Paris, a Trojan, absconded with Helen, a Greek; we also know . . .
> that this war will be perpetrated yet again and again through successive
> erotic transgressions in that future which is our past and also (unless we
> use signs properly) the future of England itself: the *Troilus* as an English
> poem is both history and potential prophecy. [11]

What I have tried to do in these pages is to draw up a plan for an interpretation of the *Troilus* that would take into account both the text and the historical context. Because Gower's *Vox Clamantis* displays the relationship of free
individual choice, the service of Venus, and the welfare of the state very
clearly, I have in essence asked for—and sometimes attempted—a "Gower-

ian" reading of the *Troilus*. If we bear in mind what Chaucer and Gower thought about the love of self and the love of country, about brotherly love, wedded love, unwedded love, love of friends, love of family, and love of God, we shall find in the *Troilus* a poem that may be read on its own terms as condemning lovers and their love, but also as a great poem in praise of other loves.

Notes

Abbreviations

AM	*Annuale Mediaevale*
ChauR	*The Chaucer Review*
E&S	*Essays and Studies*
EETS	Early English Text Society
EIC	*Essays in Criticism*
ELH	*English Literary History*
ELN	*English Language Notes*
ES	*English Studies*
JEGP	*Journal of English and Germanic Philology*
M&H	*Medievalia et Humanistica*
MLN	*Modern Language Notes*
MLQ	*Modern Language Quarterly*
MP	*Modern Philology*
MS	*Mediaeval Studies*
N&Q	*Notes and Queries*
NLH	*New Literary History*
NM	*Neuphilologische Mitteilungen*
PL	*Patrologia Latina*
PLL	*Papers on Language and Literature*
PMASAL	*Papers of the Michigan Academy of Science, Arts, and Letters*
PMLA	*Publications of the Modern Language Association of America*
PQ	*Philological Quarterly*
RES	*Review of English Studies*
SP	*Studies in Philology*
TSLL	*Texas Studies in Literature and Language*

Preface

1. All quotations are from *The Works of Geoffrey Chaucer*, ed. F. N. Robinson, 2nd ed. (Boston, 1957), and will be cited by abbreviation in the text. Italics have occasionally been added for emphasis.

2. C. S. Lewis, *The Allegory of Love* (New York, 1958), pp. 197, 43. First published in 1936. Walter Clyde Curry, "Destiny in Troilus and Criseyde," reprinted in *Chaucer Criticism: Troilus*

and Criseyde and the Minor Poems, ed. Richard J. Schoeck and Jerome Taylor (Notre Dame, 1961), II, 69. Henceforth this volume will be cited as Schoeck and Taylor, II.

3. Howard Rollin Patch, *On Rereading Chaucer* (Cambridge, Mass., 1939), pp. 57, 60–61.

4. John P. McCall, *Chaucer Among the Gods: The Poetics of Classical Myth* (University Park, Pa., 1979), pp. 30–35, 98.

5. Monica E. McAlpine, *The Genre of Troilus and Criseyde* (Ithaca, N.Y., and London, 1978), pp. 148–217.

6. *The Book of Troilus and Criseyde*, ed. Robert Kilburn Root (Princeton, 1926), p. 1; James Lyndon Shanley, "The *Troilus* and Christian Love," Schoeck and Taylor, II, 136–46; D. W. Robertson, Jr., "Chaucerian Tragedy," Schoeck and Taylor, II, 86–121, and his redaction of the essay in *A Preface to Chaucer* (Princeton, 1962), pp. 472–503; Roger Sharrock, "Second Thoughts: C. S. Lewis on Chaucer's *Troilus*," *EIC*, 8 (1958): 123–37. Sharrock perhaps belongs with those who find a qualification of the praise of earthly love, but it is so qualified I have placed him with Root, Robertson, and Shanley. His words are that the poem is "tender in its recognition of the limited human goodness of passionate love . . . but agonizingly aware of its limitations" (p. 128).

7. This interpretation has been advanced by H. A. Kelly, John B. Maguire, and Karl P. Wentersdorf. None of the critics adequately deals with the problem of the disparagement of earthly love at the end of the poem, which would seem strikingly inappropriate if the love of Troilus and Criseyde had been wedded rather than illicit love. Because married love is "figured" (*ParsT*, 922) by the marriage between Christ and the Church, it is hard to imagine its being condemned as "wordly vanyte" (V, 1837). For other objections see chapter 4, n. 37. The works referred to are Henry Ansgar Kelly, *Love and Marriage in the Age of Chaucer* (Ithaca and London, 1975), pp. 49–67, 217–42, 286–331; "Clandestine Marriage and Chaucer's 'Troilus'," *Viator*, 4 (1973): 435–57; John B. Maguire, "The Clandestine Marriage of Troilus and Criseyde," *ChauR*, 8 (1974): 262–78; Karl P. Wentersdorf, "Some Observations on the Concept of Clandestine Marriage in *Troilus and Criseyde*," *ChauR*, 15 (1980): 101–26.

8. Ida L. Gordon, "The Narrative Function of Irony in Chaucer's *Troilus and Criseyde*," in *Medieval Miscellany Presented to Eugène Vinaver*, ed. F. Whitehead, et al. (Manchester, 1965), pp. 149–50.

9. Charles Dahlberg, "Love and the *Roman de la Rose*," *Speculum*, 44 (1969): 568–84; *The Romance of the Rose*, trans. Charles Dahlberg (Princeton, 1971), pp. 1–27; Robertson, *Preface*, pp. 196–207, 361–65; Rosemond Tuve, *Allegorical Imagery: Some Mediaeval Books and Their Posterity* (Princeton, 1966), pp. 239–80; John V. Fleming, *The Roman de la Rose: A Study in Allegory and Iconography* (Princeton, 1969).

10. *Boccaccio's Two Venuses* (New York, 1977).

11. Oxford, 1970.

Chapter I

1. *The Filostrato of Giovanni Boccaccio*, trans. Nathaniel Edward Griffin and Arthur Beckwith Myrick (Philadelphia, 1929), pp. 127, 115. Subsequent citations and translations will be from this edition, with the general practice of citing longer passages in translation. For greater clarity I have used the Italian names whenever referring to the Italian poem, even when citing the translation. I have followed Griffin and Myrick in using the spelling *Troilo*, although it is *Troiolo* in most editions.

2. C. S. Lewis, "What Chaucer Really Did to *Il Filostrato*," Schoeck and Taylor, II, 19; Thomas A. Kirby, *Chaucer's Troilus: A Study in Courtly Love* (Gloucester, Mass., 1958), p. 93 (first published 1940); Sanford B. Meech, *Design in Chaucer's Troilus* (Syracuse, 1959), p. 387; Robert P. apRoberts, "Love in the *Filostrato*," *ChauR*, 7 (1972): 1. An essay similar to C. S. Lewis', but finding more irony, is Ian C. Walker's "Chaucer and *Il Filostrato*," *ES*, 49 (1968): 318–26.

3. *The Book of Troilus and Criseyde by Geoffrey Chaucer*, ed. Robert Kilburn Root (Princeton, 1926), p. xlix.

4. One of the few scholars to study Boccaccio's poem within its own terms of reference is Mi-

chael H. Blechner. In an as yet unpublished essay, "Foolish Love in Boccaccio's *Il Filostrato*," delivered to the Tenth Conference on Medieval Studies, Western Michigan University, May 6, 1975, Blechner argues persuasively that Boccaccio does not glorify the love between Troilo and Criseida, but attacks it, portraying Troilo as a follower of irrational love who becomes foolish, idolatrous, and unpatriotic as a result. The essay regrettably did not come to my attention until after my own study of Boccaccio was completed. I am grateful to him for letting me read a copy of the text of his speech. Robert Hollander's admirable study of all of Boccaccio's minor works (*Boccaccio's Two Venuses*) also takes an unsentimental view of the *Filostrato* and like Blechner's shorter piece was not available to me until after my own work was completed. I am grateful to him for letting me read his book in manuscript.

5. *Contributo agli studi di Giovanni Boccaccio* (Turin, 1887). I follow Griffin's summary of the love affair.

6. *Chaucer's Troylus and Cryseyde Compared with Boccaccio's Filostrato*, ed. and trans. William Michael Rossetti (London, 1873), Chaucer Society nos. 57 & 59, p. 1; Karl Young, *The Origin and Development of the Story of Troilus and Criseyde* (London, 1908), Chaucer Society, ser. 2, no. 40, pp. 28–30, 40; A. Lytton Sells, *The Italian Influence in English Poetry: From Chaucer to Southwell* (Bloomington, Ind., 1955), pp. 38–41; Herbert G. Wright, *Boccaccio in England from Chaucer to Tennyson* (London, 1957), p. 59; Mario Praz, *The Flaming Heart* (Gloucester, Mass., 1966), p. 79 (first published 1958); Meech, *Design*, pp. viii, 5–6; Paul G. Ruggiers, "The Italian Influence on Chaucer," in *Companion to Chaucer Studies*, ed. Beryl Rowland, rev. ed. (Toronto, 1979), p. 172; Howard Schless, "Transformations: Chaucer's Use of Italian," in *Geoffrey Chaucer*, ed. Derek Brewer (Columbus, Ohio, 1975), p. 208. This is not a complete list. Ruggiers' contribution to the *Companion* has a very useful bibliography. Two standard works on Chaucer and Boccaccio that do *not* talk about the autobiographical element in the Italian writer are Hubertis M. Cummings' *The Indebtedness of Chaucer's Works to the Italian Works of Boccaccio* (New York, 1965), first published 1916, and Mungo MacCallum, *Chaucer's Debt to Italy* (Sydney, 1934).

7. *The Works of Geoffrey Chaucer* (Boston, 1957), p. 386; "Love in the *Filostrato*," p. 10.

8. Giuseppe Billanovich, *Restauri Boccacceschi* (Rome, 1947); Vittore Branca, "Profilo Biografico," in *Tutte le opere di Giovanni Boccaccio*, ed. Vittore Branca (Verona, 1967), I, 26–28. See also *Opere*, II, 3–4; *Boccaccio, The Man and His Works*, trans. Richard Monges (New York, 1976), pp. 1–86; Walter Pabst, *Venus als Heilige und Furie in Boccaccios Fiammetta-Dichtung* (Krefeld, 1958); Bernhard König, *Die Begegnung im Tempel: Abwandlungen eines literarischen Motivs in den Werken Boccaccios* (Hamburg, 1960). The latter work, which brilliantly explores the presumed meeting of Boccaccio and his Fiammetta in church as a *topos* deriving from classical and earlier medieval literatures, shows how interesting Boccaccio can be when we go beyond autobiographical criticism.

9. "Schemi litterari e schemi autobiografici," in *Boccaccio Medievale* (Florence, 1964), p. 170n. Piero Boitani is one of the few Chaucerian scholars to acknowledge Branca's autobiographical dicta, but his analysis of the *Filostrato* is conventional. See *Chaucer and Boccaccio*, Medium Aevum Monographs, n.s. no. 8 (Oxford, 1977).

10. Branca notes of Boccaccio's celebrated "conversion" in later life that the presumed licentiousness of his early works is not mentioned in the actual documents ("Profilo Biografico," pp. 124–25). I cannot, however, agree with Branca's assessment of Andreas' treatise as a "compendio casistica erotico-sociale" (*Opere*, I, 153). Recent historical research on courtly love indicates that the treatise could be considered a practical application of moral theory only insofar as the immoral desires of the first two books are shown to be unsuccessful in practice or to bring about undesirable consequences.

11. On Boccaccio and the *Romance of the Rose* see: Lisi Cipriani, "The *Roman de la Rose* and Chaucer," *PMLA*, 22 (1907): 571–95; L. F. Benedetto, "Il *Roman de la Rose* e la letteratura italiana," *Beihefte zur Zeitschrift für romanische Philologie*, 21 (1910): 124; Otto Löhman, *Die Rahmenerzählung des Decameron* (Halle, 1935), pp. 99, 104; Edith G. Kern, "The Gardens in the *Decameron* Cornice," *PMLA*, 66 (1951): 505–23.

12. "Guillaume de Machaut's Erotic 'Autobiography': Precedents for the form of the *Voir-Dit*," in *Studies in Medieval Literature and Languages in Memory of Frederick Whitehead*, ed. W. Rothwell, et al. (Manchester, 1973), pp. 133–52.

13. *Opere*, II, 856.

14. *Giovanni Boccaccio* (Bari, 1972), pp. 72–98.

15. apRoberts, p. 9, n. 12.

16. apRoberts, pp. 1, 3 (two mentions), 4, 26. Boccaccio uses the phrase only once in his long poem; apRoberts uses it five times in his short article.

17. On the similarities see Griffin and Myrick, pp. 61–63; Muscetta, p. 83.

18. Dorothy L. Sayers, *Introductory Papers on Dante* (London, 1964), pp. 155–66; Mark Musa, *Dante's Vita Nuova: A Translation and an Essay* (Bloomington, Ind., 1973), pp. 89–210. Musa would probably not go so far as I do in calling the *Vita Nuova* a satire on youthful passion. Musa sees the poem as portraying "the development of the young Dante's love from preoccupation with his own feelings to enjoyment of Beatrice's excellence . . ." (p. 168). Cf. Rocco Montano's illuminating chapter "Dante Personaggio," in *Storia della poesia di Dante* (Florence, 1965), I, 368–76. On the deletion of religious imagery in the first edition see Charles S. Singleton, *An Essay on the Vita Nuova* (Cambridge, Mass., 1958), p. 4.

19. Musa, pp. 172–73. He also reminds us (p. 209n) that Leo Spitzer had long ago suggested that the third spirit's Latin had some barbarisms, deliberately placed there by Dante for comic effect. "Bemerkungen zu Dantes 'Vita Nuova,'" *Travaux du Séminaire de Philologie Romane*, 1 (1937): 162–208.

20. Musa, pp. 169–70.

21. J. B. Leishman, *The Monarch of Wit: An Analytical and Comparative Study of the Poetry of John Donne* (London, 1951), p. 147.

22. Dorothy Everett has suggested that the flattering reference to the lady's discernment was meant "to turn her attention away from those features of the tale which were not so appropriate to the situation: particularly from the infidelity of the heroine" (*Essays on Middle English Literature* [Oxford, 1955], p. 117). I would agree that certain features are very inappropriate, but would interpret the inappropriateness as deliberately introduced for comic effect.

23. *The Consolation of Philosophy*, trans. Richard Green, The Library of Liberal Arts (Indianapolis and New York, 1962), p. 26. Italics mine. Subsequent quotations in modern English translation will be from this text.

24. The passage on happiness and misery is also adduced by Francesca of Rimini in Dante's *Commedia*, in *Inferno* V. While most commentators have found her reminiscence of the happiness of former times ("del tempo felice") rather touching, it should be remembered that for her the ephemeral pleasure of adultery brought about eternal damnation. Like the character Boethius, she cannot distinguish between true and illusory happiness. Boccaccio himself comments dryly on the degree of adulterous felicity she enjoyed, which was sufficient to cause her to call "felice il tempo il quale aveva nella presente vita, per rispetto a quello che era nella dannazione perpetua . . ." (*Il Comento sopra la Commedia di Dante Alighieri*, ed. A. Penna [Florence, 1831], II, 59). Robert Hollander brilliantly analyzes the scene in terms of a series of quotations that show "the misuse of literature that promotes the sin of lust in Francesca" (*Allegory in Dante's Commedia* [Princeton, 1969], p. 112).

25. *Opere*, II, 8. Griffin, p. 71.

26. Meech, *Design*, p. 20.

27. In this section I transcribe Branca's quotations from the Latin text, but have used Parry's translation for my own quotations. Andreas Capellanus, *The Art of Courtly Love*, trans. John Jay Parry (New York, 1959).

28. *The Art of Courtly Love*, p. 204.

29. Branca says that I, 36 is only "il primo dei numerosi riflessi" of the precept codified by Andreas, that love made public seldom endures, and he cites II, 8; II, 25–26; II, 74; II, 116; II, 140–41; III, 9–10; II, 15; III, 43; IV, 153. The passages, though, like I, 36, tend to be about discovered love being disgraceful or vexatious rather than coming to an end. Some passages, like IV, 153, are closer to Andreas' rule 13 than others, but Branca's list is too elastic to prove very much.

30. *The Art of Courtly Love*, p. 191.

31. Dante Alighieri, *La Vita Nuova e le Rime*, ed. Mario Pazzaglia (Bologna, 1965), chap. VII. Cf. Musa, p. 182n.

32. *Vita Nuova*, chap. XXX.

33. *Expositio super Jeremiam*, *PL*, 111, col. 1185. A few other late commentaries exist, but Rabanus' is a standard.

34. Although the absence of mountains near Troilo's home city of Troy had led earlier critics to find an autobiographical explanation for them, Branca notes that the mountains are literary and traditional, although he does not trace them back to the Psalms.

35. The biblical echo here is a bit distorted, and it might be argued that its existence is tenuous. Branca notes the similarity of two contemporary poems, but of course that does not necessarily obviate an ultimately scriptural source (*Opere*, II, 856, n. 60). Some support for the idea that Boccaccio is using a scriptural echo playfully may be found in the fact that the rhetorician Boncampagno (†1240) wrote a love poem beginning with a very precise quotation from I Cor. 13: "Si linguis angelicis loquar et humanis." Of the poem's scriptural and liturgical allusions Dronke says "these are not in any way parodistic or blasphemous: they are not there to establish an incongruity but to overcome one." However, Wimsatt has an analysis much closer in perspective to the interpretation of Boccaccio advanced in the text here. He argues that Boncampagno's lyric is a "witty tale" showing a "sublime ideal" existing "only in the deluded lover's mind." Troilo, I think, is a deluded lover whose misappropriation of St. Paul's imagery is a witty touch by Boccaccio. See further Peter Dronke, *Medieval Latin and the Rise of the European Love Lyric*, 2nd ed. (Oxford, 1968), I, 318, and James I. Wimsatt, "Chaucer and the Canticle of Canticles," in *Chaucer the Love Poet*, ed. Jerome Mitchell and William Provost (Athens, Ga., 1973), p. 82. For the definitive treatment of "Si linguis angelicis . . ." see D. W. Robertson, Jr., "Two Poems from the *Carmina Burana*," *The American Benedictine Review*, 27 (1976): 45–59.

36. *Opere*, II, 470. Branca's note to *Filostrato* III, 80, remarks that Boccaccio uses Hercules to justify love in the *Amorosa Visione* and the *Fiammetta*, but does not address itself to the issues raised by the *Teseida*. Branca notes a different tone in Boccaccio's use of Hercules in *De casibus* I, 18. Ultimately Hercules' degeneration from manhood to effeminacy may be found in Ovid's *Heroides* IX. Medieval moralizations of that passage may be found in John of Garland's *Integumenta Ovidii*, and in the *Romance of the Rose*, ll. 9191–9202. For an illuminating discussion of the two aspects of Hercules see Richard L. Hoffman, *Ovid and the Canterbury Tales* (Philadelphia, 1966), pp. 41–44. For an excellent treatment of Hercules in the *Amorosa Visione* see Janet Levarie Smarr, "Boccaccio and the Choice of Hercules," *MLN*, 92 (1977): 146–52.

37. *Opere*, II, 853, n. 78.

38. Muscetta, *Boccaccio*, p. 83.

39. On Chaucer and Canticles see D. W. Robertson, Jr., "The Doctrine of Charity in Medieval Literary Gardens," *Speculum*, 26 (1951): 45; Robert E. Kaske, "The *Canticum Canticorum* in the *Miller's Tale*," *SP*, 59 (1962): 479–500; James I. Wimsatt, "Chaucer and the Canticle of Canticles," in *Chaucer the Love Poet*, pp. 66–90. I do not mean to gloss Boccaccio with Chaucer, who of course wrote later. The playful use of Scripture in medieval Latin poetry prior to Boccaccio's time has been studied by others such as Wimsatt. See also Robertson's article on the "Si linguis angelicis" mentioned in note 35, and his essay "The 'Partitura Amorosa' of Jean de Savoie," *PQ*, 33 (1954): 1–9. For the playful use of secular poetry we have the example of Dante himself, who humorously cannibalized some of his own more extravagant efforts in the *Vita Nuova*, as discussed earlier.

40. See D. W. Robertson, Jr., *A Preface to Chaucer* (Princeton, 1962), pp. 491–92; Gordon, *Double Sorrow*, pp. 38–39. This passage will be discussed in more detail in chapter 4.

41. See *Opere*, II, 856, n. 61.

42. Quotations from and translations of the *Commedia* are from Dante Alighieri, *The Divine Comedy*, trans. Charles S. Singleton, 6 vols. (Princeton, 1970–75).

43. Remember that the heroine's ignoble birth clashes with the address to the "nobilissima donna" of the *Proemio*. Even allowing for a general rather than social significance for "nobilissima," there still is a contrast between the donna of the *Proemio*, who is encouraged to find parallels with herself in "every good thing" possessed by Criseida, and Criseida herself, who seems to lose whatever good thing she might have had. For another reference to the disparity of station of the lovers see II, 76.

44. Note further Troilo's remarkable praise of the woman whose "corruption" he has accomplished as the cause "d'ogni mio valore" (IV, 51).

45. For an analysis of truth and falsehood, fidelity and betrayal in Chaucer's version, see John P. McCall, "Troilus and Criseyde," in *A Companion to Chaucer*, pp. 456–58.

46. Branca notes that true nobility was discussed by theologians of the time as well as by poets and essayists. He also calls attention to the occurrence of the idea in Andreas Capellanus. The

high-minded defense of true nobility immediately preceding the eight dialogues of proposed seduction in Andreas might have given Boccaccio the hint for a similarly humorous situation—one
wherein moral sentiments are uttered in immoral surroundings. A variation on this theme occurs
in Chaucer's *Wife of Bath's Tale,* in which the foul old hag quotes Dante on true gentility only in
order to gain "maistrie" in marriage. Although female domination in marriage appealed to the
old hag and to the Wife of Bath, it is contrary to Christian teaching.

47. For a passing reference to her wicked father's treachery, see IV, 128.

48. apRoberts, p. 1.

49. *The Vision of William Concerning Piers the Plowman* . . . , ed. Walter W. Skeat (Oxford,
1886), II, 31. William Langland, *Piers the Plowman,* trans. J. F. Goodridge (Harmondsworth,
Middlesex, 1959), p. 319.

50. *John Gower: Moral Philosopher and Friend of Chaucer* (London, 1965), p. 221.

51. Lewis, "What Chaucer Really Did to *Il Filostrato*," Schoeck and Taylor, II, 17; Fisher,
p. 215.

52. Fisher, p. 208.

53. Chaucer also received an annuity from John of Gaunt from 1374 onwards. On the whole he
seems to have been very, very highly connected. I mainly follow the account in Robinson's edition, pp. xxi–xxii. See also *Chaucer Life-Records,* ed. Martin M. Crow and Clair C. Olson (Oxford, 1966), pp. 553–68 and passim.

54. On London and New Troy see D. W. Robertson, Jr., *Chaucer's London* (New York, 1968),
pp. 2–3 and 221; John P. McCall and George Rudisill, Jr., "The Parliament of 1386 and Chaucer's Trojan Parliament," *JEGP,* 58 (1959): 284, n. 25. All quotations from the *Vox Clamantis*
will be from *The Major Latin Works of John Gower,* trans. Eric W. Stockton (Seattle, 1962), and
will be cited by page number in the text.

55. John P. McCall, "The Trojan Scene in Chaucer's *Troilus*," *ELH,* 29 (1962): 263–75. Cassandra refers to "the accursed love, by which we are all to be undone" (VII, 86).

56. For an analysis of Bishop Brinton's sermons on these topics see Robertson, *Chaucer's London,* pp. 67–69. Gower, as noted above, thought significantly that it was Venus who had attracted
the allegiance of the people. Bishop Bradwardine specifically noted with regard to the Scots that
it was the carnality of the king and of the nobles, who were "maxime venerei reputantur," that
brought defeat to the people. See Heiko Oberman and James A. Weisheipl, O.P., "The *Sermo
Epinicius* Ascribed to Thomas Bradwardine (1346)," *Archives d'histoire doctrinale et littéraire du
moyen âge,* 25 (1958): 328.

57. For example in Criseyde's dream of the eagle and in the image of Love who "bigan his
fetheres so to lyme" (I, 353).

58. Cf. Morton W. Bloomfield, "Distance and Predestination in *Troilus and Criseyde*,"
Schoeck and Taylor, II, 196–210, who similarly emphasizes the distance of the narrator from the
narrative, but who aligns Chaucer the narrator with Troilus after the betrayal as one unhappy in
love (p. 202).

59. Although Chaucer's invocation, "Thesiphone, thow help me for t'endite / Thise woful
vers, that wepen as I write" (I, 6–7), might be interpreted as showing a weeping narrator, it is
more likely the verses that weep. Root and others so render it, partly because that is the sense in
Boccaccio. For Tisiphone as "carnal delight, which very often Drives the lecherous mad," see
Joan Morton Jones, "The Chess of Love: Old French Text with Translation and Commentary,"
Ph.D. diss. Nebraska 1968, p. 459, and cf. Robertson, *Preface,* p. 474.

60. Troilus' extravagant humility may derive from the self-abasement of Amant to the God of
Love. Cf. "'My lyf, my deth is in youre hond'" (*RR,* 1955). In Boccaccio's poem it is only when
Criseida must leave that Troilo says she holds the key to his life and death, and in the comparable
passage Chaucer omits part of the phrasing. See *Filostrato* IV, 143 and *T&C,* IV, 1497–98.

61. Criseida's cognizance that Troilo is of royal blood in *Filostrato* II, 72, is elaborated in
T&C, II, 644, 708.

62. Note to *Filostrato* II, 49–56; p. 57.

63. Chaucer repeats Boccaccio's comment that Troilo was not proud in spite of his royal blood
(*Filostrato* III, 93; *T&C,* III, 1800–1801). The only omission by Chaucer of a reference to the
hero's nobility by Boccaccio is Chaucer's decision to exclude Cassandra's complaint that Troilo, a
king's son, is wasting himself on an ignoble lady—the daughter of an evil priest (*Filostrato* VII,

87). However, the idea of unequal backgrounds is not so important to Chaucer as the concept of a ruler who is himself ruled by passion.

64. Elizabeth Salter, "'Troilus and Criseyde': A Reconsideration," in *Patterns of Love and Courtesy: Essays in Memory of C. S. Lewis*, ed. John Lawlor (Evanston, Ill., 1966), p. 102.

65. Young, *Origin and Development*, p. 180. Hubertis M. Cummings, in *The Indebtedness of Chaucer's Works to the Italian Works of Boccaccio* (New York, 1965; first published 1916), argues that Chaucer seldom satirizes the emotions of his characters; yet Cummings discovers "almost luxurious indulgence in [Troilus'] emotions" (p. 96).

66. See p. 199 of Stockton's translation. Both Gower and Chaucer probably took the images of humility and bird-catching from the *Romance of the Rose*. Cf. the *Romaunt*, ll. 1620–24, 1955. This supposition does not affect the argument in the text, which is that Chaucer uses the images with an implied moral, whereas Gower uses them in a situation where the moral is overt.

67. Fisher, *Gower*, pp. 208, 230.

68. Ibid., p. 288.

Chapter II

1. Fisher also finds a destinal element in Troilus' falling in love: *Gower*, p. 230. The other citations are from: P. M. Kean, "Chaucer's Dealings with a Stanza of *Il Filostrato* and the Epilogue of *Troilus and Criseyde*," *Medium Aevum*, 33 (1964): 39; Salter, "Reconsideration," p. 81; Peter Heidtmann, "Sex and Salvation in *Troilus and Criseyde*," *ChauR*, 2 (1968): 250; Donald W. Rowe, *O Love, O Charite! Contraries Harmonized in Chaucer's Troilus* (Carbondale and Edwardsville, Ill., 1976), p. 3.

2. All quotations are from *The Book of Theseus: Teseida delle Nozze d'Emilia by Giovanni Boccaccio*, trans. Bernadette Marie McCoy (Sea Cliff, N.Y., 1974), pp. 196–98 for Mars; pp. 199–207 for Venus. For an excellent discussion of these glosses, their authorship, and their significance, see Robert Hollander, *Boccaccio's Two Venuses* (New York, 1977), pp. 56–65 and notes. For earlier discussions of the glosses see D. W. Robertson, Jr., *A Preface to Chaucer* (Princeton, 1962), pp. 106n, 110, 260n, 370–71; Chauncey Wood, *Chaucer and the Country of the Stars* (Princeton, 1970), p. 68.

3. Ll. 1944, 1968, 1969, 1955.

4. On the significance of sleeve-basting see Graham D. Caie, "An Iconographic Detail in the *Roman de la Rose* and the Middle English *Romaunt*," *ChauR*, 8 (1974): 320–23.

5. The French is "Touz li mondes va cele voie, / c'est li dex qui touz les desvoie" (*Le Roman de la Rose*, ed. Felix Lecoy [Paris, 1965], ll. 4311–12). Reason's further qualification, that the God of Love does not mislead the perverted, who are presumably misled in another way, reinforces the general meaning: heterosexuality is a road of the force of love. The cupidinous physical love that is under the aegis of the God of Love misleads people from the right road of controlled heterosexuality, while homosexuality pursues another road altogether. Thus Dahlberg translates, "The whole world travels that road. He is the God who turns them all from their road" (*The Romance of the Rose*, trans. Charles Dahlberg [Princeton, 1971], p. 95). On the lover's progress from physical desire to cupidity see Dahlberg, "Love and the *Roman de la Rose*," *Speculum*, 44 (1969): 568–84.

6. *Vox Clamantis*, Bk. V, chap. 3 in *The Major Latin Works of John Gower*, trans. Eric W. Stockton (Seattle, Wash., 1962), p. 199. Fisher fails to note the double movement here and describes it as a "passage on the overmastering power of love . . ." (*Gower*, p. 229). For a superb analysis of Gower's attitude toward love in one of his later works, see the introduction to *Confessio Amantis*, ed. Russell A. Peck (New York, 1968), pp. xi–xxix.

7. That one cannot fight with Cupid and win was still a commonplace in the Renaissance, as may be seen in Spenser's "March" eclogue in *The Shepheardes Calendar*. Cf. ll. 103–4, "Thomalin I pittie thy plight. / Perdie, with Love thou diddest fight" (*The Complete Poetical Works of Spenser*, ed. R. Neil Dodge [Boston, 1936], p. 17).

8. *Vox Clamantis*, Bk. V, chap. 4, p. 201; chap. 5, p. 202; chap. 8, p. 208; chap. 6, p. 202.

9. *Vox Clamantis*, Introduction, p. 20. Professor Fisher (*Gower*, pp. 229–30) sees these chapters in the *Vox* as a "moralistic treatment" that is "in contrast" with Chaucer's "elevation of courtly love" in the *Book of the Duchess*. Fisher's further development of the differences, in which Chaucer is supposed to make the love of Troilus and Criseyde a "manifestation of the universal creative urge of natural love" seems to me to miss the point made in the *Romance* and by Boccaccio: sexual urges are natural but must be ordered by marriage. Fisher's reference to "Chartrian naturalism" to explain Chaucer's attitude is now somewhat dated. For a detailed analysis of the differences between Chartrian naturalism that denies any emphasis on sexual license in the latter, see John V. Fleming, *The Roman de la Rose: A Study in Allegory and Iconography* (Princeton, 1969), pp. 185–249.

10. For an account of Chaucer's modification of a clear biblical analogy in Gower into a seemingly realistic detail in the General Prologue, see Chauncey Wood, "The Sources of Chaucer's Summoner's 'Garleek, Oynons, and eek Lekes'," *ChauR*, 5 (1971): 240–44. For a broader discussion of the differences between the two writers see Fisher, *Gower*, pp. 206–8. Although he does not treat *Vox Clamantis*, there is a useful discussion of Gower and Chaucer in John Peter, *Complaint and Satire in Early English Literature* (Oxford, 1956), pp. 1–59.

11. Bernard F. Huppé and D. W. Robertson, Jr., *Fruyt and Chaf: Studies in Chaucer's Allegories* (Princeton, 1963), pp. 115–16; J. A. W. Bennett, *The Parlement of Foules: An Interpretation* (Oxford, 1957), pp. 84–86.

12. "The Venus of Alanus de Insulis and the Venus of Chaucer," in *Philological Essays: Studies in Old and Middle English Language and Literature in Honour of Herbert Dean Meritt*, ed. James L. Rosier (The Hague, 1970), p. 191.

13. "Champertors be they that move Pleas and Suits, or cause them to be moved either by their own Procurement, or by others, and sue them at their proper Costs, for to have part of the Land in variance, or part of the Gains." *Statutes of the Realm* (London, 1810), I, 145. There is a more elaborate description of champarty (along with a prohibition of it) at I, 360. Cf. pp. 33, 95, 139, 145, 216. I am grateful to D. W. Robertson, Jr., for calling my attention to the legal status of champarty.

14. See Robertson, *Preface*, p. 92, and Richard L. Hoffman, *Ovid and the Canterbury Tales* (Philadelphia, 1966), pp. 71–77.

15. Charles Muscatine, *Chaucer and the French Tradition: A Study in Style and Meaning* (Berkeley and Los Angeles, 1957), p. 185.

16. See further Chauncey Wood, "Chaucer and *Sir Thopas*: Irony and Concupiscence," *TSLL*, 14 (1972): 394–95 and n. 12, which attempts to refute Dorothy Bethurum Loomis, "Chaucer's Point of View as Narrator in the Love Poems," *PMLA*, 74 (1959): 511–20.

17. For an excellent study of the nature of love in the *Legend*, see Edmund Reiss, "Chaucer's *fyn lovyng* and the late Medieval Sense of *fin amor*," in *Medieval Studies in Honor of Lillian Herlands Hornstein*, ed. Jess B. Bessinger, Jr., and Robert R. Raymo (New York, 1976), pp. 181–91.

18. In *The Boke of Cupide*, also known as *The Cuckoo and the Nightingale*, the same general situation obtains that has been outlined here. The power and virtue of Cupid are claimed, but the undesirability of serving him and the possibility of not doing so are insisted upon by the Cuckoo, who will not "in loves yoke to drawe. / For louers be the folke that lyven on lyve / That most disese han, and most unthrive" (ll. 140–42). The Cuckoo further maintains that "With such a lorde wolde I neuer be, / For he is blynde and may not se" (ll. 201–2). The text cited is from V. J. Scattergood, "*The Boke of Cupide*—An Edition," *English Philological Studies*, 9 (1965): 47–83. For a very different interpretation from the one offered here see David E. Lampe, "Tradition and Meaning in *The Cuckoo and the Nightingale*," *PLL*, 3 (1967): 49–62.

19. One should note that "vertuous" in this context may only mean "powerful." It is so translated by Daniel Cook in his edition. However, I prefer Krapp's translation of "virtue," which preserves the parallel ironies between line 254, in which Love is "so vertuous" by nature, and 259, in which Love is said to lead lovers "so wel." See *Troilus and Criseyde*, ed. Daniel Cook (New York, 1966), and *Troilus and Cressida*, trans. George Philip Krapp (New York, 1932).

20. For slightly different interpretations see Robertson, *Preface*, pp. 476–77, who says that this is good advice provided the love acquired is properly channeled, and Gordon, *Double Sorrow*, p. 67, who finds ambiguity where I find irony. Another superficially unequivocal statement about love's power occurs later in the poem when Criseyde praises "'the excellence / Of love, ayeins the which that no man may / Ne oughte ek goodly make resistence'" (III, 988–90). The

circumstances, though,—Criseyde is in bed with Troilus and in the process of yielding to him—suggest that she is not an altogether impartial speaker.

21. One of the very few critics to give proper recognition to the woe suffered by Troilus—and by lovers generally—is Edmund Reiss. See "Chaucer's Courtly Love," in *The Learned and the Lewed: Studies in Chaucer and Medieval Literature*, ed. Larry D. Benson (Cambridge, Mass., 1974), pp. 107–9.

22. The conclusion that "the naive narrator is another blind man leading blind men to their fates" is unwarrantedly literal, unless we posit a naive narrator who gives way to a wise narrator at the end of the poem. See G. T. Shepherd, *"Troilus and Criseyde,"* in *Chaucer and Chaucerians*, ed. D. S. Brewer (University, Ala., 1966), p. 73.

23. A good introduction to the issue of Chaucer's use of Boethian materials in the *Troilus* may be obtained from the series of chapters and articles reprinted in *Chaucer Criticism: Troilus and Criseyde and the Minor Poems*, ed. Richard J. Schoeck and Jerome Taylor (Notre Dame, 1961), vol. II. In "Destiny in *Troilus and Criseyde*," Walter Clyde Curry argues that it is "inevitable . . . that Troilus should love" (p. 55, cf., p. 41). Howard R. Patch, in "Troilus on Determinism," asserts to the contrary that Troilus, in uttering some Boethian passages, is "giving way to his feelings rather than to his intellect, with all the solemnity of his despair in a situation on which the poem as a whole sheds ironic light" (p. 77). Patch accordingly thinks that Troilus "gives himself up a willing victim to the Court of Love" (p. 78). D. W. Robertson, Jr., in "Chaucerian Tragedy," points out that the passages from the *Consolation of Philosophy* that Troilus utters are in fact taken from "the false reasoning of the speaker . . . omitting Philosophy's answer" (p. 112), an insight that appeared almost simultaneously in Theodore A. Stroud's "Boethius' Influence on Chaucer's *Troilus*," which says that Troilus' "ensuing soliloquy on predestination actually lifts a long passage from 'Boethius'' climactic challenge to the position which Philosophy had advanced" (p. 124). Patch had anticipated the direction of these approaches in "Troilus on Predestination," in which he contrasted Troilus and the character Boethius. See the reprint in *Chaucer: Modern Essays in Criticism*, ed. Edward Wagenknecht (New York, 1959), pp. 369–71. Morton W. Bloomfield, in "Distance and Predestination in *Troilus and Criseyde*," asserts that Chaucer "makes his chief character awake to the fact of predestination towards the end of the story" (p. 206), which, Bloomfield argues, allies him with the narrator, for whether or not Chaucer himself was a predestinarian (Bloomfield thinks he was), the narrator of the story perforce knows how it ends, and in that sense sees the characters as predestined.

In addition to the essays in the Schoeck and Taylor collection, one should note the following: John Huber, in "Troilus' Predestination Soliloquy," *NM*, 66 (1965): 120–25 argues correctly that Troilus is more eager than Boethius to rule out free will, although Huber is not quite so precise about the nature and function of the differences between the two as are Stroud and Robertson. Charles A. Owen, Jr., in "The Problem of Free Will in Chaucer's Narratives," *PQ*, 46 (1967), in an approach somewhat similar to Bloomfield's, notes that while the reader and author know the outcomes of love and war from the start, nevertheless "the characters live in ignorance of what their choices and their evasions of choice will inevitably bring to pass" (p. 440). Joseph J. Mogan, Jr., in "Free Will and Determination in Chaucer's *Troilus and Criseyde*," *Journal of Research in Western Languages and Literatures*, 2 (1969), contends that "the answer to the problem of free will and determinism in Chaucer's poem will depend upon how much free will, if any, inheres in the convention of courtly love" (p. 160). My own treatment sees a defence of the freedom of the will as common in literary treatments of love—if not of courtly love. I am grateful to Professor Mogan for sending me a copy of his essay, which is very difficult to obtain. There is a careful analysis of both the Boethian speeches and their implications in David Sims, "An Essay at the Logic of *Troilus and Criseyde*," *Cambridge Quarterly*, 4 (1969): 125–49. Peter Elbow, in *Oppositions in Chaucer* (Middletown, Conn., 1975), while accepting Robertson's and Stroud's point about Troilus' appropriations from Boethius being cries of "erroneous despair" (p. 62), nevertheless maintains that in a "deeper sense . . . Troilus is *right* to say that all is necessary and men lack free will" (p. 57). For a treatment of the problem somewhat similar to that put forward by Bloomfield and C. A. Owen, see Peter Christmas, *"Troilus and Criseyde*: The Problems of Love and Necessity," *ChauR*, 9 (1975): 285–96.

24. One should compare Singleton's notes to canto 5 of the *Inferno* with his exposition of the passages on love and free will in *Purgatorio*. Francesca's claim that love is ineluctable, that no one may withstand its power, is indicative of her flawed reasoning. The contrast between her position and Vergil's is a silent comment on why she is among the damned.

25. See Dahlberg's note to 17,101.

26. Fleming, *Roman de la Rose*, p. 55.

27. Fleming, pp. 202–3.

28. See above, n. 23.

29. It is clear from the context that Gower does not distinguish between fate and Fortune in this book of the *Vox Clamantis*. Stockton's note (p. 377) that Gower is "at heart . . . a fatalist" is not very convincing.

30. *The Sermons of Thomas Brinton, Bishop of Rochester* (1373–1389), ed. Mary Aquinas Devlin (London, 1954), II, 216. Cf. D. W. Robertson, Jr., *Chaucer's London* (New York, 1968), pp. 67–69. Although nothing specific is said, it seems likely that both Brinton and Gower feared that Englishmen were becoming like—*horribile dictu*—Frenchmen. That the French were doomed to be defeated at Crécy because of their Venereal allegiances was a point made emphatically in 1346 by Thomas Bradwardine. See Heiko Oberman and James A. Weisheipl, O. P., "The *Sermo Epinicius* Ascribed to Thomas Bradwardine (1346)," *Archives d'histoire doctrinale et littéraire du moyen âge*, 25 (1958): 323–24. One may compare with this Gower's despair that "the French sins now clamor to take possession of our households" (p. 258).

31. George R. Coffman, "John Gower in His Most Significant Role," in *Elizabethan Studies and Other Essays in Honor of George F. Reynolds*, University of Colorado Studies, ser. B., Studies in the Humanities, II, no. 4 (Boulder, Colo., 1945), pp. 52–61.

32. A promising approach to the issue of the dedication, which differs from the view presented here in its conception of the narrator, is by Frank H. Whitman, "*Troilus and Criseyde* and Chaucer's Dedication to Gower," *Tennessee Studies in Literature*, 18 (1973): 1–11.

Chapter III

1. Cited by Caroline F. Spurgeon, *Five Hundred Years of Chaucer Criticism and Allusion, 1357–1900* (New York, 1960), II, 177.

2. Spurgeon, *Allusion*, II, 276; II, 112.

3. Critical estimate of the poem prior to the nineteenth century is difficult to assess, since Henryson's unflattering continuation of the story of Criseyde was commonly believed as late as 1650 to have been written by Chaucer (Spurgeon, *Allusion*, III, 1). Moreover, the vagueness of many of the early judgments makes it impossible to know the precise reasons for the opinions ventured. Sidney's well-known praise of the *Troilus* was based on Chaucer's ability to "see so clearly" (Spurgeon, *Allusion*, I, 122), but that does not help us to know how Sidney read the poem. It may well be that in the Renaissance the *Troilus* was commonly treated as a simple love story, since one often encounters treatments of the first three books alone. Cf. Spurgeon, *Allusion*, I, 177–78, 203–7. For a detailed analysis of the history of the *Troilus* see Alice K. Miskimin, *The Renaissance Chaucer* (New Haven and London, 1975), pp. 156–225.

4. *The System of Courtly Love Studied as an Introduction to the Vita Nuova of Dante* (Boston, 1896). Discussions abound of the ennobling effect of courtly love in medieval literatures other than English. For an example see Frederick Goldin, *The Mirror of Narcissus in The Courtly Love Lyric* (Ithaca, N. Y., 1967).

5. William George Dodd, *Courtly Love in Chaucer and Gower* (Gloucester, Mass., 1959), pp. 129–30. First published in 1913.

6. *The Book of Troilus and Criseyde*, ed. Robert Kilburn Root (Princeton, 1926), p. xlviii. Those who believe that Troilus is improved by love commonly write about his "ennoblement." I have collected a sizeable number of examples. There are more than a few critics who do not share this view. It is rare, however, for them to address the issue of love's effects in terms of "ennoblement" or lack of it. A well-argued essay of the latter sort is by Edmund Reiss, "Troilus and the Failure of Understanding," *MLQ*, 29 (1968): 131–44.

7. Thomas A. Kirby, *Chaucer's Troilus: A Study in Courtly Love* (Baton Rouge, 1940), p. 279.

8. Alexander J. Denomy, C.S.B., "The Two Moralities of Chaucer's *Troilus and Criseyde*," Schoeck and Taylor, II, 148.

9. Sanford Brown Meech, *Design in Chaucer's Troilus* (Syracuse, 1959), p. 165.

10. Alfred David, "The Hero of the *Troilus*," *Speculum*, 37 (1962): 573; Donald R. Howard, *The Three Temptations* (Princeton, 1966), pp. 101–2, 152.

11. The principal spokesman for an ironic reading of Andreas is D. W. Robertson, Jr. See "The Subject of the *De amore* of Andreas Capellanus," *MP*, 50 (1953): 145–61; *A Preface to Chaucer* (Princeton, 1962), pp. 391–448; "The Concept of Courtly Love as an Impediment to the Understanding of Medieval Texts," in *The Meaning of Courtly Love*, ed. F. X. Newman (Albany, 1968), pp. 1–18. See also John F. Benton, "The Court of Champagne as a Literary Center," *Speculum*, 36 (1961): 551–91; "Clio and Venus: An Historical View of Medieval Love," in *The Meaning of Courtly Love*, pp. 19–42; E. Talbot Donaldson, "The Myth of Courtly Love," in *Speaking of Chaucer* (London, 1970), pp. 154–63; Christopher Kertesz, "The *De Arte (Honeste) Amandi* of Andreas Capellanus," *TSLL*, 13 (1971): 5–16. A useful article on Latin puns in Andreas is by Betsy Bowden, "The Art of Courtly Copulation," *M&H*, 9 (1979): 67–85. There is a good bibliography of writings of all persuasions in *The Meaning of Courtly Love*. In addition to the essays listed above propounding an ironic approach, there are several important essays with a different point of view that have appeared since Newman's collection. In addition to those by Douglas Kelly and Francis L. Utley, which will be cited later, Michael D. Cherniss, while finding considerable humor in Andreas, nevertheless contends that Andreas describes "the ennobling effect of love" in "The Literary Comedy of Andreas Capellanus," *MP*, 72 (1975): 228.

12. At one time I thought I had been the first to discover the evidence to be discussed, but I find that I have been anticipated by Robertson, *Preface*, p. 85, n. 59.

13. Andreas Capellanus, *The Art of Courtly Love*, trans. John Jay Parry (New York, 1959), p. 28. Later in this chapter where a closer textual study occurs, I shall use Parry's translation along with the Latin text.

14. *Petri Allegherii super Dantis ipsius genitoris Comoediam Commentarium*, ed. Vincentio Nannucci (Florence, 1845), p. 89.

15. Francis L. Utley, "Must We Abandon the Concept of Courtly Love?" *M&H*, n.s. 3 (1972): 310. For a similar statement on the significance of the Condemnation, see Irving Singer, "Andreas Capellanus: A Reading of the *Tractatus*," *MLN*, 88 (1973): 1288. Singer notes without a smile that "Andreas insists that love adorns a man with the virtue of relative chastity." The most important study of the relationship between Andreas' *De amore* and the Condemnation is by Alexander Denomy, C.S.B., "The *De amore* of Andreas Capellanus and the Condemnation of 1277," *MS*, 8 (1946): 107–49, which is an expansion of an idea first stated by Martin Grabmann, "Das Werk *De Amore* des Andreas Capellanus und das Verurteilungsdekret des Bischofs Stephan Tempier von Paris vom 7. März 1277," *Speculum*, 7 (1932): 75–79. See also Peter Dronke, *Medieval Latin and the Rise of the European Love Lyric*, 2nd ed. (Oxford, 1968), I, 82–84.

16. My discussion of the Condemnation of 1277 is based upon the superb analysis by Fernand van Steenberghen, *The Philosophical Movement in the Thirteenth Century* (London, 1955). I also wish to record my debt to my late friend Julius R. Weinberg, with whom I often discussed the Condemnation.

17. *The Art of Courtly Love*, pp. 107–24.

18. Denomy, "The *De amore* and the Condemnation," pp. 108, 149.

19. For an excellent discussion of the attempts to relate the condemnation of *simplex fornicatio* to the *Romance of the Rose*, see Fleming, *The Roman de la Rose*, pp. 214–18.

20. Kirby, *Chaucer's Troilus*, p. 64, cf. p. 279. There are somewhat more guarded statements about the origin of all goodness in Andreas in Alexander J. Denomy, C.S.B., *The Heresy of Courtly Love* (New York, 1947), pp. 33–35, and Douglas Kelly, "Courtly Love in Perspective: The Hierarchy of Love in Andreas Capellanus," *Traditio*, 24 (1968): 121 and n. 7. C. S. Lewis' statement on the subject, first published in 1936, has been seminal. See *The Allegory of Love* (New York, 1958), p. 34.

21. Andreas Capellanus, *De amore*, ed. E. Trojel (Munich, 1964), p. 21. Subsequent quotations will be from this edition and will be cited in the text. Because of the verbal parallels to be discussed in this section, I include the Latin along with Parry's translation.

22. Kertesz properly notes that both *amor* and *bonus* are ambiguous here. "The *De Arte (Honeste) Amandi*," p. 9.

23. Robertson, *Preface*, p. 415.

24. Kertesz calls attention to the appositeness of Paul's letter to Timothy for an interpretation of the first dialogue (p. 9), but it is even more pertinent for the third.

25. "Amor est passio quaedam innata, procedens ex visione et immoderata cogitatione formae alterius sexus, ob quam aliquis super omnia cupit alterius potiri amplexibus et omnia de utriusque voluntate in ipsius amplexu amoris praecepta compleri" (p. 3). This is the passage cited in English earlier in the chapter that was used to define lust by Pietro di Dante.

26. A precise analogy to the humor in Andreas may be found in the *Romance of the Rose*, of which Rosemond Tuve writes that a common authorial practice is to have the real point at issue "wrapped . . . in some bland contradiction that no one on the scene recognizes as an outrage, though we are expected to" (*Allegorical Imagery: Some Mediaeval Books and Their Posterity* [Princeton, 1966], p. 241).

27. The duty of widows is expanded upon in St. Augustine's *De bono viduitatis*, available in translation as "On the Good of Widowhood" in *St. Augustine: On the Holy Trinity, Doctrinal Treatises, Moral Treatises* in *Nicene and Post-Nicene Fathers*, ed. Philip Schaff (Grand Rapids, Mich., 1956), III, 441–54.

28. Cited by Robertson, *Preface*, p. 400.

29. Lest anyone miss the joke, Andreas makes it clear a little bit later that *amor purus* and *amor mixtus* are in fact the same. See Parry's translation, p. 164. For a detailed discussion of the two see Robertson, *Preface*, pp. 436–44.

30. Kelly has argued that Andreas "keeps courtly love in perspective; he marks off clearly the area within which it is operative, and subordinates it to Christian teaching regarding carnal love" (p. 122). With this perspective in mind Kelly asserts that Andreas, in the several passages we have been discussing, insists on the benefits of courtly love while limiting them to this earthly life—hence the use of qualifying phrases like *in mundo*, *in hac vita*, and *in saeculo* (p. 121). Actually, the modifiers do not make any difference since the claim is equally fallacious for earthly or heavenly benefits. Moreover, it is not Andreas who asserts the claims, but rather a series of men who are speaking neither theoretically nor disinterestedly about the presumed benefits of the *amor* they seek. When Andreas speaks in the first person, in Book III, he says clearly that all wickedness and no good come from *amor*, and he is speaking in an earthly, not heavenly, sense: "Quum, igitur omnia sequantur ex amore nefanda, nullumque inde bonum evenire cognoscatur sed infinitas hominibus procedere poenas, cur, stulte juvenis, quaeris amare et te Dei gratia aeterna hereditate privare?" (p. 332).

31. *PL*, 6, col. 653.

32. *PL*, 42, cols. 551–72. The idea is later asserted by Boethius in the *Consolation of Philosophy*, especially in Bk. III, pr. 10. It is worth noting that the images of both the *fons* and the *radix* are used in a discussion of *De substantia dilectionis* erroneously attributed to St. Augustine. If, as seems likely, Andreas' audience was partly clerical or at least familiar with clerical humor, his outrageous statements in the dialogues about the origin of good would have been transparent enough: "Unus fons dilectionis intus saliens, duos rivos effundit: alter est amor mundi, cupiditas; alter est amor Dei, charitas. Medium quippe est cor hominis, unde fons amoris erumpit: et cum per appetitum ad exteriora decurrit, cupiditas dicitur; cum vero desiderium suum ad interiora dirigit, charitas nominatur. Ergo duo sunt rivi, qui de fonte dilectionis emanant, cupiditas et charitas: et omnium malorum radix cupiditas, et omnium bonorum radix charitas" (*PL*, 40, cols. 843–44). Cited by Robertson, "The Subject of the *De amore*," p. 149, n. 27.

33. Dante's statement about love as the source of every virtue and every deed deserving punishment is very similar to the image of a fountain with two streams in the *De substantia dilectionis* cited in the previous note. If Andreas' humor is to describe the two streams as one, to admit that love is an inborn passion but then to confine its potential to supposed good, then his humor was recognized by Jean de Meun, who used Andreas' definition of love in a similarly restricted sense. See Charles Dahlberg, "Love and the *Roman de la Rose*," *Speculum*, 44 (1969): 574.

34. *Vox Clamantis*, Bk. V, chap. 6, pp. 202–3.

35. Gaston Paris, "Lancelot du Lac," *Romania*, 12 (1883): 518–21. Paris also says that ladies justified their superiority over their lovers by "l'influence ennoblisante," that they exerted, but he seems to be speaking of "vertus sociales" rather than anything more profound. See p. 530.

36. Dodd, *Courtly Love*, p. 130, citing I, 246–52; II, 848–54; III, 22–28; III, 1800–6. Francis Lee Utley, "Chaucer's Troilus and St. Paul's Charity," in *Chaucer and Middle English Studies* *in Honour of Rossell Hope Robbins,* ed. Beryl Rowland (London, 1974), pp. 272–87. Utley actually cites more than the six passages that he calls "major points," and all will be taken up. The attempt to link the several passages describing Troilus with a medieval treatise on charity is unpromising in view of Troilus' goals and motivation, neither of which has anything to do with charity. Dodd and Utley have used multiple textual references to make their points about ennoblement. The list of those who have reached a similar conclusion based on fewer references would be far too long for inclusion here, and if one added those who do not use the specific idea of ennoblement but speak more generally about improvement or "regeneration" (cf. Dorothy Everett, *Essays on Middle English Literature* [Oxford, 1955], p. 127), the list would be overwhelming indeed. The stanzas that close Book I, describing Troilus as playing the lion in the field while simultaneously being friendly, humble, and having every supposed vice "for a vertu chaunge" (I, 1085) are cited by Utley (although not by Dodd), and have been cited by a great many others. A selective list of other commentators on these stanzas will be supplied when the passage is discussed.

37. There are as well those who do not adduce specific passages for evidence, but rather refer more generally to the action of the poem. For instance: "The lovers' identification in book III (and earlier) with the sacred law of Nature, its inevitability and high morality, its philosophical desirability, the ennobling quality of the lovers' conduct towards each other and towards others—all this summum bonum, this human felicity, deserves a different reward and resolution" (John Norton-Smith, *Geoffrey Chaucer* [London and Boston, 1974], p. 200). Because of its vagueness and generality this argument is at once hard to refute but not very compelling. For two instances of reference to Troilus' ennoblement that are less sweeping than the one cited, but also less tendentious than Dodd or Utley, see Barbara Bartholomew, *Fortuna and Natura: A Reading of Three Chaucer Narratives* (The Hague, 1966), p. 35, and E. G. Stanley, "About Troilus," *E&S*, 29 (1976): 102.

38. There is not, however, universal agreement about the absence of irony in the portrait. The major assertion of the Knight's unworthiness is by Terry Jones, *Chaucer's Knight: The Portrait of a Medieval Mercenary* (London, 1980). For a learned defense of the Knight's worthiness see Jill Mann, *Chaucer and Medieval Estates Satire* (Cambridge, 1973), pp. 106–15.

39. Utley, "St. Paul's Charity," pp. 273–75.

40. *Allegorical Imagery,* p. 259. In addition to Dahlberg's discussion of Jean de Meun's two voices, see the excellent analysis by Fleming, *Roman de la Rose,* pp. 185–87.

41. P. M. Kean, "Chaucer's Dealings With a Stanza of *Il Filostrato*, and the Epilogue of *Troilus and Criseyde*," *Medium Aevum,* 33 (1964): 39.

42. Beryl Rowland, *Blind Beasts* (Kent State, Ohio, 1971), p. 135. Chaucer himself refers to "Bayard the blynde" in *CYT*, 1413. Troilus' blindness will be discussed further in chapter 5.

43. Robertson, *Preface,* pp. 30, 194, 253–55, 476.

44. *Double Sorrow,* pp. 67, 70.

45. *Double Sorrow,* p. 71. See further Gordon's discussions on pp. 139–40: "The medieval doctrine of love, which serves throughout as the touchstone for the irony, posited a 'natural law' of love by which sexual love can be comprehended in *caritas* in a harmonious relation, if the love is for the right reasons." Again it is regrettable that the author does not specify that marriage was the sole "harmonious relation" envisioned in medieval thought. On Nature, Grace, and sexuality, see Fleming's lucid discussion, *Roman de la Rose,* pp. 185–210.

46. Stephen A. Barney, "Troilus Bound," *Speculum,* 47 (1972): 452.

47. These arguments on the importance of pride have received welcome support in the excellent article by J. D. Burnley, "Proud Bayard: 'Troilus and Criseyde', I. 218," *N&Q,* 23 (1976): 148–52. Burnley's emphasis on Troilus' lack of prudence is well taken, but I would relate it in turn to his self-love. As a footnote to the whole discussion it bears noting that Dante associates Troy's submission to Fortune with the city's pride in *Inferno* 30:13–15.

48. Fleming, p. 93.

49. For a discussion of Cupid and the Well of Narcissus see Robertson, *Preface,* pp. 90–98.

50. This stanza and the two first lines of the next, "Now sith it may nat goodly ben withstonde, / And is a thing so vertuous in kynde," have been taken unironically by Kean and Salter as mentioned in chapter 2, n. 1. Denomy writes: "in these passages the poet sets forth the theory of the irresistibility of love and of its ennobling power" ("The Two Moralities of Chaucer's

Troilus and Criseyde," Schoeck and Taylor, II, 151). See also Kirby, *Courtly Love*, pp. 247–48, and cf. Kean's later treatment in *Chaucer and the Making of English Poetry* (London and Boston, 1972), I, 125–28, which treats this and several other passages.

51. *Confessio Amantis* IV, 2296–99, in *The English Works of John Gower*, ed. G. C. Macaulay, EETS, Extra Series nos. 81–82 (London, 1901), I, 363. Cf. the often useful essay by J. A. W. Bennett, "Gower's 'Honeste Love,'" in *Patterns of Love and Courtesy: Essays in Memory of C. S. Lewis*, ed. John Lawlor (Evanston, Ill., 1966), pp. 107–21. An excellent essay that compares Gower's "honest love" with *fin' amors* is by Edmund Reiss, "*Fin' Amors*: Its History and Meaning in Medieval Literature," in *Medieval and Renaissance Studies*, no. 8, ed. Dale B. J. Randall (Durham, N.C., 1979), pp. 74–99.

52. Utley, "Troilus and St. Paul's Charity," p. 276.

53. On the date see John Norton-Smith, "Chaucer's *Etas Prima*," *Medium Aevum*, 22 (1963): 117–24. For a recent employment of the banishment of pride, envy, and avarice as evidence of Troilus' ennoblement, see John Gardner, *The Poetry of Chaucer* (Carbondale and Edwardsville, Ill., 1977), pp. 107–8.

54. See *RR*, 8355–8455; 9493–9678 in Dahlberg's translation. For an excellent discussion of the Golden Age in the *Romance* see Fleming, pp. 144–50.

55. Rosemond Tuve perceptively notes that in fact the religious language undercuts "the elegant amorist with his cover-up jargon and his pathetic triviality" (*Allegorical Imagery*, p. 264).

56. *Allegory of Love*, p. 126.

57. On the complementary nature of the figures see Dahlberg's notes, p. 359. An early commentator refers to the portraits as "vicia sive defectus [quod] non participant ad actum de dilectione et ideo dicitur esse extra murum" (cited by Fleming, p. 32). For further discussion see D. W. Robertson, Jr., "The Doctrine of Charity in Medieval Literary Gardens: A Topical Approach through Symbolism and Allegory," *Speculum*, 26 (1951): 40 and n. 71; Dahlberg, "Love and the *Roman de la Rose*," *Speculum*, 44 (1969): 582.

58. On true and false virtues see D. W. Robertson, Jr., "The Subject of the *De amore* of Andreas Capellanus," *MP*, 50 (1953): 157–59, citing *Civitas Dei*, Bk. 19, chap. 5, and Alanus de Insulis' treatise on virtues and vices edited by O. Lottin in *MS*, 12 (1957): 27. Another useful text is St. Augustine, *On Christian Doctrine*, trans. D. W. Robertson, Jr., Library of Liberal Arts (New York, 1958), p. 91.

59. For a fine treatment of the use and abuse of the idea of gentility in the poem, which nevertheless does not discuss the instance analyzed here, see Alan T. Gaylord, "*Gentilesse* in Chaucer's *Troilus*," *SP*, 61 (1964): 19–34.

60. Neither Skeat, Root, nor Robinson notes any of these parallels.

61. Robert Archibald Jeliffe, *Troilus and Criseyde: Studies in Interpretation* (n.p., Folcroft Library, 1970; first published 1956), pp. 239–40. For similar responses to this passage see Kirby, *Courtly Love*, p. 252; Dorothy Bethurum Loomis, "Chaucer's Point of View as Narrator in the Love Poems," Schoeck and Taylor, II, 226; Alfred David, "The Hero of the *Troilus*," 573; Donald Howard, *The Three Temptations*, p. 112. For incisive remarks on the difference between what the passage claims for Troilus and what he actually does, see Gordon, *Double Sorrow*, pp. 56–57. She also notes that in I, 1793–99 Troilus' speech (but not necessarily his action) is equivocally about love and virtue (p. 85).

62. "Five-Book Structure in Chaucer's *Troilus*," *MLQ*, 23 (1962): 297–308.

63. Heiko Oberman and James A. Weisheipl, O. P., "The *Sermo Epinicius* Ascribed to Thomas Bradwardine (1346)," *Archives d'histoire doctrinale et littéraire du moyen âge*, 25 (1958): 295–329. Cf. Robertson, *Chaucer's London*, p. 128.

64. For details see Alan T. Gaylord, "A 85–88: Chaucer's Squire and the Glorious Campaign," *PMASAL*, 45 (1960): 341–61.

65. Gower had expressed the identical idea earlier in *Mirour de l'Homme*, ll. 23, 893–904. In Fisher's translation the passage reads: "O knight, I speak to you, you who labor in errantry in Russia or Tartary. The reason for your going I do not know. Three causes I discern, two of which aren't worth an alder-berry: The first is, if I may say so, because of my prowess or pride . . . or else; 'It is for my lady, that I may have her love' . . ." (*John Gower*, p. 259).

66. Two of the passages asserting that lovers flee vice, which are among those cited by Dodd, have not been treated in detail in this chapter. One is found in Antigone's song in Book II and should be read in that context. Antigone says that love has put her in "'the righte lif,'" that it has

caused her to "'flemen alle manere vice and synne,'" and that it is the force that "'dooth me so to vertu for t'entende'" (II, 851–53). However, Antigone also acknowledges that some people call love "vice" or "thraldom," which she puts down to envy, delicacy, or impotence—being "right nyce" or "unmyghty." The only people who would say these things, she feels, are those who never bent Cupid's bow (II, 855–61). Of course, the narrator is one such, and in view of this and her protesting overmuch, one can hardly accept her view as definitive even if Criseyde finds it persuasive. For a detailed, if somewhat different, interpretation see Sister Mary Charlotte Borthwick, F.S.C.P., "Antigone's Song as 'Mirour' in Chaucer's *Troilus and Criseyde*," *MLQ*, 22 (1961): 227–35. The other passage is part of the invocation of Venus that stands as the Prologue to Book III, which says plainly enough that Venus causes people to resign vices (III, 25), but does not specify which Venus is meant. This passage will be treated in more detail in the next chapter.

67. For more on the two hunts, although not with reference to the *Troilus*, see Robertson, *Preface*, pp. 263–64.

68. "Hector the Second: The Lost Face of Troilostratus," *AM*, 16 (1975): 52–62.

69. Chaucer alludes to this idea later in the poem in a passage distinctly modified from Boccaccio's version. Chaucer has Troilus address the God of Love about the loss of Criseyde, whom he has bought at a price. The parodically religious language also includes a reference to grace:

> "O verrey lord, O Love! O god, allas!
> That knowest best myn herte and al my thought,
> What shal my sorwful lif don in this cas,
> If I forgo that I so deere have bought?
> Syn ye Criseyde and me han fully brought
> Into youre grace, and bothe oure hertes seled,
> How may ye suffre, allas! it be repeled?"   [IV, 288–94]

70. That secret or concealed love in medieval literature was regularly expressed as morally wrong is the thesis of Edmund Reiss, "Chaucer's *deerne love* and the Medieval View of Secrecy in Love," in *Chaucerian Problems and Perspectives: Essays Presented to Paul E. Beichner, C.S.C.*, ed. Edward Vasta and Zacharias P. Thundy (Notre Dame, Indiana, 1979), pp. 164–79. A very different approach, which sees secrecy and dissimulation in the poem as representing a literary, conventional cause (for secrecy) and a social, English effect (the need to dissimulate) is by Barry Windeatt, "'Love that Oughte Ben Secree' in Chaucer's *Troilus*," *ChauR*, 14 (1979): 116–31.

71. For some of the material on brotherly love I am indebted to my former student Eleanor McCulloch, who addressed the topic in her 1969 McMaster University M.A. thesis, "Chaucer's 'Female Pantheon' in *Troilus and Criseyde*," pp. 39–49. In addition to the specific deceptions of Deiphebus and Criseyde there is a wider strain of more profound betrayal that runs throughout the poem. Those who have written on it have contributed significantly to our understanding of the poem. See John P. McCall, "Troilus and Criseyde," in *Companion to Chaucer Studies*, rev. ed. (Toronto, 1979), pp. 456–58; John Speirs, "Chaucer (I) *Troilus and Criseyde*," *Scrutiny*, 11 (1942): 96 and n. 3; W. F. Bolton, "Treason in Troilus," *Archiv*, 203 (1967): 255–62.

72. The text of the poem does not say that Pandarus invents Poliphete or Horaste, or that he invents their relationships to Criseyde. The circumstances, however, strongly indicate that he does one or the other. The major editors of the poem, Skeat, Root, and Robinson, do not address the issue. Many interpreters, however, have stated that Pandarus fabricates either the people or the circumstances. For a few examples see Meech, *Design*, p. 51; Robert G. Cook, "Chaucer's Pandarus and the Medieval Ideal of Friendship," *JEGP*, 69 (1970): 418–19; Bert Dillon, *A Chaucer Dictionary: Proper Names and Allusions* (Boston, 1974), s.v.v. "Horaste" and "Polyphoetes." Cook's article gives an excellent account of the lies Pandarus tells.

73. See Lonnie J. Durham, "Love and Death in *Troilus and Criseyde*," *ChauR*, 3 (1968): 11. Cf. Donald R. Howard, "Experience, Language and Consciousness: *Troilus and Criseyde*, II, 596–931," in *Medieval Literature and Folklore Studies: Essays in Honor of Francis Lee Utley*, ed. Jerome Mandel and Bruce A. Rosenberg (New Brunswick, N.J., 1970), pp. 188–89. For the eagle as symbol of Troilus the potentially dangerous warrior, see Joseph E. Gallagher, "Criseyde's Dream of the Eagle: Love and War in *Troilus and Criseyde*," *MLQ*, 36 (1975): 115–32.

74. Many critics have taken these images *in bono*. Compare, for example, Meech's remarks on

Troilus: "He plays the lion against the Greeks. He is the glorious eagle of her dream, a sparrowhawk in the act of love as she is the lark. He is the well of worthiness, small wonder that, as in the source, he proves sweet to her" (*Design in Chaucer's Troilus*, p. 410).

75. Thomas A. Van, "Imprisoning and Ensnarement in *Troilus* and *The Knight's Tale, PLL*, 7 (1971): 3–12; Barney, "Troilus Bound," *Speculum*, 47 (1972): 445–58.

76. Galatians 5:1. Cf. Galatians 4:1–5, and Romans 6:3–7, 17–18.

77. Cf. *ParsT*, 132 and 277; *SecNT*, 345–47; *MLT*, 570–71. Most of the Chaucerian references have been noted by Barney, "Troilus Bound," p. 450, n. 25, but his handling of the theme is somewhat different. Note too that Christ also functions as opener of the gates of hell, an analogous action.

78. In the *Consolation* the uses of the yoke, bridle, or chain *in malo* far outnumber the uses *in bono*. Thus the good bridle and good yoke mentioned in the text should be contrasted with the bad yoke of Bk. III, m. 1 already cited, with the bad yokes of Bk. II, pr. 1 and m. 7, and with the bad bridle of Bk. I, m. 7. I cannot find any good chains *per se* in the *Consolation* with the possible exception of the "destinal cheyne" of Bk. V, pr. 2. Bad chains, however, abound. In addition to the "hevy cheynes" of Bk. I, m. 2 cited in the text, cf. the chains of Bk. I, m. 4 and Bk. III, m. 10. Three more chains *in malo* in the *Consolation* will be discussed in the text as they are specifically libidinous. On chain imagery in the *Troilus* and other Chaucerian poems see John Leyerle, "The Heart and the Chain," in *The Learned and the Lewed: Studies in Chaucer and Medieval Literature*, ed. Larry D. Benson (Cambridge, Mass., 1974), pp. 113–45. Leyerle concentrates on the good chain.

79. McCall, "Five-Book Structure," passim.

80. Remarkably, neither Skeat, Root, nor Robinson notes this clear indebtedness. For a very different treatment of the religious elements in the poem see A. C. Spearing, *Chaucer: Troilus and Criseyde* (London, 1976), pp. 23–27.

81. Cf. Thomas W. Ross, *Chaucer's Bawdy* (New York, 1972), p. 166. For a later usage in precisely the same sense see "The Court of Love," wherein the scorner of love, like Troilus, becomes a worshipper of Venus and vows to be "the chief post of thy feith" (*Chaucerian and Other Pieces*, ed. Walter W. Skeat [Oxford, 1957], l. 1189).

82. On providence and purveiaunce see the *Consolation* in Chaucer's translation, Bk. IV, pr. 6.

83. The possibility of an obscene pun on "penaunce" is not suggested by Ross, but seems warranted in this instance. A clearer occurrence may be found elsewhere in the *Troilus* when it is said of the hero that, trusting in Criseyde's promise to return:

> . . . the grete furie of his penaunce
> Was queynt with hope, and therwith hem bitwene
> Bigan for joie th'amorouse daunce.   [IV, 1429–31]

There is, of course, an additional pun here on "queynt." One may also compare Dorigen's decision to marry Arveragus because she "Hath swich a pitee caught of his penaunce" (*FranklT*, 740). The pun is very clearly established by the time of the Renaissance. Donne uses it in the elegy "Going to Bed": ". . . cast all, yea, this white lynnen hence, / There is no pennance due to innocence" (*The Complete Poetry of John Donne*, ed. John T. Shawcross [New York, 1968], p. 58, ll. 45–46), while Shakespeare uses it in Henry VIII, I, iv, 15–18, with an additional pun on *confessor*. See Eric Partridge, *Shakespeare's Bawdy* (London, 1968), s.v. "confessor." For the reference to John Donne I am indebted to my colleague Graham Roebuck.

84. For the historical background of direct and ironic statement in late medieval poetry, see Charles Dahlberg, "The Narrator's Frame for *Troilus*," *ChauR*, 15 (1980): 85–100.

85. For background on the medieval theories of contraries see Chauncey Wood, "Speech, the Principle of Contraries, and Chaucer's Tales of the Manciple and the Parson," forthcoming in *Medievalia*, 6 (1980): 209–29.

Chapter IV

1. On "stuwe" (III, 601, 698) in the sense of "brothel," see Ross, *Chaucer's Bawdy*, pp. 214–15. The Summoner's reference to "wommen of the styves" (*FrT*, 1332), is convincing evidence that the word could be used in this sense by Chaucer.

2. I follow Root in reading "seint" rather than "blisful" in III, 705. On the superiority of readings from the *beta* group see Daniel Cook, "The Revision of Chaucer's *Troilus*: The *Beta* Text," *ChauR*, 9 (1974): 51–62. The idea of Venus as a "saint" in the parodic religion of love may have been suggested to Chaucer by the *Romance of the Rose*. Cf. "my modir, seint Venus" in the Middle English *Romaunt*, l. 5953.

3. The significance of the date has been debated. See Robertson, "Chaucerian Tragedy," Schoeck and Taylor, II, 101; John P. McCall, "Chaucer's May 3," *MLN*, 76 (1961): 201–5; George R. Adams and Bernard S. Levy, "Good and Bad Fridays and May 3 in Chaucer," *ELN*, 4 (1966): 245–48.

4. See Robertson, "Chaucerian Tragedy," p. 107, and *Preface*, p. 488. On music and the two Venuses see *Preface*, pp. 124–37.

5. That kissing is a warrant of ultimate bedding is at least as old as Ovid. For kissing as "ernest of the remenaunt" see *RR*, 3677–80. Kisses were also used to seal contracts of fealty and marriage in the Middle Ages, and in that sense Pandarus praises in religious terms what he perceives as the sexual "contract" he has been arranging.

6. For the glove as sexual symbol see Fleming, *Roman de la Rose*, pp. 85–86.

7. The literal as well as figurative centrality of the seduction scene is discussed by Thomas B. Hanson, "The Center of *Troilus and Criseyde*," *ChauR*, 9 (1975): 297–302. The article by Robert P. apRoberts, "The Central Episode in Chaucer's *Troilus*," *PMLA*, 77 (1962): 373–85, is in fact devoted to the degree of Criseyde's acquiescence before the fact rather than to centrality per se.

8. In order to account for the many possible roles of Venus, medieval mythographers refer to two Venuses, to three Venuses, and distinguish her functions in different myths and in various astrological situations. The existence in the Middle Ages of not only a "good" and a "bad" Venus but of several species of nonsexual Venus was necessitated by her extraordinary variety in classical antiquity. At one time or another Venus was related to everything from sacred prostitution to modesty in matrons (Venus Verticordia); from a basic religious force to the mother of Rome (Venus Genetrix); from the Lucretian creative force to the goddess of victory (Venus Victrix). See Robert Schilling, *La Religion Romaine de Vénus* (Paris, 1954).

9. On the two Venuses see: Robertson, *Preface*, pp. 124–27, 370–73; Richard L. Hoffman, *Ovid and the Canterbury Tales* (Philadelphia, Pa., 1966), pp. 12–19; Wood, *Chaucer and the Country of the Stars*, pp. 67–73; Earl G. Schreiber, "Venus in the Medieval Mythographic Tradition," *JEGP*, 74 (1975): 519–35; George D. Economou, "The Two Venuses and Courtly Love," in *In Pursuit of Perfection: Courtly Love in Medieval Literature*, ed. Joan M. Ferrante and George D. Economou (Port Washington, N.Y., 1975), pp. 17–50; Robert Hollander, *Boccaccio's Two Venuses* (New York, 1977), passim, but see especially pp. 59–60 and 158–60.

10. Donald W. Rowe, *O Love, O Charite! Contraries Harmonized in Chaucer's Troilus* (Carbondale and Edwardsville, Ill., 1976), pp. 92–94. An essay similar to Rowe's book in that it finds "sexuality and charity . . . in one continuum" is by Davis Taylor, "The Terms of Love: A Study of Troilus's Style," reprinted in *Chaucer's Troilus: Essays in Criticism*, ed. Stephen A. Barney (Hamden, Conn., 1980), esp. p. 240.

11. Gordon, *Double Sorrow*, pp. 30–33.

12. *On Christian Doctrine*, pp. 87, 101–2.

13. See Tuve, *Allegorical Imagery*, p. 261. The joke is the opposite in Andreas Capellanus, where love is defined as lust at the outset, and a pretense is made that no other definition exists.

14. It is worth remarking here that the *Hous of Fame* presents a kind of mirror image of the *Troilus*. In the former poem Venus promotes the cause of Aeneas, who is inconstant in his relations with Dido, while in the latter, Venus grants the implorations of Troilus who is "falsed" by Criseyde. In both poems Venus is primarily linked with the male protagonist but has some minor connections with the female principal. Criseyde alludes to Venus, and Venus may be the cause of Dido's loving Aeneas as well as the other way around in view of the ambiguity of the lines describing her role: "She made Eneas so in grace / Of Dido, quene of that contree" (*HF*, 240–41). Dido is encountered again in the *Parlement of Foules* along with Helen, Cleopatra, Pyramus and Thisbe, Troilus himself, and many others who are depicted on the walls of the Temple of Venus. Some idea of the significance of these portraits of mostly unhappy events may be gained from Chaucer's linking the manner of their loves with the manner of their deaths: "Alle these were peynted on that other syde, / And al here love, and in what plyt they dyde" (*PF*, 293–94).

15. That the Temple of Venus in the *Knight's Tale* shows "the destructive power of earthly desire" and is little different from those of Mars and Diana is ably shown by Edmund Reiss,

"Chaucer's Parodies of Love," in *Chaucer the Love Poet*, ed. Jerome Mitchell and William Provost (Athens, Ga., 1973), p. 39. See also *Country of the Stars*, pp. 72–78 on the association of Venus with death in the *Knight's Tale* and *Troilus*.

16. That the stanza is about generation and not worthiness I argue in "On Translating Chaucer's *Troilus and Criseyde*, Book III, 12–14," *ELN*, 11 (1973): 9–14.

17. In the *Filostrato* Criseida is specifically childless, but Chaucer prefers to leave the matter in doubt (I, 132–33). It is clear, though, that whatever interest Criseyde may have had previously in procreation, it is not an issue in her affair with Troilus.

18. *Ovid and the Canterbury Tales*, pp. 56–60.

19. See further John P. McCall, "The Trojan Scene in Chaucer's *Troilus*," *ELH*, 29 (1962): 263–75. It should be noted that Chaucer here departs from Boccaccio, who says that Venus sent Jove to earth when she asked for first one thing and then another (III, 76). For a very different reading of Jove's function in the *Troilus*, in which Venus represents a "civilizing influence" on both Jove and Mars, and in which Troilus' love for Criseyde is a manifestation of God's [i.e., Jove's] "love as it appears on earth," see Dorothy Bethurum Loomis, "The Venus of Alanus de Insulis and the Venus of Chaucer," in *Philological Essays: Studies in Old and Middle English Language and Literature in Honour of Herbert Dean Meritt*, ed. James L. Rosier (The Hague, 1970), p. 195.

20. See Alan T. Gaylord, "Friendship in Chaucer's *Troilus*," *ChauR*, 3 (1969): 239–64; Robert G. Cook, "Chaucer's Pandarus and the Medieval Ideal of Friendship," *JEGP*, 69 (1970): 407–24; Leah Rieber Freiwald, "Swych Love of Frendes: Pandarus and Troilus," *ChauR*, 6 (1971): 120–29.

21. See McCall, "The Trojan Scene," pp. 263–64.

22. For the significance of the strife between the rulers and their parliament see John P. McCall and George Rudisill, Jr., "The Parliament of 1386 and Chaucer's Trojan Parliament," *JEGP*, 58 (1959): 276–88.

23. I am indebted to Eleanor McCulloch for directing my attention towards this important theme, and to D. W. Robertson, Jr. for one of the details. See chapter 3, note 71 for McCulloch's thesis.

24. Although her uncle, Troilus, and later Diomede, are all interested in exploiting Criseyde, not everyone so behaves. Hector twice defends her (I, 113–23; IV, 176–214), and Deiphebus volunteers to be her "champioun" (II, 1427) in response to Pandarus' factitious story of Criseyde's persecution.

25. For fishing see V, 777. The idea that Venus reveals the *invisibilia* of private parts is put into an amusing context of religious language by Jean de Meun in the closing verses of the *Romance*. This might be Chaucer's source for the idea. See Fleming's fig. 42 and the discussion below in this chapter.

26. In his notes Robinson suggests that the language used here echoes that often addressed to the Virgin. However, "lady bright" is used frequently by Chaucer in a secular sense (indeed Criseyde is so addressed), and Venus' "benignitee" seems no more than coincidentally similar to the phrasing of the Prioress' prayer to the Virgin. Nevertheless, that the poet styles himself a "clerc" acting in "reverence" of those who serve Venus is part of the larger scheme of religious imagery.

27. *Chaucer and the Country of the Stars*, p. 49. For a somewhat different view see Daniel C. Boughner, "Elements of Epic Grandeur in the *Troilus*," Schoeck and Taylor, II, 186–95. Although Calliope is not always identified as the muse of epic poetry in the Middle Ages, she is so specified by Fulgentius, one of the earliest and most influential of the mythographers. See *Fulgentius the Mythographer*, trans. Leslie George Whitbread (Columbus, Ohio, 1971), p. 43. It is tempting to think that Chaucer had Fulgentius in mind. In the Prologue to his *Mythologies* Fulgentius invokes the Muses, among them "friendly Calliope" the "queen of eloquence" (p. 43). In his conversation with her, Fulgentius is obliged for the second time in his Prologue to disclaim any intention of writing erotic poetry. Calliope accordingly offers the aid of Philosophy and Urania for his serious purpose. Later, Calliope appears to him "tall beyond the average look of mortal men" (p. 47) and reminds Fulgentius of his philosophical goals. It may be that Chaucer, like Fulgentius, invoked Calliope not only as the epic Muse and not only because of her pride of place among the Muses (as the one who responds in the contest with the Pierides), but also as a Muse of philosophy rather than eroticism. Her great height in Fulgentius' version is

reminiscent of Lady Philosophy in the *Consolation*, Bk. 1, pr. 1, and Fulgentius' overall presentation of her suggests an anti-Venus. Chaucer's selection of her to close his Prohemium to Venus would be, accordingly, ironically enriched in that he asks the philosophical, epic, non-erotic muse to help him describe "the gladnesse / Of Troilus, to Venus heryinge" (III, 47–48). There is no evidence that Chaucer knew Fulgentius, but he knew Dante, who invokes both the planet Venus and Calliope, the muse of epic, at the opening of the *Purgatorio*, in which he will describe the ascent of souls to Heaven. The ironic contrast with Troilus' ascent to his heaven of love is obvious.

28. While there is much to admire in Allen C. Koretsky's study of the apostrophes in the poem, I cannot agree with him that Troilus' two apostrophes in Book III "present an exalted conception of love" ("Chaucer's Use of the Apostrophe in *Troilus and Criseyde*," *ChauR*, 4 [1971]: 253).

29. For an example see P. M. Kean, *Chaucer and the Making of English Poetry* (London, 1972), I, 127, where Troilus' apostrophe of III, 1744, ff. is thought to be similar to the Prohemium and to III, 1802 ff., all giving us "assurance of the ennobling power love exerts on Troilus."

30. See, for example, Meech, pp. 19, 126.

31. Robertson, "Tragedy," Schoeck and Taylor, II, 100.

32. Cf. Job 3:10; Canticles 5:14. Ross' excellent analysis of the erotic language of Book III does not discuss this particular image. Michael E. Cotton's contention that the "texture of the poetry" runs counter to Troilus' "rapturous panegyrics" and to the "heavenly" terminology is correct; I offer different examples. See "The Artistic Integrity of Chaucer's *Troilus and Criseyde*," *ChauR*, 7 (1972): 37–43.

33. Parts of this scene may be instructively compared and contrasted with Dante's encounter with Beatrice and his subsequent ascent to Heaven. Both Dante and Troilus are rebuked by their ladies—Dante for his inconstancy (*Purg.* 30:73–74), and Troilus for Pandarus' report of his belief in Criseyde's inconstancy. Troilus says he is "nought to blame" (III, 1085), faints, and is tossed into bed, while Dante confesses his guilt, is forgiven, and falls asleep to a hymn (*Purg.* 31:34–42; 32:61–69). Dante is vouchsafed a vision of the future of the Church and the Empire, drinks of the river of Eunoë, and is born again to rise to heaven with his eyes fixed on the sun and Beatrice by his side (*Purg.* 33, passim; *Par.* I, passim). Troilus awakens with his shirt opened and Criseyde kissing him. Pandarus takes away the light, Troilus grabs Criseyde when "sodeynly avysed" (III, 1186), delights in the "hevene" of her body, and apostrophizes Love and Charity.

34. If we assume that in the earlier prayer to the planetary deities Venus' father refers to Saturn, then it follows that Troilus is here thanking the same deities he earlier asked for help.

35. The Cytherean Venus also represents the fleshly aspect of Venus in the *Knight's Tale*, 1936–37, 2215, 2223. It is from Cytherea that Venus arrives in the closing scenes of the *Romance of the Rose* to help Amant by shooting a flaming arrow at what, in at least one illumination, are depicted as flaming genitalia. (See Tuve, fig. 100.) The claim by George D. Economou that Cytherea represents the good as opposed to the concupiscent Venus throughout Chaucer's works depends upon Troilus' confused hymn for part of its proof (*The Goddess Natura in Medieval Literature* [Cambridge, Mass., 1972], pp. 137–38). The argument of J. A. W. Bennett in *The Parlement of Foules: An Interpretation* (Oxford, 1957), p. 56, that in the *Parlement* "Cytherea can hardly be anything but the benevolent planet of a christianized cosmology" is also unconvincing. The firebrand that accompanies the goddess in the *Parlement* is surely a sign of the concupiscent Venus as it is in the English version of the *Romaunt*, l. 3705, and as it is in the concupiscent marriage of January and May in the *Merchant's Tale*. Bennett notes these passages but does not seem to find them running counter to his claim for a benevolent Cytherea. That Troilus hails Venus as the "wel-willy planete" (III, 1257), is mildly ironic considering all the woe he suffers because of Venus' influence in his horoscope (II, 684–85).

36. See the previous note and Robert P. Miller, "The Myth of Mars' Hot Minion in Venus and Adonis," *ELH*, 26 (1959): 470–81.

37. C. S. Lewis says that Book III is "in effect a long epithalamium." However, he grants that there is the "thinnest partition" between theirs and wedded love. *The Allegory of Love* (New York, 1958), pp. 196–97. See also A. Leigh DeNeef, "Robertson and the Critics," *ChauR*, 2 (1968): 229–30; John Maguire, "The Clandestine Marriage of Troilus and Criseyde," *ChauR*, 8 (1974): 262–78. Maguire notes that Criseyde pledges her "trouthe" in III, 1111, and compares this with the plighting of troth in a medieval marriage ceremony (pp. 271–72). However, a marriage requires that the participants agree to marry one another, as is illustrated by the marriage document Maguire adduces. Criseyde's pledging of her "trouthe," on the other hand, is simply her affirmation that she is not angry: "'Iwys, my deere herte, I am nought wroth, / Have here my trouthe!' and many another oth" (III, 1110–11). This line does not and cannot have anything to do with marriage. The use of "trouthe" in avowals is a commonplace in Middle English, and there are dozens of instances of its use in that sense in Chaucer's writings. The precise phrase "have here my trouthe" may be found in *KnT*, 1610 and *PardT*, 755 in nonmatrimonial contexts, and other examples could be adduced. Maguire further contends that Troilus' address to Criseyde as "'wommanliche wif'" (III, 106, 1296) is additional evidence for a matrimonial union. It seems rather to be part of the larger pattern of Troilus' linguistic inaccuracy, and underscores Troilus' inability to confront and name the true nature of his and Criseyde's relationship. There are two more extensive studies of the asserted phenomenon of clandestine marriage by Henry Ansgar Kelly: "Clandestine Marriage and Chaucer's *Troilus*," *Viator*, 4 (1973): 435–57; *Love and Marriage in the Age of Chaucer* (Ithaca and London, 1975). Kelly is energetic and resourceful in showing that clandestine marriages, based on mutual consent, were both valid and widespread in medieval England. He is less successful in his attempts to show that several occur in Chaucer. Indeed, with the supposed clandestine marriage in the *Troilus*, Kelly is forced to plead that it is so secret it was not only hidden from the Trojans but also from Chaucer's own audience (*Love and Marriage*, p. 240). In his essay on the marriage in *Viator*, Kelly argues that Hymen, god of marriage, is invoked, rings are exchanged, and vows of truth (the presumed equivalent of trothplight) are exchanged. This overlooks some important qualifications: Hymen is invoked along with the Cytherean Venus who usually represents lechery; the exchange of rings is undercut by the partial modifier, "pleyinge entrechaungeden hire rynges" (III, 1368); the vows seem not to be considered binding by either of the participants since neither presents it as a fait accompli to prevent the exchange of Criseyde for Antenor. For a rebuttal of the suggestion made by Kelly (*Love and Marriage*, p. 328) and others that Troilus goes to Heaven as a reward for loving, see *Chaucer and the Country of the Stars*, pp. 180–91, where it is argued that Troilus is remanded for a very long time to a place of penance or purification in the eighth sphere, a place much more like purgatory than like Heaven. For a more general response to Kelly's book see the review by Derek Brewer in *RES*, 28 (1977): 194–97. On secrecy see Edmund Reiss, "Chaucer's *deerne love* and the Medieval View of Secrecy in Love," p. 170. A recent article by Karl P. Wentersdorf, "Some Observations on the Concept of Clandestine Marriage in *Troilus and Criseyde*," *ChauR*, 15 (1980): 101–26, goes over some of the same ground covered earlier by Maguire and Kelly. While Wentersdorf plays down the significance of Troilus' addressing Criseyde as "'wommanliche wif'" (III, 106, 1296), he nevertheless insists that "the phrase 'they were oon' is surely an intentional echo of the biblical concept of man and wife as 'one flesh'" (p. 115). This is very tenuous. Chaucer uses the idea of man and woman being "aton" in a distinctly nonmatrimonial context in the *Reeve's Tale*, l. 4197. Critics who argue for a clandestine marriage in the *Troilus* ignore the intention of the principals. As Hugh of St. Victor noted in his *De sacramentis*, "those who consent only to the mingling of the flesh, in view of such a consent cannot still be called consorts. For both fornicators and adulterers do this, from whom the phrase, conjugal chastity, is recognized to be far removed" (*On the Sacraments of the Christian Faith*, trans. Roy J. Deferrari [Cambridge, Mass., 1951], p. 329). Although no marriage takes place in the *Troilus*, the echoes of the marriage ceremony are there for a purpose: to remind us of the ultimate expression of "trouthe" between individuals, which is modelled upon Christ's marriage to the Church. Thus the poem's closing invocation of the "sothfast Crist" (V, 1860) who "nyl falsen no wight" (V, 1845) supplies the paradigm for genuine "trouthe" and also for marriage. Moreover, insofar as the proper relationship between a sovereign and his subjects was perceived as a marriage, the lack of a proper marriage in Old Troy is proleptic of the troubles in New Troy. Gower comes at this point directly when he says in *Vox Clamantis* that "Useful doctrine is unwelcome, but the delight of Venus' prattlings is quite a joy to the ear. Now love is lust and adultery is married . . ." (p. 259).

38. On the more general issue of inappropriate language in the poem, see the admirable essay by Adrienne Lockhart, "Semantic, Moral, and Aesthetic Degeneration in *Troilus and Criseyde*," *ChauR*, 8 (1973): 100–118.

39. See, for example, Root's 1926 edition. The same passage from the *Paradiso* was later used in much more appropriate circumstances by Chaucer in the Second Nun's *Invocacio ad Mariam*.

40. Gordon, *Double Sorrow*, pp. 34–35.

41. Observed by Gordon, p. 38.

42. Gordon, p. 36.

43. B. G. Koonce, *Chaucer and the Tradition of Fame: Symbolism in the House of Fame* (Princeton, 1966), p. 92; J. A. W. Bennett, *Chaucer's Book of Fame: An Exposition of 'The Hous of Fame'* (Oxford, 1968), pp. 15–24; Meg Twycross, *The Medieval Anadyomene: A Study in Chaucer's Mythography*, Medium Aevum Monographs, n.s. no. 1 (Oxford, 1972), p. 88.

44. For Oiseuse's iconographic—and moral—background, see Fleming, pp. 73–80.

45. In addition to the general similarity between the Venuses of the two poems and the specific similarity of the "religious" attitudes towards sexuality of Amant and Troilus, the scene of Troilus' infatuation is reminiscent of Amant's experiences and of the Well of Narcissus as noted in chapter 3. Troilus is several times called "proud," he is hit with an arrow fired by the God of Love, Love begins to lime his feathers (I, 353), he makes a mirror of his mind in which he sees Criseyde (I, 365–66), and he says he has been caught in a "snare" (I, 506). In the *Romance*, Amant, like the proud Narcissus, gazes into the Mirror Perilous, where Cupid, Venus' son, sets his snares to capture lovers, not deigning to hunt any other bird. In the mirror Amant sees the rose, and soon he is shot by an arrow fired by the God of Love. Although it is only later in the poem that Troilus is overtly linked with Venus, and only at the end of the *Romance* that Venus comes directly to the aid of Amant, nevertheless Venus was favorable in Troilus' nativity (II, 684–95), and she ultimately controls the garden that Amant enters at the beginning of the poem.

46. The idea that a poet's employment of an iconographic description without its moralization implies a rejection of the moralization (a position most firmly stated by Jean Seznec, who thought that Petrarch did this because he was a humanist and a man of taste), must remain a red herring until its supporters explain how images can be so neatly cut off from their contextual meanings. When Chaucer furnishes the Summoner with a diet of garlic, onions, and leeks, it is incontrovertible that Chaucer wishes to convey both the scriptural source and its meaning: otherwise he is merely saying that the Summoner eats like some people in the Bible, which is nonsense. For Seznec's remark see *The Survival of the Pagan Gods*, trans. Barbara F. Sessions (New York, 1961), p. 174. For the Summoner see my article, "The Sources of Chaucer's Summoner's 'Garleek, Oynons, and eek Lekes,'" *ChauR*, 5 (1971): 240–44.

47. *Arthurian Legends in Medieval Art* (New York, 1938), p. 70 and fig. 135. The picture is reproduced without discussion by J. A. W. Bennett, *The Parlement of Foules*, plate 2b. Seznec discusses but does not reproduce the work in *Survival of the Pagan Gods*, p. 206, n. 64.

48. Note too that Pride figures importantly in Pope's imagery as it does in the illustrations that are to be discussed.

> And now, unveiled, the Toilet stands display'd,
> Each silver Vase in mystic order laid.
> First, rob'd in white, the Nymph intent adores,
> With head uncover'd, the Cosmetic pow'rs.
> A heav'nly Image in the glass appears,
> To that she bends, to that her eyes she rears;
> Th'inferior Priestess, at her altar's side
> Trembling, begins the sacred rites of Pride.

(*Poetical Works*, ed. Herbert Davis [London, 1966], ll. 121–28). For a brilliant analysis of the unheroic events of the *Troilus*, in spite of its epic form, see Thomas E. Maresca, *Three English Epics* (Lincoln, Neb., and London, 1979), pp. 143–98.

49. *Allegorical Imagery*, p. 260 on the "commandments"; p. 261 on the lover's pliancy.

50. *KnT*, 1101–2; *T&C*, I, 425–26. There are similar phrases in both the *Teseida* and the *Filostrato*, which I believe function in the same way. On John the carpenter's pride see John J. O'Connor, "The Astrological Background of the *Miller's Tale*," *Speculum*, 31 (1956): 125.

51. For a clear example see Jean Seznec, *Survival of the Pagan Gods*, plate 80. Cupid is sometimes depicted with clawed or taloned feet, but the artistic intention is to suggest by this that he is a devil. See Erwin Panofsky, *Studies in Iconology* (New York, 1962), p. 115. Panofsky's interpretation of the lying-in tray is that the knights depicted therein are Venus' "victims" (p. 115, n. 65).

52. See, for example, *Fulgentius the Mythographer*, trans. Leslie George Whitbread (Columbus, Ohio, 1971), p. 73. Note too Boethius' "wikkide cheynes" of the "desceyvable delyt of erthly thynges" residing in man's thoughts in Bk. III, m. 10. For further discussion see Robert P. Miller, p. 478; Robertson, *Preface*, pp. 105, 394, 499, 478; *Chaucer and the Country of the Stars*, pp. 138–39; supra, chapter 3, n. 78.

53. The Loomises contend that the rays stream from Venus' "body," while Seznec says they come from her "womb" (p. 206, n. 64). Gordon more accurately notes that most of them emanate from the "pudendum" (p. 134). Alfred E. Hamill and Ulrich Middeldorf comment on the significance of gazing at Venus' pudendum in two Renaissance paintings in letters in *The Art Bulletin*, 29 (1947): 65–67. The picture's emphasis on the pudendum is heightened by the placement of Venus in a mandorla, which has an obviously vaginal shape. *In bono* the vaginally shaped mandorla is used for Christ, and represents the eternal Incarnation of the Word. See the analysis printed with the frontispiece, "Alpha and Omega"–Bib. Nat. MS Lat. 9438, in *By Things Seen: Reference and Recognition in Medieval Thought*, ed. David L. Jeffrey (Ottawa, 1979).

54. Joan Morton Jones, "The Chess of Love: Old French Text with Translation and Commentary," Ph.D. diss. Nebraska 1968, p. 459.

55. Meech, *Design*, p. 220.

Chapter V

1. Robertson, *Preface*, p. 248.

2. Ibid., p. 249.

3. For example, Edward Wagenknecht, *The Personality of Chaucer* (Norman, Okla., 1968), p. 88; Matthew Corrigan, "Chaucer's Failure with Women: The Inadequacy of Criseyde," *Western Humanities Review*, 23 (1969): 114. In a generally perceptive essay on the narrator's attitude toward the heroine, E. Talbot Donaldson, by professing that he himself loves Criseyde, takes psychological criticism to the critic (*Speaking of Chaucer* [London, 1970], p. 71). For a more effusive reaction ("I do hereby and herewith bequeath to Criseyde, the perfect symbol of woman, my love for as long as I may"), see Neil D. Isaacs, "Further Testimony in the Matter of *Troilus*," *Studies in the Literary Imagination*, 4 (1971): 27. People who "love" literary characters would not have astonished anyone in the Middle Ages, when literary characters themselves were described as loving rosebuds (like Amant), statues (like Pygmalion), or their own images (like Narcissus). Even so, it will doubtless be of more general usefulness if critics concentrate on analyzing their subjects rather than on self-analysis. For more temperate considerations of Criseyde see Alfred David, "Chaucerian Comedy and Criseyde," and Mark Lambert, "*Troilus*, Books I–III: A Criseydan Reading," both in *Essays on Troilus and Criseyde*, ed. Mary Salu, *Chaucer Studies* III (Cambridge and Totawa, N.J., 1979), pp. 90–104, 105–25. In spite of the plethora of gushy remarks on Chaucer's Criseyde and Boccaccio's Criseida, it is worth noting that exceptions to the rule have been around for more than half a century. Henri Hauvette, for example, thought Boccaccio's treatment of his heroine more satiric than that of either Troilo or Pandaro. See *Boccace: Étude Biographique et Littéraire* (Paris, 1914), p. 85.

4. For a rare instance of character reversal consider Chauntecleer, easily "ravysshed" by "flaterie" (*NPT*, 3324), whose experiences finally teach him to overcome his blind pride.

5. It is possible to overstress the complexity of Criseyde's makeup, as when Charles Muscatine says "her ambiguity is her meaning" (*Chaucer and the French Tradition* [Berkeley and Los Angeles, 1957], p. 164).

6. Lewis, *Allegory of Love*, pp. 185–90. Some fourteen years before the appearance of Lewis' book, R. K. Root had called attention to Criseyde's "slydynge corage" in *The Poetry of Chaucer* (Boston, 1922), p. 114. Arthur Mizener's objection to Root's interpretation is that it puts the whole burden of clarifying Criseyde's motives upon a half line located near the end of the poem. See "Character and Action in the Case of Criseyde," reprinted in *Chaucer: Modern Essays in Criticism*, ed. Edward Wagenknecht (New York, 1959), p. 349. However, as noted in the text, it would be easy enough to adduce more evidence. Significantly, Mizener does not attempt to refute Lewis' more detailed argument.

7. For more detailed analyses of this aspect of Criseyde, see: Susan Schibanoff, "Argus and Argyve: Etymology and Characterization in Chaucer's *Troilus*," *Speculum*, 51 (1976): 647–58;

Peggy A. Knapp, "The Nature of Nature: Criseyde's 'Slydyng Corage,'" *ChauR*, 13 (1978): 133–40; David Aers, "Criseyde: Woman in Medieval Society," *ChauR*, 13 (1979): 177–200.

8. Ida L. Gordon, "Processes of Characterization in Chaucer's *Troilus and Criseyde*," in *Studies in Medieval Literature and Language in Memory of Frederick Whitehead*, ed. W. Rothwell, et al. (Manchester, 1973), p. 130.

9. One of the rare essays noting Criseyde's deficiency in fortitude, although not in moral or theological terms, is by Maureen Fries, "'Slydynge of Corage': Chaucer's Criseyde as Feminist and Victim," in *The Authority of Experience: Essays in Feminist Criticism*, ed. Arlyn Diamond and Lee R. Edwards (Amherst, Mass., 1977), p. 58.

10. Mizener repeatedly claims that Criseyde is prudent, in spite of her own testimony to the contrary ("Character and Action," pp. 349, 353, 354).

11. Griselda's husband, Walter, is also prudent. On the other hand, Chaucer says that a character is prudent several times when it is reasonably clear that his meaning is the opposite, and he is being ironic. Thus the lecherous Monk of the *Shipman's Tale* is said to be prudent, and the Man of Law's praise of rich merchants as being prudent presumably reflects his and not Chaucer's ideas on the subject. Note too that when Placebo wishes to flatter January he praises his prudence—a quality conspicuously absent in the self-indulgent January. On Prudence's importance for *The Canterbury Tales*, see the admirable essay by Elisabeth Lunz, "Chaucer's Prudence as the Ideal of the Virtuous Woman," *Essays in Literature—Western Illinois University*, 4 (1977): 3–10.

12. It has long been known that Chaucer's source for the three-eyed Prudence is Dante's *Purgatorio*, XXIX, 132. Recently it has been suggested that Dante's somewhat cryptic lines would have made a greater impact on Chaucer had he read them in a glossed and illustrated manuscript, and indeed such manuscripts were available. See Lloyd J. Matthews, "Chaucer's Personification of Prudence in *Troilus* (V, 743–749): Sources in the Visual Arts and Manuscript Scholia," *ELN*, 13 (1975–76): 249–55.

13. It is ably argued by Susan Schibanoff that the audience is encouraged by the poem to exercise prudence in order to evaluate the actions of the characters. "Prudence and Artificial Memory in Chaucer's *Troilus*," *ELH*, 42 (1975): 507–17.

14. For Criseyde's pride note her "chere, / Which somdel deignous was" (I, 289–90). She considers herself one of the best and most beautiful women in Troy (II, 746–47), and complacently imagines how the company would glorify her if they knew she had the power of life and death over the great Troilus (II, 1590–94).

15. Boccaccio elsewhere writes that widows, because of their former experience in love, are the more easily disposed toward that passion. See *Boccaccio on Poetry*, ed. and trans. Charles G. Osgood (New York, 1956), p. 68. It follows that Boccaccio's portrayal of Criseida in the *Filostrato* is as easily understood in literary as in personal terms. Chaucer's heroine does, of course, have her share of passion too. See E. Talbot Donaldson, "Briseis, Briseida, Criseyde, Cresseid, Cressid: Progress of a Heroine," in *Chaucerian Problems and Perspectives: Essays Presented to Paul E. Beichner, C.S.C.*, ed. Edward Vasta and Zacharias P. Thundy (Notre Dame and London, 1979), pp. 3–12.

16. *Lydgate's Siege of Thebes*, ed. Axel Erdmann, EETS, e.s. no. 108 (London, 1911), I, 123: ll. 2981–83. Of course, Chaucer could not have known Lydgate's work, but the moral seems implicit in the story. Statius does not directly charge the Greeks with imprudence, but Lydgate may have picked this up from medieval *scholia*. In the French version, which Chaucer did know, Amphiarus' death is a warning to the Greeks that they are being punished for their sins: "Pour nos pechiez Dex nos apele, / et par son flael nos flaele." Taking that sense of the story, Criseyde should be very cautious about her actions, for as Amphiarus' death was a warning to the Greeks, so should it be a warning to Criseyde. Significantly, Pandarus urges her "'Do wey youre book'" (II, 111), and it is not heard of again. The story of Thebes, however, is later recapitulated by Cassandra. On Chaucer's knowledge of the French version see B. A. Wise, *The Influence of Statius on Chaucer* (New York, 1967), p. 9. For the text see *Le roman de Thèbes*, ed. Guy Raynaud DeLage (Paris, 1966), I, 167: ll. 5329–30. For an excellent interpretation of the function of the "Siege of Thebes" in Chaucer's *Troilus*, see Alice B. Miskimin, *The Renaissance Chaucer*, pp. 199–205. Essentially Miskimin argues that the "Siege of Thebes" tells a cautionary story about men and gods at strife, yet the work is twice rejected, by Pandarus and Troilus, as irrelevant or untrue. This, in turn, intensifies the meaning of the tale for Chaucer's audience. Another fine treatment of the Theban background is by David Anderson, "Theban History in Chaucer's *Troilus*," *Studies in the Age of Chaucer*, 4 (1982): 109–33. For a very different approach to the incident see Alain Renoir, "Thebes, Troy, Criseyde, and Pandarus: An Instance of Chaucerian Irony," *Studia Neophilologia*, 32 (1960): 14–17.

17. "Chaucerian Tragedy," Schoeck and Taylor, II, 102.

18. The *locus classicus*, of course, is Abelard's Preface to the *Sic et non*. Leif Grane has observed that while Abelard leaves the "solution" of contrasting passages to the reader, Abelard nevertheless shows the "proper direction." See *Peter Abelard: Philosophy and Christianity in the Middle Ages*, trans. Frederick and Christine Crowley (London, 1964), p. 88.

19. On Chaucer's change of a very clear allusion in Gower to a much less transparent detail of description in *The Canterbury Tales*, see my article "The Sources of Chaucer's Summoner's 'Garleek, Oynons, and eek Lekes,'" *ChauR*, 5 (1971): 240–44.

20. Criseyde asks Pandarus how he fares in "loves daunce" (II, 1106), and the lovers are said to begin "for joie th'amorouse daunce" (IV, 1431).

21. For a discussion of medieval ideas about widowhood see Robertson, *Preface*, p. 483, and chapter 3, n. 27.

22. On the ruby and the ring see *Chaucer's Bawdy*, s.v. "hol." Gordon's generally fine analysis of the passage probably errs in perceiving a reference on the literal level to the relationship between wisdom and rubies. Although the pertinent passages in the King James version specify rubies, the Vulgate passages do not mention gems at all (Proverbs 3:15, 8:11; Job 28:18). See Gordon, *Double Sorrow*, pp. 136–37.

23. Robertson discusses these terms in his essay "The Subject of the *De amore* of Andreas Capellanus," *MP*, 50 (1953): 152.

24. See further the admirable article by Adrienne R. Lockhart, "Semantic, Moral and Aesthetic Degeneration in *Troilus and Criseyde*," *ChauR*, 8 (1973): 100–118.

25. Dahlberg's translation, p. 99 (l.4645).

26. Dahlberg's translation, p. 116 (ll. 5692–5762).

27. Criseyde's failures in reasoning show her vulnerability to passion, as is the case with Amant. Her failures in logic in particular may have been introduced by Chaucer for the amusement of some of his friends—especially the logician Ralph Strode to whom, along with Gower, the poem is dedicated. On the "philosophical" Strode's reputation as a logician, see Robertson, *Chaucer's London*, p. 201.

28. It has been contended by Maguire that this line can as easily be interpreted to signify that Criseyde is free to accept the attentions of Troilus as that it means she rejects marriage (Maguire, "The Clandestine Marriage," p. 270). However, Maguire's claim is not entirely convincing. Criseyde first observes that she stands "'unteyd in lusty leese / Withouten jalousie,'" then says no husband will say "'chek mat'" to her—one of the troubles with husbands being their proclivity towards jealousy. The probable meaning of the passage is that she does not suffer from marital jealousy in her widowed state and will not risk marriage, which might well bring her a jealous husband.

29. Tuve, *Allegorical Imagery*, p. 261.

30. For St. Augustine and Cicero on *passio* see Robertson, "The Subject of the *De Amore*," p. 152.

31. Criseyde's "sin" is mentioned by C. S. Lewis, *The Allegory of Love*, p. 184; Robert P. apRoberts, "Criseyde's Infidelity and the Moral of the *Troilus*," *Speculum*, 44 (1969): 393.

32. *The Art of Courtly Love*, p. 185, rule 17. apRoberts calls Criseyde's acceptance of Diomede "the unpardonable sin against the canons of love" (p. 397), while C. S. Lewis says that "by the code of courtly love it is unpardonable" (p. 184).

33. Lewis, *The Allegory*. The central theme of apRoberts' essay is that Criseyde is "perfect" in the first four books but commits a "gross sin" in the final book.

34. Robert Mannyng, *Robert of Brunne's Handlyng Synne*, ed. Frederick J. Furnivall, EETS, o.s. nos. 119 and 123 (London, 1901; 1903), p. 99. See also "What Vows Should Not Be Kept" in Hugh of Saint Victor, *On The Sacraments of the Christian Faith*, trans. Roy J. Deferrari (Cambridge, Mass., 1951), p. 371. There is a comprehensive consideration of oaths by Alan T. Gaylord, "The Promises in *The Franklin's Tale*," *ELH*, 21 (1964): 342–57.

35. "The People in Chaucer's *Troilus*," reprinted in Wagenknecht, *Chaucer: Modern Essays in Criticism*, p. 341.

36. Ibid., pp. 342–43. Kean, while finding that "the woman who can be influenced once can be influenced again—and more quickly," combines this observation with what I think to be an overestimation of Criseyde's "worth." See Kean, *Chaucer and the Making of English Poetry*, I, 133.

37. Bartlett Jere Whiting, *Chaucer's Use of Proverbs* (Cambridge, Mass., 1934), p. 75; R. M. Lumiansky, "The Function of the Proverbial Monitory Elements in Chaucer's *Troilus and Criseyde*," *Tulane Studies in English*, 2 (1950): 5–48.

38. For Gaylord, Cook, and Freiwald see chapter 4, n. 20. On Pandarus' lying see Robertson, "Chaucerian Tragedy," esp. p. 105; McCall, "Troilus and Criseyde," in the *Companion*, p. 452; W. F. Bolton, "Treason in *Troilus*," p. 258; Anthony E. Farnham, "Chaucerian Irony and the Ending of the *Troilus*," *ChauR*, 1 (1967): 209–11.

39. "Pandarus and the Fate of Tantalus," *Orbis Litterarum*, 24 (1969): 5. In spite of these negative facts there are some defenses of Pandarus, the most vigorous of which is by Eugene E. Slaughter, "Chaucer's Pandarus: Virtuous Uncle and Friend," *JEGP*, 48 (1949): 186–95. Almost as adulatory as Slaughter is Mary Grant Robbie, "Three-Faced Pandarus," *California English Journal*, 3 (1967): 47–54. Nevill Coghill in *The Poet Chaucer* (New York, 1967), argues that Pandarus is much like Chaucer himself (p. 55). Recently John Gardner has gone so far as to call Pandarus "the true lover of Troilus" (*The Poetry of Chaucer*, p. 129).

40. Alan T. Gaylord, "Uncle Pandarus as Lady Philosophy," *PMASAL*, 46 (1961): 571–95.

41. Kean, I, 148.

42. Cited by Fleming, p. 172. Peraldus' essay is one of the sources of the *Parson's Tale*.

43. Since Troilus and Pandarus call each other "brother" with some frequency, this passage may recall Matthew 5:22 on the extreme undesirability of calling one's brother "thou fool."

44. That Prudence's sententiousness is intended to be parodic has in fact been argued—indeed such an argument has probably been made more often than the argument for satire in Pandarus' use of proverbs. For a typical interpretation of the *Melibee* as a parody of Chaucer's own tendency to overuse proverbs, see Trevor Whittock, *A Reading of the Canterbury Tales* (Cambridge, 1968), pp. 214–17. For an opposite view of the *Melibee* see Chauncey Wood, "Chaucer and 'Sir Thopas': Irony and Concupiscence," *TSLL*, 14 (1972): 401–3. For a study of Pandarus' use of proverbs with conclusions quite different from those advanced here, see Karla Taylor, "Proverbs and the Authentication of Convention in 'Troilus and Criseyde,'" in *Chaucer's Troilus: Essays in Criticism*, ed. Stephen A. Barney (Hamden, Conn., 1980), pp. 277–96. Elaine Tuttle Hanson, "'The Sothe for to Seyne': Uses and Abuses of Proverbial and Sententious Discourse in Chaucer's *Troilus and Criseyde*," forthcoming in a *Festschrift* for Sherman Kuhn, notes that the proliferation of proverbs in *Troilus* makes them ineffectual, and Pandarus sometimes uses the same maxim for opposite purposes.

45. Sanford Brown Meech, "Chaucer and an Italian Translation of the *Heroides*," *PMLA*, 45 (1930): 110–28. *Epistole Eroiche di Ovidio Nasone*, ed. Vincenzo Monti (Milan, 1842), p. 42.

46. Mary-Jo Arn takes a different approach to the incident of Oenone's letter. Her conclusion, that Pandarus is a parody of the figure of the good teacher/physician, dovetails with this interpretation of him as an evil counselor. See "Three Ovidian Women in Chaucer's *Troilus*: Medea, Helen, Oënone," *ChauR*, 15 (1980): 1–10.

47. Editors and translators vary in their interpretation of this line, some relating it to hunting, others to playing at games. Either interpretation can be linked with other imagery in the poem. I should argue, however, that the line would refer to "*the* game" or "*a* game" if play were intended. Cf. "'For the have I bigonne *a* gamen pleye'" (III, 250).

48. Troilus also goes along with Pandarus' fictional account of the jealous "Horaste" (III, 795–98) because it is better for his purposes to deceive Criseyde than it would be to tell her the truth: "And for the lasse harm, he moste feyne" (III, 1158).

49. I cannot agree with Haldeen Braddy that Pandarus has sexual relations with Criseyde. Braddy's reading of the line "God foryaf his deth" (III, 1577) as referring to Pandarus' "death" of sexual orgasm is possible but not probable. Since Pandarus is described as one who knows every step of love's dance but who nevertheless hops behind in it (III, 694; II, 1107), we should imagine him in his relationship with Criseyde as one in whom the spirit is willing but the flesh weak. His interest in Criseyde is sexual, and symbolic of wrong loving, but it is doubtful that there is a physical consummation. Beryl Rowland's interpretation—that Pandarus is like Tantalus—is probably nearer the mark than Braddy's reading. See Braddy, "Chaucer's Playful Pandarus," *Southern Folklore Quarterly*, 34 (1970): 71–81, and Rowland, "Pandarus and the Fate of Tantalus," pp. 3–15.

50. "The People in Chaucer's *Troilus*," Schoeck and Taylor, II, 339.

51. *Design in Chaucer's Troilus*, p. 414.

52. On blind Fortune see Howard R. Patch, *The Goddess Fortuna in Mediaeval Literature* (Cambridge, Mass., 1922), pp. 38, 44, 96.

53. The pejorative connotations of the blindness and darkness of ignorance may be traced back from Boethius to Plato's allegory of the cave and ultimately to the worship of Apollo. For the Christian Middle Ages blindness could be associated with an intellectual failing, as in Boethius, or with a moral one, as in the numerous biblical references to blindness. In John 8:12 Christ says "Ego sum lux mundi: qui sequitur me, non ambulat in tenebris, sed habebit lumen vitae." As a consequence the interpretation of Christ's curing the blind, for example, in Luke 18:31–43, regularly relates the blind man to the human race, condemned to blindness because of the fall, and given sight by Christ's grace. See, for example, the *Glossa ordinaria*, PL, 114, cols. 324–25. The conversion of Saul is another *locus classicus* (Acts 9:1–19; 22:5–16; 26:12–18). The idea is so pervasive as to defy meaningful documentation. For the blind Synagogue, an interesting offshoot from this general tradition, see Émile Mâle, *The Gothic Image*, trans. Dora Nussey (New York, 1958), pp. 188–90, and Robertson, *Preface*, p. 189 and fig. 55.

54. Discussions of blindness in the *Troilus* are less common than one would expect. Some of the explicit imagery of blindness is noted by Meech, *Design in Chaucer's Troilus*, pp. 301–19, but without intensive analysis. There is a very good but brief discussion in John P. McCall, "The Trojan Scene," p. 271. Helen Storm Corsa, *Chaucer: Poet of Mirth and Morality* (Notre Dame, Ind., 1964), pp. 45–48, adduces a promising Boethian background for her discussion, but confines herself mainly to the metaphorical blindness of the three principals. P. M. Kean notes the blindness of passion in the poem, but does not discuss either blind Cupid or blind Fortune. Her contention that blind love can describe something desirable seems wide of the mark. On the other hand, her discussion of "blynde entencioun" (I, 211) and "blynde lust" (V, 1824) in terms of Boethius' *Consolation* Bk. V, m.3 and Bk. V, pr. 2 and 3 is admirable (I, 150–61). The best treatment of the subject, which appeared after my own study had been written, is by Julia Ebel, "Troilus and Oedipus: The Genealogy of an Image," *ES*, 55 (1974): 15–21.

55. Erwin Panofsky, "Blind Cupid," in *Studies in Iconology* (New York, 1962), pp. 112–13. A useful text by Pierre Bersuire, cited by Panofsky on p. 106, n. 38, has been translated by D. W. Robertson, Jr., ed., in *The Literature of Medieval England* (New York, 1970), p. 289: "Briefly, the poets wish to depict two blind deities, Cupid and Fortune. For Cupid, or love as it is called, is so blind that it sometimes undertakes the impossible, as is clear in the example of Narcissus, who loved his shadow unto death. In the same way we see vile persons love noble persons and vice versa. Fortune is also said to be blind when it provides for the unworthy and deprives the worthy. As St. Paul says [Romans 11:25], 'blindness has happened in Israel.'"

56. *Filostrato*, V, 56–57.

57. On Juno *pronuba* see Hoffman, *Ovid and the Canterbury Tales*, pp. 56–60.

58. For example, by Isidore of Seville, Rabanus Maurus, the second and third Vatican mythographers, "Thomas Walleys," (actually Pierre Bersuire), and Boccaccio. The texts are all cited by Panofsky, *Studies in Iconology*, pp. 105–7.

59. For Boccaccio's text (*Gen. deor.*, IX, 4) and other evidence see Panofsky, *Studies*. Panofsky remarks of the blindfold that "in the fourteenth century the blindness of Cupid had so precise a significance that his image could be changed from a personification of Divine Love to a personification of illicit Sensuality, and vice versa, by simply adding, or removing, the bandage" (p. 121). Panofsky's assertions about the "good" Cupid in the later Middle Ages, particularly the example he believes he finds in the Prologue to Chaucer's *Legend of Good Women*, are less convincing than his well-documented interpretation of the sensual Cupid.

60. See Patch, *The Goddess Fortuna*, p. 11.

61. "Chaucerian Tragedy," in Schoeck and Taylor, II, 86–121; *Preface*, pp. 472–503.

62. Root notes that the idea that a fool can sometimes advise a wise man *is* proverbial. In the context of the other images of blindness, though, the proverb is just silly. In this sense Pandarus is reminiscent of the blind guides of Matt. 23:24, who strain at gnats and swallow camels. Pandarus spouts proverbs on a hit-or-miss basis throughout the poem, and in view of his general role he is certainly not to be considered as an imparter of wisdom, albeit he sometimes parrots Lady Philosophy in inappropriate circumstances.

63. For a more detailed discussion of Chaucer's narrative pose as one unable in love see chapter 2.

64. "On the *Thebaid*," in *Fulgentius the Mythographer*, trans. George Leslie Whitbread (Columbus, Ohio, 1971), p. 240.

65. For a well-argued defense of the opposite point of view—that Troilus does *not* arrive at fuller comprehension among the spheres—see Edmund Reiss, "Troilus and the Failure of Understanding," *MLQ*, 29 (1968): 131–44.

66. For the tradition and its employment in Dante see John Freccero, "*Paradiso* X: The Dance of the Stars," *Dante Studies*, 86 (1968): 85–111.

67. Other imagery of this general sort is common in the Middle Ages. St. Cecilia is etymologically the way for the blind or the contrary of blindness in the Prologue to the *Second Nun's Tale*, while the opposite side of the coin may be found in Dante's description of Hell as the "cieco mondo" in *Inf.* IV, 13.

Epilogue

1. For an essay identifying numerous instances of infidelity in the poem, but which finds Troilus' "trouthe" to the unfaithful Criseyde to be evidence of his Christ-like nature, see Barbara Newman, "'Feynede Loves,' Feigned Lore, and Faith in Trouthe," in *Chaucer's Troilus: Essays in Criticism*, ed. Stephen A. Barney (Hamden, Conn., 1980), pp. 257–75.

2. Stephanie Yearwood, "The Rhetoric of Narrative Rendering in Chaucer's *Troilus*," *ChauR*, 12 (1977): 27; Thomas H. Bestul, "Chaucer's *Troilus and Criseyde*: The Passionate Epic and its Narrator," *ChauR*, 14 (1980): 366–78; Michael Olmert, "Troilus in *Piers Plowman*: A Contemporary View of Chaucer's *Troilus and Criseyde*," *The Chaucer Newsletter*, 2 (1980): 14; Thomas E. Maresca, *Three English Epics: Studies of Troilus and Criseyde, The Faerie Queene, and Paradise Lost* (Lincoln, Nebraska, and London, 1979), pp. 143–96. For a very early "judgmental" statement about Chaucer's "revulsion" at the "unsound morals" of the characters, see Karl Young, "Chaucer's Renunciation of Love in *Troilus*," *MLN*, 40 (1925): 270–76.

3. John M. Steadman, *Disembodied Laughter: Troilus and the Apotheosis Tradition* (Berkeley and Los Angeles, 1972), p. 124; Charles Dahlberg, "The Narrator's Frame for *Troilus*," *ChauR*, 15 (1980): 85.

4. Steadman, *Disembodied Laughter*, p. 106.

5. For a brilliant and detailed critique of the fondness for complexity among critics of the *Troilus*, see Alan T. Gaylord, "The Lesson of the *Troilus*: Chastisement and Correction," in *Essays on Troilus and Criseyde*, ed. Mary Salu, *Chaucer Studies III* (Cambridge and Totowa, N.J., 1979), pp. 23–42. Critical estimates of the *Troilus* as simultaneously expressing contradictory viewpoints are too numerous for meaningful documentation. However, here are two samples: ". . . the lines in which Chaucer condemns the world . . . poignantly enhance the very thing he is repudiating" (E. T. Donaldson, *Chaucer's Poetry: An Anthology for the Modern Reader* ([New York, 1958], p. 980); ". . . even the polar opposition in the Epilog of heavenly to mundane affection cannot obliterate our memories of the fine if soon withered fruits which the latter yielded to the hero" (Meech, *Design*, p. 427). That Chaucer was at war with his sources is the thesis of Salter's essay, "A Reconsideration." Edward Wagenknecht, who tentatively advances some simultaneously opposed views in the poem, nevertheless cautions us about Chaucer: "I doubt very much that he could ever have agreed with Keats that 'the only means of strengthening one's intellect is to make up one's mind about nothing'" (*The Personality of Chaucer* [Norman, Okla., 1968], p. 133).

6. Dorothy L. Sayers, *Introductory Papers on Dante* (London, 1954), p. 208.

7. Lee W. Patterson, "Ambiguity and Interpretation: A Fifteenth-Century Reading of *Troilus and Criseyde*," *Speculum*, 54 (1979): 323. Patterson's essay is nevertheless an important one.

8. Joan Morton Jones, "The Chess of Love: Old French Text with Translation and Commentary," (Ph.D. diss., Nebraska, 1968), part 3, p. 568.

9. *Commentum duplex in Boetium de consolatione philosophie* (Lyons, 1498), fol. 154. Cited by Steadman, *Disembodied Laughter*, p. 133, n. 31.

10. "Form and Social Statement in *Confessio Amantis* and *The Canterbury Tales*," *Studies in the Age of Chaucer*, I (1979): 27. J. A. W. Bennett, although finding an important strain of "courtoisie" in the *Confessio*, nevertheless notes that "'Honeste love' in wedlock, *caritas* in the commonwealth, are wholly compatible ideals. . . ." ("Gower's 'Honeste Love,'" in *Patterns of Love and Courtesy: Essays in Memory of C. S. Lewis*, ed. John Lawlor [Evanston, Ill., 1966], p. 121). The best treatment of this complex subject is by Russell Peck, who writes of the close of the *Confessio*, "The concluding prayer for the State of England grows naturally out of the romance plot as Gower fuses his great social theme with Amans' story. . . . Having regained his sense of personal kingdom he now prays, as poet, for common profit, right use of memory, and good governance" (*Kingship and Common Profit in Gower's Confessio Amantis* [Carbondale and Edwardsville, Ill., 1978], p. 182).

11. Eugene Vance, "Mervelous Signals: Poetics, Sign Theory, and Politics in Chaucer's *Troilus*," *NLH*, 10 (1979): 313. Another valuable essay that assesses the overall tone of the poem is by Melvin Storm, "Troilus, Mars, and Late Medieval Chivalry," *Journal of Medieval and Renaissance Studies*, 12 (1982): 45–65.

Index

Chauncey Wood is Professor of English, McMaster University. He has published *Chaucer and the Country of the Stars: Poetic Uses of Astrological Imagery* and numerous articles, many of them on Chaucer.

Of related interest

Spenser and the Motives of Metaphor
A. Leigh DeNeef

Kinde Pitty and Brave Scorn
John Donne's Satyres
M. Thomas Hester

Gentle Flame
The Life and Verse of Dudley, Fourth Lord North
Dale B. J. Randall

Jonson's Gypsies Unmasked
Background and Theme of The Gypsies Metamorphos'd
Dale B. J. Randall

"This Poetick Liturgie"
Robert Herrick's Ceremonial Mode
A. Leigh DeNeef